MUSIC

and

MUSICIANS

in

EARLY

AMERICA

MUSIC
and
MUSICIANS
in
EARLY
AMERICA

———

Irving Lowens

W · W · NORTON & COMPANY · INC · NEW YORK

Dedicated to the memory of

RICHARD S. HILL
(1902–1961)

friend, teacher, colleague

CONTENTS

---—»» «« ——---

ILLUSTRATIONS

PREFACE

THE FOLLOWING ARTICLES and papers dealing with various aspects of the history of music in early America and the history of early American music (by no means identical areas) are selected from an output extending over a period of more than 15 years. Upon rereading them with this volume in mind, I was astonished to discover how frequently I had composed small variations on the same themes, and since no book reader should be subjected to quite so much repetition, I have used the blue pencil boldly. In some instances, I have also corrected factual errors, altered clumsy formulations, and added the results of more recent scholarship in footnotes. It turns out, then, that the alterations are rather substantial, and the versions reprinted here should be understood to supersede the originals.

ACKNOWLEDGMENTS

————⋙ ⋘————

I AM INDEBTED to the following for permission to use previously published materials, in altered form, in this volume:

The Theodore Presser Company, Bryn Mawr, Pa., for "Music in the American Wilderness," published in *Etude*, LXXIV, 7 (September 1956);

Journal of the American Musicological Society, Otto E. Albrecht, business manager, Philadelphia, Pa., for "John Wyeth's *Repository of Sacred Music, Part Second:* A Northern Precursor of Southern Folk Hymnody," in V, 2 (Summer 1952); for "The Origins of the American Fuging Tune," in VI, 1 (Spring 1953); for "The Bay Psalm Book in 17th-Century New England," in VIII, 1 (Spring 1955); for "Writings About Music in the Periodicals of American Transcendentalism (1835–50)," in X, 2 (Summer 1957); and for "Andrew Law and the Pirates," in XIII, 1–3 (1960);

Journal of Research in Music Education, Allen P. Britton, editor, Ann Arbor, Mich., for "*The Easy Instructor* (1798–1831): A History and Bibliography of the First Shape-Note Tune-Book," I, 1 (Spring 1953); and for "John Tufts's *Introduction to the Singing of Psalm-Tunes* (1721–1744): The First American Music Textbook," in II, 2 (Winter 1954);

Harry Dichter, Philadelphia, Pa., for "Benjamin Carr's *Federal Overture* (1794)," reprinted from the facsimile edition of the only known copy (Philadelphia: Musical Americana, 1954).

Notes, William Lichtenwanger, editor, Washington, D.C., for "Daniel Read's World: The Letters of an Early American Composer," in IX, 2 (March 1952);

Bulletin of the New York Public Library, David V. Erdman, editor, New York, N.Y., for "The Musical Edsons of Shady: Early American Tunesmiths," in LXV, 4 (April 1961);

Ellen Stone Honoré, New York, N.Y., for "The First Matinee Idol: Louis Moreau Gottschalk," in *Musicology,* I, 4 (Fall 1947); for "The Triumph of Anthony Philip Heinrich," in *Musicology,* II, 1 (Spring 1948); and for "William Henry Fry: Fighter for American Music," in *Musicology,* II, 2 (Fall 1948);

Dr. Martin Just, co-editor, Würzburg, Germany, for the English translation of "Amerikanische Demokratie und die amerikanische Musik von 1830 bis 1914," as published by the Gesellschaft für Musikforschung in the *Bericht über den Internationalen Musikwissenschaftlichen Kongress, Kassel, 1962* (Kassel: Bärenreiter-Verlag, 1963).

Robert S. Paul, editor, *The Hartford Quarterly,* Hartford, Conn., for "The Warrington Collection: A Research Adventure at Case Memorial Library," in the Hartford Seminary Foundation *Bulletin,* 12 (January 1952);

Lee H. Bristol, Jr., President, Westminster Choir College, Princeton, N.J., for "The American Tradition of Church Song," as published in *Of Hymns and the Choral Service* (Princeton, NJ.: Westminster Choir College, 1964).

Chapter 6 was written originally in collaboration with Professor Allen P. Britton, Associate Dean, School of Music, University of Michigan, Ann Arbor, Mich. The version in this book was revised by me alone, with his permission.

I owe Dr. Britton considerably more than this bald credit might imply, however. We have been cultivating the same musicological berry-patch together for more than a decade now, and the single joint study published in this volume is by no means our only common effort. The crystallization of many of my ideas about the history of music in this country is due in large part to the extensive correspondence between us over the years. Only one other living person has influenced me so deeply and taught me so much—my constant co-worker (and wife), Violet E. Lowens.

Of course, there are many others whose cooperation made my own work possible. Much of my research was undertaken in the Library of Congress in the years before I became a member of the LC family. I must make special mention of my past and present colleagues there, who have helped to turn many a chore into a pleasant task—the late Richard S. Hill, Harold Spivacke (Chief, Music Division), Edward N. Waters (Assistant Chief, Music Division), William Lichtenwanger (Head, Reference Section, Music Division), Frederick R. Goff (Chief, Rare Book Division), Frank C. Campbell (at present Assistant Chief, Music Division, New York Public Library), and Donald W. Krummel (at present Head, Reference Services, Newberry Library). A second research home for me always has been the American Antiquarian Society in Worcester, Mass., where the late Clarence S. Brigham made me feel that I was master of all I surveyed, a tradition followed by his successor, the present Director of AAS, Clifford K. Shipton. I have also made good use of research facilities at the New York Public Library, the New-York Historical Society, Brown University, Harvard University, Yale University, the Hartford Theological Seminary, the New Haven Colony Historical Society, the Newberry Library, and the University of Michigan.

The following individuals have either helped me with various problems in person or replied to letters of inquiry from me:

Charles A. Anderson (Presbyterian Historical Society), Ford W. Battles (Hartford Seminary Foundation), Geraldine Beard (New-York Historical Society), Marion E. Brown (John Hay Library, Brown University), Edwin H. Carpenter (California Historical Society), Avis G. Clarke (American Antiquarian Society), Sidney Robertson Cowell (Shady, N.Y.), Charles E. Hughes, Jr. (City Archivist, Philadelphia, Pa.), William A. Jackson (Houghton Library, Harvard University), Mary V. Jennings (New York State

Library), Joyce Ellen Mangler (Brown University), Absley E. Pearce (Charleston, S.C., Library Society), Morris L. Radoff (State Archivist, Annapolis, Md.), Elizabeth de W. Root (Case Memorial Library, Hartford Theological Seminary), Robert C. Sale (State Librarian, Hartford, Conn.), Brooks Shepard, Jr. (Librarian, School of Music, Yale University), Lewis M. Stark (Rare Book Room, New York Public Library), Harry R. Warfel (University of Florida).

To all these, as well as to many others not mentioned above, I am profoundly grateful.

music, and heard music. It would have been a singular thing indeed if the nearly 18,000 Britishers who made up the population
of New England by 1640 had made no music at all on this side
of the Atlantic. Obviously, they did make music, and since voices
took up no extra room in the crowded holds of the tiny ships that
crept across the ocean, it is safe to assume that at least the vocal
music of the old country, both secular and sacred, must have been
fairly commonplace here.

Among the dissenting sects from which the settlers of the New
England colonies were largely drawn, vocal music meant mostly
the singing of psalms, however. As good Calvinists, Pilgrims and
Puritans followed the Biblical injunction "to sing praise unto the
Lord, with the words of David." So that they could carry out this
"ordinance" of their faith, a metrical version of the psalms designed for singing was ordinarily bound in with their Bibles. The
Pilgrims used a new translation by Henry Ainsworth; the Puritans used the Sternhold and Hopkins translation, already almost
a century old and officially sanctioned by the Anglican Church.

Both psalters were provided with "apt notes to sing them with-
all," and doubtless many of the original settlers knew how to read
musical notation. In regard to the Pilgrims, there is Governor
Winslow's flat statement that many of the congregation, at the
time they left Leyden, were "very expert in music." Thomas
Symmes (about whom more later) wrote about the Plymouth
Church that "till about 1682, their excellent custom was to sing
without reading the line." In view of the difficulty of the Ainsworth tunes, the fact that the Pilgrims did not "line out" for more
than 60 years after the foundation of their church is a pretty
good indication of their continuing musical literacy. Among the
Puritans, however, "lining out" seems to have been commonplace
as early as 1647, when John Cotton referred to the practice as a
necessary evil so that those "who want either books or skill to
reade, may know what is to be sung, and joyne with the rest in
the dutie of singing." The clear implication that there were at
least some who did *not* lack "either books or skill to reade" music

is worth noting, and a look at the inventories of estates left by first-generation Puritan settlers bears this out.

But even those Pilgrims and Puritans who *were* musically illiterate must have known many psalm-tunes by heart, since their religion *required* them to sing the psalms—all of the psalms. There are 15 distinct meters in the Ainsworth psalter and 17 in the Sternhold and Hopkins, and each meter must be sung to a different tune. The minimum repertory was therefore 15 tunes for the Pilgrims and 17 for the Puritans. In reality it was doubtless somewhat larger in the first years, but the 17th century saw a progressive shrinkage of variety as the older generation died out, and the new generations were not equipped with the musical skills of the first settlers.

The earliest commentator on the 17th-century American musical scene was the Rev. Thomas Symmes, a graduate of Harvard's class of 1698 who liked to add after his name "Philomusicus." Perhaps more than any other single individual, the sharp-tongued Symmes was responsible for the start of the celebrated New England "singing war" of the 1720s. Writing at a time when musical literacy had virtually disappeared in the population at large, Symmes (then minister at Bradford, Mass.) fired the first gun of the war in his *The Reasonableness of Regular Singing* (Boston, 1720). This was a spirited argument in favor of the necessity of learning to read music and a slashing attack on the old fogies who refused to change their ways. Since Symmes took great pleasure in referring to his opponents as "Anti-Regular-Singers" (frequently abbreviated "A.R.S.es"), the violence of the reaction was hardly surprising. He continued the battle, with no less wit and vigor, in his *Utile Dulci, or A Joco-Serious Dialogue, Concerning Regular Singing* (Boston, 1723). He plainly demonstrated that what the "A.R.S.es" thought was a radical "new way" of singing the psalms (by note rather than by rote) was really the "old way" of the founding fathers, insisting that music "was study'd, known and approv'd of in our College, from the very foundation of it." Since the original freshman class at Harvard began work in 1638, the antiquity of formal music education in New England is quite remarkable. To prove his assertion, Symmes adduced Harvard's "musical theses, which were formerly printed; and . . . some writings containing some tunes, with directions for singing by note . . . and these are yet in being though of more than sixty-years' standing." Exasperatingly enough, Symmes's documentation, apparently antedating 1660, has never been located.

Harvard's contemporary historian, Samuel Eliot Morison, has called attention to the existence of two commonplace books that provide strong evidence of singing and some musical knowledge in the student body during this early period. Both, curiously enough, pertain to secular songs rather than psalm-tunes. The first in point of time was kept by Seaborn Cotton (A.B., 1651), son of John Cotton, the patriarch of New England. Young Seaborn jotted down three English ballads in their entirety (as well as parts of others) in versions so different from those in print that it would be fair to assume that he heard them sung at college and recorded them from memory rather than from some printed broadside or ballad-sheet. The later notebook, belonging to Elnathan Chauncey (A.B., 1661), is of even greater musical significance. Elnathan too copied ballads—and also copious selections from the amorous poems of Spenser and Herrick—but the real prize is several bars of an unidentified tune, the earliest known instance of music notation set down by a New Englander.

There is also plenty of evidence of instrumental as well as vocal music-making in Harvard. Michael Wigglesworth, future author of America's first best-seller, the horrendous *Day of Doom* (Boston, 1662), but then a tutor at the College, recorded in his diary under date of June 25, 1653, that he had heard a student "in the forenoon with ill company playing music, though I had solemnly warned him yesterday of letting his spirit go after pleasures." What instruments were the "ill company" and the misguided student playing? Wigglesworth does not tell us. Perhaps the request of freshman Josiah Flynt in 1660 that his uncle send him a fiddle from London provides us with a clue. Perhaps it was a "treble viall" such as that mentioned in the will of Nathaniel Rogers in 1661; perhaps it was a "base vyol" which, together with many books of music, the "noted musician" Edmund Browne left to posterity upon his death in 1678; perhaps it was just a plain "violl" or a "gittarue" such as those owned by John Foster, a classmate of would-be fiddler Flynt.

The first reference to the existence of any musical instrument in New England occurs in an account of a visit to Plymouth in 1627 by Isaac de Rasières, secretary of the Dutch colony at Manhattan. De Rasières remarks in passing that the Pilgrims "assemble by beat of drum, each with his firelock or musket, in front of the captain's door."

Slightly more tuneful is the jew's harp, a favorite item of barter rather frequently mentioned in early records. Just why the Indians found it irresistibly attractive is not very clear, but it certainly was a popular instrument. A bill from William Pynchon of Roxbury dated March 17, 1635, to John Winthrop, Jr. (to cite only one early instance) includes a charge for "4 doz. Jewes harpes at 12d. doz." The trumpet too was heard in the American wilderness. At Windsor, Conn. a platform was constructed on top of the meetinghouse in 1638 "to walk conveniently to sound a trumpet or a drum to give warning to meeting," according to the town records.

As Percy Scholes has pointed out, when the notorious Rev. Samuel Peters invented the "Blue Law" stating that "no one shall read Common-Prayer, keep Christmas or Saints-days, make minced pies, dance, play cards, or play on any instrument of music," in his fairy-tale history of Connecticut, he judiciously excepted the drum, trumpet, and jew's harp in order to maintain some semblance of credibility.

By far the most spectacular early reference to musical instruments occurs in the inventories of the goods of two neighboring New Hampshire "plantations" taken approximately ten years after they were originally settled. At "Newitchwanicke, 1d of Julie, 1633 . . . in the Great House, 15 recorders and hoeboys" were listed, while "at Pascattaquack 2d Julie, 1633," one day later, there were no less than "hoeboys and recorders 26" and "1 drume"!

Even from the scanty evidence available, it would seem almost certain that music was an important ingredient of New England's culture during the initial 50 or so years of its settlement. It is perhaps a good idea to ponder over the fact that in the year 1700, Boston, with a population of less than 7,000, was second only to London in the number of books published in the entire English-speaking world, easily besting such centers of learning as Oxford and Cambridge.

This alone should give us pause before we make the unwarranted assumption that there was little musical activity here during the 17th century. Surely, the colonists demonstrated extraordinary intellectual vitality and thrust in other fields—is there any reason why music should have been excluded from the range of their interests?

MUSIC

2

---·≫≪·---

THE BAY PSALM BOOK
IN 17th-CENTURY NEW ENGLAND

THE BAY PSALM BOOK, first book-length product of a printing press in British North America, is an imprint of prime importance to the student of early American music history. This psalter was the axis about which New England's psalmody revolved for more than a century. If it is perhaps less interesting from a strictly musical point of view than the Ainsworth psalter brought over from Holland by the Pilgrims, or the Sternhold and Hopkins brought over from England by the Puritans, it must be remembered that its influence on this side of the Atlantic was infinitely greater. It alone left a permanent mark upon our culture. To see the beginnings of music in this country clearly, to see the logic of 18th-century developments, we must go to this source. The purpose of this study is to point out a few of the things that its provenance, bibliography, and metrical patterns can tell us about 17th-century psalmody in New England.

By way of introduction to the subject, it might be well to redefine briefly the Puritan attitude towards music, particularly in view of renewed controversy concerning the validity of the well-known and generally accepted Scholes thesis. In July, 1951, an important article by Cyclone Covey appeared in the *William and Mary Quarterly*[1] in which the author advanced the idea that

1. "Puritanism and Music in Colonial America," *William and Mary Quarterly*, 3rd Ser., VIII (1951), 378–88. Mr. Covey later elaborated his ideas further in "Did Puritanism or the Frontier Cause the Decline of Colonial Music," *Jour. of Research in Mus. Ed.*, VI (1958), 68–78.

Scholes had considerably overstated the case in favor of the Puritans. Covey seriously questioned Scholes's interpretation of the evidence and virtually advocated a return to the discredited view of the Puritan as *diabolus in musica.* A lively correspondence involving Clifford K. Shipton of the American Antiquarian Society, Walter Muir Whitehill of the Boston Athenaeum, and Mr. Covey was published in a later issue of the same journal.[2]

The truth seems to lie somewhere between Scholes's perhaps slightly overenthusiastic apologia for Puritanism and Covey's rigid rejection of his conclusions. The Puritan attitude towards music, in essence, was this: music was fine in its place, but its place was a small one in the Puritan cosmos. So long as music was confined to singing the praises of God in the church or at home, the Puritan was one of its most enthusiastic partisans—if its performance conformed to his interpretation of the Scriptures. As to secular music, it was "lawful" and "admitted," but it was a dangerous toy with which to meddle. It was generally regarded by most educated Puritans as pretty much of a waste of time, as an expendable in the Puritan scale of values. This attitude was admirably summed up in a letter written in 1661 by a future president of Harvard to his nephew, Josiah Flynt, then a freshman at the college. The young man had asked his uncle to send him a fiddle from London. "Musick I had almost forgot," replied Leonard Hoar.

I suspect you seek it both to soon and to much. This be assured of that if you be not excellent at it Its worth nothing at all. And if you be excellent it will take up so much of your mind and time that you will be worth little else; And when all that excellence is attained your acquest will prove little or nothing of real profit to you unless you intend to take upon you the trade of fidling [3]

—unthinkable, of course, for one of God's future ministers. But although Hoar would not buy a fiddle for the potentially holy

2. *William and Mary Quarterly,* 3rd Ser., IX (1952), 128–36.
3. Letter to Josiah Flynt dated March 27, 1661, in *Mass. Hist. Soc. Collections,* 1st Ser., VI (1799), 106.

Josiah, his sisters—mere females—apparently fell into a different category. Hoar went on to say that he *had* procured "the Instruments desired" for them—he unfortunately does not tell us what these were—"for whom tis more proper and they also have more leisure to looke after it." [4]

If the Puritans were no more than lukewarm in their enthusiasm for mere fiddling—an attitude, by the way, that is hardly uncommon even today—they were unquestionably ardently devoted to psalm-singing. Like the non-dissident members of the Church of England, in church they sang in unison unaccompanied, as was the Calvinist custom. They used as singing-book the officially sanctioned Sternhold and Hopkins metrical translation of the psalms, some edition of which containing tunes was invariably bound into their copies of the Bible. At home, however, the more cultured Puritans may well have sung the psalms in harmony, perhaps even with instrumental accompaniment if the instrument were available. It is difficult to account otherwise for the presence, among the belongings of the first settlers, of such books as Thomas Ravenscroft's 1621 *Whole Booke of Psalms* "composed into 4 parts by sundry Authors," [5] Richard Allison's 1599 *Psalmes of David* [6] with the tune designed "to be sung and plaide upon the Lute, Orpharyon, Citterne or Bass Violl, seuerally or altogether," and an unidentified "Iohnson's psalmes in meeter," [7] possibly an unknown psalter compiled by the Edward Johnson who contributed a madrigal to the *Triumphs of Oriana* as well as several psalm-tune settings to Thomas Est's 1592 *Whole Booke of Psalmes.*

But scholarly Puritans were dissatisfied with the official trans-

4. *Ibid.*
5. A copy of Ravenscroft owned by Gov. John Endecott (*ca.* 1589–1665) is in the Massachusetts Historical Society.
6. Inventory of the library of William Brewster (1643), quoted in Thomas Goddard Wright, *Literary Culture in Early New England, 1620–1730* (New Haven, 1920), p. 261.
7. Wright, p. 263.

lation because they felt that too many liberties had been taken
with the meaning of the original Hebrew. To quote the cadenced
words of John Cotton, one of the compilers of the *Bay Psalm Book,*
they were unhappy about Sternhold and Hopkins because

> it is not unknowne to the godly learned that they have rather presented
> a paraphrase than the words of David translated according to the rule
> 2 *chron.* 29. 30.[8] and that their addition to the words, detractions from
> the words are not seldome and rare, but very frequent and many times
> needles[s], . . . and that their variations of the sense, and alterations
> of the sacred text too frequently, may iustly minister matter of offence to
> them that are able to compare the translation with the text; of which
> failings, some iudicious have oft complained, others have been grieved,
> wherupon it hath bin generally desired, that as wee doe inioye other,
> soe (if it were the Lords will) wee might inioye this ordinance also in its
> native purity . . .[9]

It was not for nothing that the Puritans were so named.

THUS it came about that a committee of 30 New England divines,
more distinguished for their piety and learning than for their
poetic gifts, undertook to prepare a more literal metrical translation. *The Whole Booke of Psalmes Faithfully Translated into
English Metre*—with the accent on "faithfully"—was finally
printed at Cambridge, Massachusetts, in 1640 on a small press
procured as an "appendage of Harvard College" in an edition of
1,700 copies. Virtually every congregation in the Massachusetts
Bay Colony immediately adopted the psalter. In this manner, it
came to be known as the *Bay Psalm Book,* although it was never
so designated on the title page.

Despite the Puritan love for psalm-singing, an inevitable consequence of the use of the new psalm-book was a pronounced limita-
tion upon the number and variety of psalm-tunes that could be
sung to its words. It was a regular part of the Puritan regimen

---

8. "Moreover, Hezekiah the king, and the princes commanded the Levites
to sing praise unto the Lord, with the words of David. . . ."
9. *The Whole Booke of Psalmes* [*Bay Psalm Book*] (1640), fol. **2ᵛ.

and an "ordinance" of the sect to sing through the entire book of psalms "in course," that is, in sequence. Since the Sternhold and Hopkins version employed no less than 17 metrical schemes, it is logical to assume that the psalm-tune repertory of the first Puritan settlers was at least large enough to embrace the complete psalter. The *Bay Psalm Book,* on the other hand, following a trend towards metrical simplification already quite evident in England, accomplished its purpose with only six metrical patterns. So far as music was concerned, the elimination of 11 metrical schemes had the practical result of pronouncing the death sentence in New England upon almost all the old long Genevan tunes. When the *Bay Psalm Book* supplanted Sternhold and Hopkins here, later generations of Puritans were automatically limited to singing only those psalm-tunes which conformed to its six meters.

That the compilers of the *Bay Psalm Book* were aware of this can perhaps be inferred from a careful reading of the "admonition to the Reader" added, seemingly as a space-filler, to the final page of the first edition. These few sentences spell out the tunes to be used for the six metrical patterns in the psalter. In the first paragraph, it is explained that the psalms in common meter (three-fourths fall into this category) "may be sung in very neere fourty common tunes; as they are collected, out of our chief musicians, by *Tho. Ravenscroft*." The compilers are doubtless referring to the 39 four-line common-meter tunes found in Ravenscroft's *Whole Booke of Psalms* (1621). These tunes were then replacing in everyday use in England the 16th-century eight-line common-meter tunes, although the official Sternhold and Hopkins psalters lagged behind the times and for the most part included only the older tunes. However, of the 39 tunes of this type in Ravenscroft, to our knowledge only 16 had previously appeared in print anywhere; the remaining 23 were apparently published there for the first time. It therefore would seem most unlikely that the new tunes, at any rate, were familiar to the New England Puritans as a whole. The citation of Ravenscroft—evidently his collection must have been fairly well known here—thus appears to be a reference to a source where as many as "very neere fourty common tunes" *might be found*, a bibliographical footnote, rather than a factual report of just what common-meter psalm-tunes were being sung by Massachusetts Puritans in 1640. In essence, it was an attempt to enlarge the psalm-tune repertory. In the light of what we know about later New England circumstances—scarcity of music, increasing musical illiteracy, the decline in congregational participation in the service, to mention but a few—the attempt was predestined to fail.

In the second paragraph of the "admonition," three tunes are cited for use with short-meter psalms. Although they too are to be found in Ravenscroft, it will be noted that the readers are referred not to that collection but rather to "our english psalm books," which can only mean the everyday Sternhold and Hopkins psalters.

The third paragraph similarly specifies three tunes for long-meter texts, but here a curious comment is added: "which three tunes aforesaid, comprehend almost all this whole book of psalmes, as being tunes most familiar to us." On the surface, this observation seems to be entirely incomprehensible. How could three long-meter tunes, even if they were those "most familiar" to the Puritans, "comprehend" a psalter in which the long-meter psalms were only 9 per cent of the total? If the word "tunes" is understood to mean "meters," however, everything becomes plain. The comment now reads: "which three *meters* aforesaid [i.e., common-, short-, and long-meters], comprehend almost all this whole book of psalmes, as being *meters* most familiar to us." In terms of figure, 94 per cent of the psalms are thus "comprehended."

The last three paragraphs specify one tune each for the three remaining meters.

Thus, if the "very neere fourty common tunes" are understood to refer to the 39 four-line common-meter tunes in Ravenscroft, 48 psalm-tunes in all are mentioned. These can be accurately a complete list is appended.[10]

The second edition of the *Bay Psalm Book* is nothing more than an English reprint of the first, it need not detain us here. The third edition—virtually a new book—must, however, be briefly examined.

This third edition, of which 2,000 copies were printed in 1651, appears to have come about primarily as a result of dissatisfaction with the text as an instrument for singing. Although the committee of 30 excused the crudity of their verse by explaining that "Gods Altar needs not our pollishing," [11] a decade of experience in singing from the *Bay Psalm Book* caused a change in mind. "It was thought," Cotton Mather wrote coyly half a century later, "that a little more of Art was to be employ'd upon them [i.e., the psalms]: And for that Cause, they were committed to Mr. *Dunster,* who Revised and Refined this Translation; and (with some Assistance from one Mr. *Richard Lyon . . .*) he brought it into the Condition wherein our Churches have ever since used it." [12] Dunster and Lyon overhauled the original from stem to stern, smoothing out the versification, adding alternative versions of certain psalms and appending to the book a group of 36 newly translated "other Scripture-Songs" traditionally included in English psalters. They even abandoned the old title and called the new edition *The Psalms Hymns and Spiritual Songs of the Old and New Testament faithfully translated into English metre for the use, edification, and comfort of the saints in publick and private, especially in New England.* The third edition proved to be the definitive one. In this form, the *Bay Psalm Book* (or the *New*

10. The following list of numbers are those assigned to the tunes in Maurice Frost, *English & Scottish Psalm & Hymn Tunes, c. 1543–1677* (London, 1953). Common-meter tunes: 42, 121, 247, 243a, 248, 242, 239a, 240, 19, 251, 238, 229, 249, 109, 237, 232, 111, 250, 205, 236, 231, 202, 203, 207, 206, 204, 208, 209, 241, 228, 234, 239b, 129, 233, 103, 227, 243b, 172a, 246a; short-meter tunes: 230, 65, 45; long-meter tunes: 71, 114, 178; hallelujah-meter tune: 174; 6-8's meter tune: 180; 12-8's meter tune: 125.

11. *Bay Psalm Book* (1640), fol. **3ᵛ.

12. *Magnalia Christi Americana* (London, 1702), III, 100.

England Psalm Book, as the third and later editions came to be called) held the field until Thomas Prince brought out the last revision in 1758, well over a century later. It even extended its influence into England and Scotland, where at least 40 editions were printed. Except for the Sternhold and Hopkins, Tate and Brady, and Watts versions of the psalms, no psalter in English ever achieved greater popularity.

Analysis of the metrical changes made by Dunster and Lyon shows a continuing trend in the direction of a smaller psalm-tune repertory. The increasing reliance upon the common-meter text and the resultant decrease in the number of essential psalm-tunes is demonstrated in the following table:

Table I

THE 150 PSALMS AND THEIR METERS

Numbers of Psalms in Three Psalm Books

Meter	Sternhold & Hopkins	Bay Psalm Book (1640)	Bay Psalm Book (1651)
CM	128	112	125
SM	5	14	8
LM	2	15	14
HM	1	6	2
6 8's	2	2	1
12 8's	1	1	0
4 10's, 2 11's	1	0	0
4 5's, 6565	1	0	0
6 6's, 667667	1	0	0
6 6's	1	0	0
866877	1	0	0
668668	1	0	0
5 10's	1	0	0
888866	1	0	0
4 12's, 2 10's	1	0	0
7676	1	0	0
8 10, 8 10	1	0	0
	150	150	150

Summarizing, we find that in 1651, the proportion of psalms in common meter has been increased from 75 per cent to 83 per cent. Long-meter texts are present in about the same proportion, but psalms in three of the other meters are sharply reduced in number and one meter is entirely eliminated.[13]

Thus, the shrinkage of the psalm-tune repertory in New England can be documented as early as 1651. All evidence points to the fact that this process continued steadily at least until the 1690s. During this decade, a plateau appears to have been reached when the number of psalm-tunes in use changed very little. It was not until the 1720s that the fortunes of New England congregational song took a decided turn for the better, due in large part to the rise of the singing-school movement.

But the plateau was at least some improvement in that the decline was halted. What was it to which we can attribute the stabilization of the situation? It was undoubtedly the appearance of an edition of the *Bay Psalm Book* containing psalm-tunes in musical notation. The earliest *known* such edition is the ninth of 1698,[14] which includes a selection of 13 psalm-tunes in two-part arrangements and a few rudimentary instructions for their proper performance. Nine of the 13 are four-line common-meter tunes; a single specimen takes care of each of the four remaining meters.

Although we do not know who was responsible for this choice, the exact sources from which the musical materials in the ninth edition of the *Bay Psalm Book* were borrowed can be identified. One would perhaps suspect that the anonymous compiler would turn to the most popular musical psalter of the day, John Playford's *Whole Book of Psalms*, but instead, surprisingly enough, he turned to a textbook. He consulted Playford's *Brief Introduc-*

13. If the 36 Scripture songs of the supplement are included in the analysis, the proportion of common-meter texts is even greater; 85 per cent. It is also illuminating to note that while the first edition of the *Bay Psalm Book* utilizes six meters and the third five, the supplement makes use of only four.

14. Boston, Printed by B. Green, and J. Allen, for Michael Perry, under the West-End of the Town house. 1698.

tion to the Skill of Musick, the standard English theoretical treatise of the latter part of the 17th century. Furthermore, when one tries to pin down the particular edition of the many-editioned Playford which served him as prototype, it becomes plain that he must have used no less than three separate editions. To each, the music section in the ninth edition of the *Bay Psalm Book* owes certain of its characteristics.

The first paragraph in this music section is quite famous:

First observe of how many *Notes* compass the *Tune* is. Next, the place of your first *Note;* and how many *Notes* above & below that: so as you may begin the *Tune* of your first *Note* as the rest may be sung in the compass of your and the peoples voices, without *Squeaking* above, or *Grumbling* below. . . . [p. 419]

It is almost invariably quoted in reference works. There seems to be something about it, particularly in the phrase "*Squeaking* above, or *Grumbling* below," which has struck historians as a singularly apt description of the primitive nature of American psalmody at the time, and it has been naturally assumed that this paragraph must have been written with the American scene specifically in mind. It may therefore put a somewhat different light on the situation to point out that these remarks are quoted, verbatim and literatim, from either the 1666 or the 1667 edition of Playford's *Brief Introduction*,[15] a work written with no reference to the American practice of psalmody. And as these editions of Playford are the only ones in which the paragraph appears in this exact form (even its capitalization and italics are used in the *Bay Psalm Book*), there can be no doubt that one of them is the exact exemplar from which it was taken. From the same source, the compiler also borrowed the notes as to whether the tunes should be sung to "Psalms Consolatory," "to Psalms of Prayer, Confession & Funerals," or "to Psalms of Praise and Thanksgiving," as well as the suggestions as to where particular tunes should be pitched.

15. London, Printed by William Godbid for John Playford, 1666, pp. 59–60. The 1667 edition is identical except for the changed date on the title page.

It will be noted that a fasola notation in which the letters FSLM are placed directly under the musical notes is found in the ninth edition of the *Bay Psalm Book*.[16] This notation does not appear in the 1666 or 1667 edition of Playford from which the introductory paragraphs were borrowed. It does, however, appear in the 1672 edition[17] in exactly the same form. As this was the only edition of Playford where the fasola notation was utilized, it too was doubtless familiar to the *Bay Psalm Book* compiler.

The tunes themselves were almost certainly taken from yet a different edition. The 1667 edition, source of the introductory remarks, lacks HACKNEY, one of the *Bay Psalm Book* tunes, includes another under a different name, and gives several others in different keys. The 1672 edition, source of the fasola notation, still omits HACKNEY and gives all the tunes without a bass. The next three known editions of Playford—those of 1674,[18] 1679,[19] and 1683 [20]—do contain all the *Bay Psalm Book* tunes in two-part arrangements; this is not true of still later editions. The 1683 edition may be eliminated from consideration because corrected misprints found only here are not followed in the *Bay Psalm Book* versions of the tunes. The *Bay Psalm Book* does follow the 1674 and 1679 editions exactly. Because the two Playford editions are identical so far as the musical notation of the psalm-tunes is concerned, it does not seem possible to isolate the specific edition used by the compiler of the *Bay Psalm Book* selection.

SUMMARIZING, it seems certain that the individual responsible for the music section of the *Bay Psalm Book*'s ninth edition must have been familiar with at least three separate editions of Playford's

16. The probable source from which John Tufts derived his letter notation in 1721. See the following chapter, pp. 50–51.
17. *An Introduction to the Skill of Musick*, 6th ed. (London, Printed by W. Godbid for J. Playford, 1672), p. 75.
18. 7th ed.
19. 8th ed.
20. 10th ed. No 9th ed. has been located, and it is doubtful that any was issued. On this point, see C. L. Day and E. B. Murrie, *English Song-Books, 1651–1702; A Bibliography* (London, 1940), p. 55.

Introduction—those of 1666 or 1667, 1672, and 1674 or 1679. Why were the editions of 1683, 1687, or 1694, not used for a book which appeared in 1698? This most unusual circumstance makes it appear unlikely that the compiler did his work as late as 1698, and the necessary knowledge of three editions of Playford makes it appear unlikely that he was a New Englander altogether.

All this points to the existence of an earlier, as yet unlocated edition of the *Bay Psalm Book* containing music—not unsuspected before—and indicates that we have perhaps been seeking it on the wrong continent. Thomas Symmes's near-contemporary testimony of an edition containing music extant before 1692 is well known. In a sermon delivered on October 12, 1722, he stated that *"Hackney,* or *St. Mary's* . . . has been in prick'd in one Edition of our Psalm Books above this 30 years." [21] There is record of the fact that the Plymouth Church abandoned the Ainsworth psalter in favor of the *Bay Psalm Book* in 1692 because of the difficulty of the Ainsworth tunes. Is it reasonable to believe that the Pilgrims would have done so had no music been available in the *Bay Psalm Book?* And, moreover, no one has located any copies of a sixth or seventh edition of the *Bay Psalm Book.*

It is also strange that Samuel Sewall, self-admittedly "a lover of Musick to a fault," [22] makes no mention of the 1698 edition in his highly detailed diary, one of the main sources of our knowledge of the social history of the period. If this were in truth the first appearance of music in the Puritan psalter, surely he would have noted it as a "remarkable." But Sewall notes no earlier edition either. Why? Perhaps because an earlier edition containing music was published in England between the years 1689 and 1691, during which time Sewall himself was visiting the homeland. During these years, he did not keep a diary; only random notes have come down to us. In view of Sewall's great fondness for psalm singing and his association with the book trade, it is not even

21. *Utile Dulci* (Boston: Printed by B. Green, for Samuel Gerrish, near the Brick Meeting House in Cornhill, 1723), p. 25.
22. *Mass. Hist. Soc. Collections,* 6th Ser., I (1886), 155.

beyond the realm of belief to think that he himself may have had something to do with the publication during the course of his English visit.

Further evidence that the missing edition was probably published in England can be found in the fact that no known editions of the *Bay Psalm Book* were published in the Colonies between the third of 1651 and the eighth of 1695. If we can assume this to be true, we can explain the peculiar provenance of the ninth edition by postulating an English compiler of the missing edition, of which the ninth edition would appear to be merely an American reprint.

We can even hazard a guess as to the probable publisher of the missing edition. This would seem to be the London bookdealer Richard Chiswell, for whom editions of the *Bay Psalm Book* are known to have been printed in 1671, 1680, and 1694. Chiswell supplied Boston booksellers with items for their stock, and invoices of shipments from 1683 through 1685 show that they included sizeable numbers of *Bay Psalm Books.*[23] Moreover, Chiswell was not a complete stranger to the psalm-tune publishing game, as his name appears in the imprint of a 1688 collection entitled *The Psalms and Hymns, usually sung in the Churches and Tabernacles of St. Martins in the Fields, and St. James's Westminster.*[24]

Out of these speculations, a picture of the missing edition emerges. We may expect to find an English edition of the *Bay Psalm Book* printed for Richard Chiswell between 1689 and 1691 containing the same music section as that found in the ninth edition printed for Michael Perry in Boston in 1698. Perhaps our British colleagues will help us to locate it.

The fact that we must look to England for a solution of this small American bibliographical problem illustrates in miniature one of the most fascinating aspects of early American cultural history—its curious duality. The story of the arts in 17th-century

23. Quoted in Wright, pp. 228, 230, 231, 234, 235, 236.
24. See Charles Humphries and William C. Smith, *Music Publishing in the British Isles* (London, 1954), p. 103.

New England is the tale of a people trying to plant in the New World the very vines whose fruit they had enjoyed in the Old, while, at the same time, it is the chronicle of the unconscious development of a totally different civilization. The 17th-century history of the *Bay Psalm Book* is a case in point, for although the psalm-tunes sung to its texts may superficially appear to be nothing more than a provincial utilization of certain music sung in the mother country, a mysterious qualitative change took place when they were sung on different soil. Here, they proved to be the seed out of which a new, uniquely American music was later to flower. They thus take on added interest and significance, and lead us to a heightened appreciation of the implications of the old New England adage, "despise not the day of small things," a proverb which might well stand as motto for musicology as a whole.

3

—— ⟫⟩ ⟨⟨⟨ ——

JOHN TUFTS'S *Introduction to the Singing of Psalm-Tunes* (1721-1744): THE FIRST AMERICAN MUSIC TEXTBOOK

ALMOST EXACTLY a century after the *Mayflower* dropped anchor at Plymouth, the Boston bookseller Samuel Gerrish offered for sale a slim pamphlet by the Rev. John Tufts,[1] pastor of the church in the Newbury, Massachusetts, second parish. If one were to choose any single event to mark the beginning of organized music education in America, it would be the publication of this modest work, containing a few pages of text outlining the rudiments of music in simple terms and a small selection of English psalm- and hymn-tunes. Before the appearance of Tufts's pamphlet, the New Englander who wanted to learn how to read music could turn to no guide published here. Thirteen crudely engraved tunes in the *Bay Psalm Book*[2] and an unknown number in the Brady and Tate *New Version of the Psalms of David*[3] were the only printed music

1. John Tufts, b. Medford, Mass., Feb. 26, 1689; d. Amesbury, Mass., Aug. 17, 1750. Grad. Harvard Univ., 1708. Minister, Newbury, Mass., 1714–1738. Retired from the ministry in 1738, moved to Amesbury, Mass., and set up as a shopkeeper there until his death. Detailed biographical sketches may be found in Frank J. Metcalf, *American Writers and Compilers of Sacred Music* (New York, 1925), pp. 13–19 and Clifford K. Shipton, *Sibley's Harvard Graduates* (Boston, 1937), V, 457–60.

2. The 9th ed. (1698), but see Chapter 2 for a discussion of a possibly earlier edition containing musical notation.

3. At least nine tunes were included in a 1713 Boston reprint of the *New Version*. Although no copy is known to the writer, one was sold at the Brinley

to which he could conveniently refer. For a variety of practical and theological reasons, the New England clergy were deeply concerned about the problem of musical illiteracy within their congregations at that time. John Tufts was the first to do something more than preach sermons about the situation, the first to write the textbook and supply the music without which the problem could never be solved.

Just how Tufts obtained his knowledge of music is not known, and it may probably be safely assumed that music was important to him only as a handmaiden of religion. Such were the times. Nevertheless, his pioneer position in the movement to improve the quality of congregational song and to enlarge its repertory made him an important musical figure. Sociologically speaking, his work in behalf of better singing was to have revolutionary consequences. From it developed a most remarkable new social institution, the New England singing-school, which was to control the destinies of native American music for well over a hundred years. Thanks to the singing-school movement and the teacher-composers who were its products, the last two decades of the 18th century were to see a tremendous upsurge of musical creativity, the uniqueness and vitality of which is only now beginning to be fully realized. After Tufts, no forward step of comparable magnitude was taken in the field of American music education until the advent of Lowell Mason in the 1820s.

To THE regret of music historians and those interested in the genesis of American music education, no copy of Tufts's crucially important work issued prior to the fifth edition of 1726 has come to light. The origins of this little pamphlet have been shrouded in mystery and confusion. Its key role in the early history of music

---

auction in 1881. For details regarding this imprint see Allen P. Britton and Irving Lowens, "Unlocated Titles in Early Sacred American Music," *Notes,* XI (1953), 37. The late Maurice Frost, in a letter to the author dated January 15, 1954, suggests that the nine tunes in the Boston reprint were probably identical to those printed on a separate leaflet designed for binding up with the 2nd (1698) English edition of the Brady and Tate *New Version.*

in America makes a clear answer to the question, "when did the first edition appear?" a matter of more than simple bibliographical interest. With the evidence now available, such an answer can be attempted—although 1710,[4] 1712,[5] 1714,[6] and 1715 [7] have been cited by reputable bibliographers as probable years of initial publication, it is extremely doubtful that Tufts's *Introduction* was issued before 1721. The earliest known reference to the actual publication of any musical work yet discovered in an American newspaper is the following advertisement from the January 2/9, 1721, *Boston News-Letter:*

A Small Book containing 20 Psalm Tunes, with Directions how to Sing them, contrived in the most easy Method ever yet Invented, for the ease of Learners, whereby even Children, or People of the meanest Capacities, may come to Sing them by Rule, may serve as an Introduction to a more compleat Treatise of Singing, which will speedily be published. To be Sold by Samuel Gerrish Bookseller; near the Brick Church in Cornhill, Price 6d.

Thus was the first American music imprint announced. "The most easy Method ever yet Invented" strongly suggests something unorthodox in the manner of presentation—probably Tufts's ingenious letter notation—and there can be little question that the advertisement refers to the Tufts book despite the fact that his name is not mentioned in it. Until indubitable evidence of earlier publication can be produced, it must be assumed that this "Small Book containing 20 Psalm Tunes" was, in fact, the genuine first edition of Tufts's pamphlet. It would appear that the tunes were printed unharmonized. The "more compleat Treatise of Singing" cited is undoubtedly a reference to Thomas Walter's considerably more elaborate *Grounds and Rules of Musick Explained* (Boston,

---

4. John W. Moore, *Complete Encyclopaedia of Music* (Boston, 1852), p. 759.

5. Shipton, p. 460.

6. George Hood, *A History of Music in New England* (Boston, 1846), p. 65. Shipton refers to a supposed edition of this year as the "second" edition.

7. Evans No. 1785.

1721), announced by Gerrish as "just published" in the *News-Letter* for May 15/22, 1721.[8]

The "Small Book" seems to have met with a cordial reception among the inhabitants of Boston, and the edition was probably completely disposed of very shortly after it was offered for sale. The following advertisement was printed less than four months later:

A Collection of 28 Psalm Tunes with Instructions for Singing them, in the easiest Method which has yet been known. To be Sold by Samuel Gerrish Bookseller in Boston. Price 6d. single, or 5sh. per dozen. [*Boston News-Letter,* April 24/May 1, 1721]

Gerrish again neglected to mention that Tufts was the author of the work, but we must remember that this information is important to us only in retrospect; at the time Tufts was an obscure country minister whose name was so little known that Gerrish probably did not consider it a material help in selling the book. When a name was well known, Gerrish used it. Thus Thomas Walter—who was Cotton Mather's nephew—had his name emblazoned in the public press as author of the *Grounds and Rules of Musick Explained* each time his book was advertised, and later on, when Tufts's fame was better established, his name too was invariably used. Regardless of Gerrish's reasoning, however, we do know definitely that the "Collection of 28 Psalm Tunes" of the April 24/May 1, 1721, advertisement was Tufts's actual work from the following notice on page 22 of Thomas Symmes's sermon, *A Discourse Concerning Prejudice* (Boston, 1722):

To be sold by *Samuel Gerrish,* Bookseller near the Brick Meeting House in Corn-Hill *Boston.* A Very plain and easy Introduction to the Art of Singing Psalm Tunes; With the Cantus or Trebles of Twenty eight Psalm Tunes, contrived in such a manner as that the Learner may attain the Skill of Singing them, with the greatest ease and Speed imaginable. By the Rev. Mr. *John Tufts.* Price 6d. or 5s. the duz.

8. Subscription for Walter's book were solicited before the publication of Tufts's *Introduction.* One of the original subscription papers, dated Nov. 12, 1720, may be found at the John Carter Brown Library in Providence.

A copy of either the first or second edition (because it was incomplete, it is impossible to determine which) was in existence as late as 1881. The writer has been unable to trace it since it was sold to an unknown bidder for $10.50 at the auction of George Brinley's famous Americana library in that year. In the catalog,[9] it is described as follows:

5885. [TUFTS (Rev. John) of Newbury.] A very Plain and Easy Introduction to the Art of Singing Psalm Tunes, pp. 4, 12 (Wants one or more leaves at the end), n.t.p., EXTREMELY RARE.
long 12mo, Boston, J. F[ranklin], for S. Gerrish, 1721.
This copy, though not quite complete, is in good condition, and retains half of its original marbled wrapper. The Introduction occupies four pages, with the imprint (as above) in colophon. The number of Tunes is sixteen. In printing them *letters* are used upon the staff instead of *notes;* F, S, L, M, for Fa, Sol, La, Mi (See Hood, p. 66.) The *Cantus* (Treble) only is given. There are no *bars,* except for marking the end of lines and verses.

Charles Evans, who was apparently unaware of the earlier 1721 edition, mistakenly assumes in his *American Bibliography* that the Brinley copy is that described in the April 24/May 1, 1721, advertisement.[10]

GERRISH evidently found a ready market for his music publications. Less than a year later, still another collection was announced:

S. Gerrish, Bookseller [has for sale] a Collection of 26 Psalm Tunes, in three Parts. Printed from a Copper Plate, Engraven very neatly and exactly, and in a fold suitable to bind with Psalm-books. There is intended also an Addition of many more Tunes, which have not yet been Printed here, done with the like Curiosity, and as speedily as possible, with an Introduction to the Art of Singing. [*Boston News-Letter,* October 8/15, 1722]

As no "easy Method" is here mentioned, it is probable that this

9. *Catalogue of the American Library of the Late George Brinley of Hartford, Conn., Part III* (Hartford, 1881), p. 164.
10. Evans No. 2297.

"Collection of 26 Psalm Tunes, in three Parts" was printed in orthodox notation, and it is very doubtful that it is another edition of Tufts's *Introduction*. In all likelihood, the tunes and harmonizations in this hitherto overlooked imprint were basically identical to those found in the 1721 edition of Thomas Walter's *Grounds and Rules*, but the 1722 collection was evidently published in the regular rather than the oblong format (i.e., "in a fold suitable to bind with Psalm-books") and may well have omitted Walter's detailed discussion of the rudiments. It was apparently intended for use in the church rather than in the singing-school.

Shortly afterward, what was unquestionably a new edition of the *Introduction*—the third—was announced by Gerrish:

> There is now preparing, and will in a short time be Published, the Singing Book with Letters instead of Notes, with the Bass to the Tunes, Correctly Engraven on Copper; with some further and useful Instructions, which will render that little Book still more acceptable and beneficial, to all that have any regard for Regular Singing: and will be sold by Samuel Gerrish near the Brick Meeting House in Cornhill, Boston. [*Boston News-Letter*, December 31, 1722/January 7, 1723]

Two weeks later in the *News-Letter*, Gerrish repeated the advertisement but prefaced it with the statement that "This Day or tomorrow will be Published, the Singing Book with Letters instead of Notes . . ." and notice of publication appeared the following week:

> Just Publish'd, & to be Sold by Samuel Gerrish, A Small Singing Book of 18 Psalm Tunes (both Trible and Bass) in the easy Method of Singing by Letters instead of Notes, first contrived by the Reverend Mr. Tufts. Neatly engraven on Copper, with suitable directions, very Useful for People even of the meanest capacities, and for Children. Price 1s. [*Boston News-Letter*, January 21/28, 1723]

These advertisements reveal that the third edition differed from those issued earlier in several important respects: the bass was added to the tunes; the work was printed from copper plates; [11] the instructions were amplified; certain tunes were omitted, or a new selection was made; the price was doubled.

Sixteen more tunes were soon added to the third edition:

This Day will be Published . . . a Second Sheet of Psalm Tunes in two Parts Neatly engraven on Copper, in the easy Method of Mr. Tufts's Singing book, and intended for an Addition to the Tunes in that Book, in which is contained all such common Tunes as were omitted in the first Sheet, and the rest are such as are esteemed the most excellent now in use, some of them never before Printed here. The whole number of Tunes contained now in this Book is 34 with Treble and Bass, (8 of which are long Tunes) which makes the quantity of 84 single Trebles, of 4 lines,[12] besides the raising the Notes, &c. . . . To be Sold by Samuel Gerrish Bookseller in Cornhill, Boston . . . for 2s. Single and 20s. a doz.

N.B. Such as please, may have the second sheet added to their books paying only for the Tunes. Others may still have the books with only the first sheet of Tunes if they desire it. [*Boston News-Letter*, March 15/22, 1723]

The amplified collection of tunes in three parts promised by Gerrish in his October 8/15, 1722, advertisement followed shortly on the heels of the enlarged third edition of the *Introduction:*

There has been Preparing, and is now Published, and to be Sold by Samuel Gerrish Bookseller in Cornhill, Boston, A Collection of Psalm

11. The identity of the engraver of the Tufts and Walter books—as well as the unlocated October 8/15, 1722 imprint—is unknown. However, as Francis Dewing is the only individual definitely ascertained to have been actively engraving on copper in Boston at that time, it seems not unreasonable to assume that some of the music plates were of his execution. Curiously enough, it is quite evident from an examination of the Tufts and Walter imprints that different hands were at work. Clearly there were unknown engravers on copper then plying their trade in Boston. The Walter book is the earliest known example of engraving on copper performed in that city.

12. If Gerrish is understood to have meant 84 staves of music each containing a setting of a complete stanza of text, his arithmetic is quite accurate. Thus, assuming that each four-line stanza was printed on a single staff (as is true of the known editions), it becomes apparent that the 26 "common" tunes (in two parts) occupied 52 staves, and the 8 "long" (or double length) tunes occupied 32, making a total of 84.

TUNES in three parts, Treble, Medius, and Bass, 28 consisting of 4 lines, Or common Tunes; and 10 more consisting of 8 lines, or double Tunes. Printed from a Copper plate, most curiously and correctly engraven, and in a Page fit to be bound up with the Common Psalm-books. Persons may have Psalm-books with these Tunes bound, for 5s. 6d. a piece. Or the Tunes Single for 3s. a set. And by the Doz. with Usual and proper Abatements, and cheaper still by the 100.

Any Person may have a Set of Tunes put into their Old Psalm-books, Paying only for the Tunes. [*Boston News-Letter*, June 20/27, 1723]

Another edition of the Tufts *Introduction*—apparently the fourth—came from the presses later the same year.

Just publish'd, and to be sold by Samuel Gerrish Bookseller in Corn-hill, Boston, A New Impression of the Small Singing-Book, in that most easy Method contrived by the Reverend Mr. Tufts, Containing 36 Psalm-Tunes, (the Trebles only) now done from Copper Plates, En-graven with great Care, and with the addition of Ten Tunes more than in the former small Edition, with some further useful Explanations, &c. Price 6s a Doz., or 9d Single. [Boston *Gazette*, November 11/18, 1723]

This advertisement is puzzling in several particulars. As the previous edition contained 34 tunes in two parts, why did Gerrish feel it necessary or desirable to issue a later edition with 36 apparently unharmonized tunes? The statement that the tunes are "now [i.e., for the first time] done from Copper Plates" makes sense only if "the former small Edition" is understood to mean the second edition—which also contained the "Trebles only" and was not printed from copper plates. But if Gerrish was in fact comparing the second and fourth editions, as seems likely, his arithmetic is rather curious in this case in view of the fact that the second edition was advertised as containing 28 tunes. Two explanations are possible: either one or the other notice contains a typographical error, or perhaps two tunes from the second edition were omitted from the fourth and 10 new ones added. In either case, the actual facts of the matter cannot be determined until a copy of the fourth edition turns up.

No OTHER musical publications were announced by Gerrish until

1726, when the following appeared in the press:

In about Ten Days will . . . be Printed from a Copper Plate, A Collection of Psalm Tunes in Three Parts, Treble Medius and Bass, with Letters instead of Notes, fit to be bound up with Psalm books; Or single, with an Introduction for the use of Learners, and will be sold by the said Gerrish . . . [Boston *Gazette*, June 27/July 4, 1726]

At first glance, this reads as if it were a fairly straightforward reference to a forthcoming fifth edition of the *Introduction*, but close reading reveals that there may be some justification for the belief that it describes a collection not compiled by Tufts, although utilizing his letter notation. The omission of Tufts's name at this late date, when his reputation in the music field must have been well established, seems to have been calculated rather than accidental. Although the evidence is admittedly slight, perhaps we can postulate another hitherto unknown early music imprint, particularly since the fifth edition (the first of which copies have survived) was not published until October, 1726, nearly four months—not "about Ten Days"—after the above advertisement was printed:

Just Publish'd, An Introduction to the Singing of Psalm Tunes in a plain and easy Method. With a Collection of Thirty Seven Tunes in Three Parts. By the Rev. Mr. Tufts. The Fifth Edition (with several excellent Tunes never before publish'd here) in a neat Character, correctly engraven on Copper Plates, & in a Fold suitable to bind up with Psalm Books. To be sold by Samuel Gerrish, Bookseller at the lower end of Cornhill, Boston, [Boston *Gazette*, October 17/24, 1726]

The actual title page of this tiny pamphlet measures 14 x 8 cm. (See Illus. 1.) On the verso of the title page is found a poem entitled "On the Divine Use of Musick," evidently reprinted without alteration from an edition of John Playford's *Whole Book of Psalms*, where it appears set to music.[13] The "Short Introduction to the Singing of PSALM-TUNES" which follows on pp. 1–9, an

---

13. According to Henry W. Foote, *Three Centuries of American Hymnody* (Cambridge, 1940), p. 98, the poem is largely a rewritten variant of a song from Ingelo's play *Bentivoglio and Urania*, first published in 1660.

important document in the history of music education in America, is given verbatim as Appendix A. "The Table of Tunes" or index occupies p. [10]. Twelve pages of music in Tufts's letter notation, printed on one side of the leaf from copper plates in truth "neatly engraven," complete the contents.

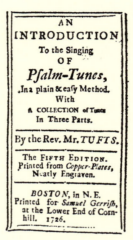

1. Title page, *An Introduction to the Singing of Psalm-Tunes* (1726) by John Tufts. Courtesy of the American Antiquarian Society.

Basically, all later editions are identical to the fifth in content. The music in Editions 5–9 was printed from identical plates; a newly engraved set, somewhat cruder in execution but containing the same tunes in the same settings, was used for Editions 10–11. Although the introductory matter was reset from edition to edition, only one important textual addition was made. This change took place in the seventh edition, where the Brady and Tate version of the 149th Psalm was added. The reason why is simple to understand. The 149 PSALM TUNE printed by Tufts is in an unusual meter not found in the *Bay Psalm Book*, for which he presumably made his selection of music. Thus, no words were readily available to which the tune could be sung, and without words the utility of the music was dubious. The publication of the text of the Brady and Tate 149th Psalm (for which the tune was originally written) neatly solved this little problem without disturbing the music plates, which were undoubtedly expensive and difficult to engrave.

It is evident from the advertisements for earlier editions of Tufts's pamphlet that the first versions of the "Short Introduction" must have differed considerably from that which is found in the fifth edition. That the fifth edition version was the definitive one is clear, however, as it was not materially altered in later editions. Here, Tufts discusses his "plain & easy" letter notation, solmization, diatonic scale steps, transpositions of *mi*, flats and sharps, his method of indicating note values, time signatures, clefs, other musical characters, and recommends the use of his exercises— "Lessons for Tuning ye Voice." In the manner in which it appears in the fifth edition, and considered as a product of its place and time, the introduction is a near miracle of condensation. It is quite obvious that Tufts was making a strong effort to write lucidly in terms as simple as possible. Generally speaking, he succeeded admirably. There can be little question that he was indeed addressing himself to "Children, or People of the meanest Capacities." In this regard, a comparison between Tufts's brief explanations and the complex and turgid essay in Thomas Walter's *Grounds and Rules of Musick Explained* is quite illuminating. The Tufts "Short Introduction" is truly an original work; it is not a mere paraphrase of an English presentation of the rudiments, as were so many later similar attempts. For this reason, it is extremely difficult to establish conclusively the exact sources of Tufts's knowledge of the theory of music. One cannot safely say much more than that he was evidently familiar with John Playford's *Introduction to the Skill of Musick* (London, 1654; many later editions) and Christopher Simpson's *Compendium of Practical Music* (London, 1665; many later editions), both of which served Tufts's era as standard works of reference.

IT IS A simpler matter to trace the origins of the letter notation claimed by Gerrish in 1723 as "first contrived by the Reverend Mr. TUFTS." Strictly speaking, the claim is not accurate, as Sirvart Poladian [14] has correctly pointed out. Miss Poladian states, however, that "it seems highly probable that the innovation ascribed to Tufts may be traced to Playford," and cites the invention of a letter notation applied to psalm-tunes intended for an instrument attributed to Playford which was widely advertised in England from around 1699 through 1715. Aside from the evident inaccuracy of crediting this particular application of letter notation to John Playford, who died in 1686 or 1687, a dozen or so years before it was publicly announced, it appears extremely unlikely that this was a probable source from which Tufts got the idea for his "plain & easy" system. As a matter of fact, the letters FSLM representing solfège syllables were printed underneath the music notes appearing in the ninth (1698) edition of the *Bay Psalm Book*, and this was unquestionably well known to Tufts. It is certainly within the realm of possibility to think that he may have conceived the simple idea of substituting the letters for the notes unaided by any other suggestion. Furthermore, letter notation as a pedagogical device had been in use in Europe for nearly a century and a half before the "Playford" application was advertised. It first occurs in a 1560 French psalter compiled by Pierre Davantes in which the syllable names are placed at the side of the notes on the staff as an aid to the novice singer. Almost simultaneously—perhaps in the same year—Pierre Vallete's psalter, which utilized a very similar notation, appeared. Ten years later, letter notation began its English career. The publisher John Day in 1570 "caused a new print of Note to be made with letters to be ioyned to euerie Note" and brought out editions of the Sternhold and Hopkins psalter making use of this "new print" in 1570, 1575, 1576, 1581, 1585, 1594, 1595, 1605, and 1608. In 1580 a letter-note edition of Phillips van Marnix's *Het Boeck der Psalmen*

14. Sirvart Poladian, "Rev. John Tufts and Three-Part Psalmody in America," *Jour. of the Amer. Musicol. Soc.*, IV (1951), 276–77.

Davids was published in Antwerp, and in the following year Dathenus' celebrated psalter (first printed in London in 1566) appeared in a letter-note edition issued at Dordrecht.[15]

Thus, it is apparent that letter notation was a familiar teaching aid in sacred music circles long before Tufts revealed his "plain & easy" system to the world, but it must also be remembered that there is no proof that he was at all aware of its long and respectable history. He may well have invented it anew.

WHERE did Tufts find the 37 tunes common to all known editions of the *Introduction?* John Playford's *Whole Book of Psalms* (London, 1677; many later editions) is almost invariably cited as the major source of his borrowings,[16] but close analysis demonstrates that only eight tunes—CAMBRIDGE (42),[17] EXETER (332b), MANCHESTER (246b), NORWICH (204), 18 PSALM TUNE (36), SABBATH HYMN (200), VENI CREATOR (1), and WORCESTER (251)— are unquestionably taken verbatim from its pages. This is sufficient to prove that Tufts was familiar with Playford's popular psalter, but as 22 tunes in the *Introduction* are found not only in Playford but also in Thomas Walter's *Grounds and Rules of Musick Explained* of 1721 and 1723,[18] with which Tufts was

15. Early systems of letter notation are discussed in some detail in John Stainer, "On the Musical Introductions Found in Certain Metrical Psalters," *Proc. of the Mus. Assoc.*, XXVII (1900), 1–50. The writer is indebted to this excellent paper for much of his information on the subject. This whole field has been generally overlooked by later musicologists. Allen P. Britton has suggested that a study of the letter notation utilized in the early psalters may well cast considerable light on the problems of musica ficta, an idea well worth further investigation.

16. See, for example, John Tasker Howard, *Our American Music*, 3rd ed. (New York, 1946), p. 13, and Leonard Ellinwood, *The History of American Church Music* (New York, 1953), p. 21. Ellinwood's citation of Ravenscroft as another important Tufts source is without any ascertainable basis in fact.

17. The numbers in parentheses following the tune names are those assigned them in Maurice Frost, *English & Scottish Psalm & Hymn Tunes, c. 1543–1677* (London, 1953). Those interested in tracing the early history in print of any of these tunes will find this definitive work invaluable.

18. It will be recalled that the music in Walter's book was printed in three-part arrangements from the outset, whereas the earliest edition of Tufts to contain three-part arrangements was the fifth of 1726.

doubtless also familiar, the full extent of his indebtedness to Playford cannot be established beyond question. The evidence in favor of either Playford or Walter as Tufts's primary source is inconclusive. Thus, Tufts follows Walter in printing CANTERBURY (19b) in G rather than in Playford's A, but he follows Playford in printing YORK (205) in G rather than in Walter's F. COMMAND-MENT (178) is identical to Walter's version; LONDON (25) to Playford's. The tunes BELLA and S. JAMES's, which do not appear in Playford, are in both Tufts and Walter, and it is possible that Tufts borrowed them from his colleague. Tufts's versions of MARTYRS (209), GLOCESTER (239c), and PENITENTIAL HYMN (186) differ from both Playford's and Walter's. The remaining tunes—S. DAVID's (235), HACKNY or S. MARY's (333a), LONDON NEW (222), OXFORD (121), PETERBOROUGH (244), 81 PSALM TUNE (132), 85 PSALM TUNE (180), 100 PSALM TUNE (114), 113 PSALM TUNE (125), 119 PSALM TUNE (99), 148 PSALM TUNE (174), SOUTH-WEL (45), WESTMINSTER (362c), and WINDSOR (129)—are iden-tical in all three collections. Between Playford and Walter, 31 of Tufts's tunes can be accounted for, but there does not seem to be any way to determine which was the more important source. How-ever, taking into consideration the fact that Tufts reprinted no less than 23 of Walter's 24 tunes, I am inclined to believe that the *Grounds and Rules of Musick Explained* must have played a sig-nificant role in shaping the musical content of the fifth and subse-quent editions of the *Introduction*.

Six tunes remain to be traced. PORTSMOUTH, ISLE OF WIGHT, and NORTHAMPTON appear to have been copied from a collection of hymn- and psalm-tunes printed for use with Simon Browne's *Hymns and Spiritual Songs* (London, 1720) which bears the fol-lowing separate title page:

A / Sett / of / Tunes in 3 Parts / (Mostly New) / Fitted to the following / Hymns / But may be sung to any / others in the same measure / By Several Hands / Frances Hoffman sculp / Sold by E^m Mathews at the Bible in Pater Noster Row.

This little known compilation, fairly certainly the work of Simon

Browne, previously has never been considered a factor in the history of early American music.[19] STANDISH, a tune which achieved no great popularity in England, was first published in the anonymously compiled *Psalm-Singer's Necessary Companion* (London, 1700). Curiously enough, the medius part in all editions of the *Introduction* through the ninth is blank; whether this was merely an oversight on the part of the engraver or Tufts's actual intention cannot be determined. The missing part was added in the re-engraved 10th edition, but as neither the early nor the late American version conforms to any contemporary English version, it appears probable that the rather unskillful arrangement was Tufts's own. The 149 PSALM TUNE (well known today as HANOVER) made its debut in the sixth edition of *A Supplement to the New Version of Psalms by Dr. Brady and Mr. Tate* (London, 1708) in a two-part arrangement. Its publication in the *Introduction* is interesting because it demonstrates that Tufts was undoubtedly familiar with this book, which contains a concisely written exposition of the rudiments of music. However, no English three-part version antedating Tufts's has been discovered, and this arrangement too is most likely his.

The 100 PSALM TUNE NEW deserves some special mention. No English publication of this tune, either before or after the appearance of the *Introduction*, is known. The question must therefore be raised: is this an American composition? If the question is answered in the affirmative—and this writer is strongly inclined to believe that it should be, for stylistic as well as historical reasons—this not unattractive psalm-tune must be considered the

19. Browne's *Sett of Tunes* is also the source of another tune which was a great favorite in 18th-century America—MEAR. This is listed as one of the 80 most popular tunes in the Southern folk hymnody tradition in George Pullen Jackson, *White Spirituals in the Southern Uplands* (Chapel Hill, 1933), p. 144. The origins of MEAR (called MIDDLESEX by Browne) have long been a matter of speculation. Some have suggested that it is an American composition, but its presence in the Browne collection conclusively establishes its English provenance. It is curious indeed that many 19th-century Southern tune-books attribute MEAR to a mysterious "Brown," although the tune was invariably published throughout the 18th century without composer attribution.

earliest authentic specimen of music composed and published in British North America. In other words, 100 PSALM TUNE NEW may well be the first American composition. Did John Tufts write it? We cannot know for certain, but it does not seem unreasonable to assume so. Thus, surprisingly enough, the ministerial compiler

2. Leaf 10, Tufts's *Introduction*. Courtesy of the American Antiquarian Society.

of the *Introduction* may well have a valid claim to be considered the first American composer as well as the author of the first American music textbook! (See Illus. 2. and 3.)

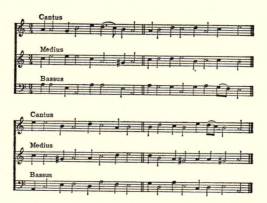

3. Transcription in modern notation, 100 PSALM TUNE NEW. Tufts's *Introduction*, 1726.

TUFTS's choice of tunes was remarkably astute. Just how good a judge of music he was is evident from the fact that no less than 18 of his 37 selections have remained in common use until contemporary times.[20] The musical influence exerted by the tunes in the *Introduction* upon later 18th-century American collections has not been fully appreciated; there is no tune-supplement published here before the Revolutionary War which does not bear, to some degree, the impress of Tufts's musical taste.

It is more difficult to assess the extent of Tufts's influence as a pedagogue because his ideas about teaching music reflect the gen-

20. To establish this point, the historical edition of *Hymns Ancient and Modern* (London, 1909) was utilized. Other modern hymnals would undoubtedly give similar results. Cf. the following numbers in *Hys. A. & M.*: 542 (S. DAVID'S), 388 (YORK), 103 (HACKNY, or S. MARY'S), 97 (WINDSOR), 344 (S. JAMES's), 409 (LONDON NEW), 462 (SOUTHWEL), 60 (BELLA), 83 (NORWICH), 125 (MARTYRS), 450 (EXETER), 336 [2] (COMMANDMENT), 217 (81 PSALM TUNE), 371 [1] (85 PSALM TUNE), 316 (100 PSALM TUNE), 335 (113 PSALM TUNE), 326 [1] (149 PSALM TUNE). The 18 PSALM TUNE is No. 586 in *The Church Hymnary* (London, 1930).

eral educational concepts of his age and not an individual system. While it is true that his "plain & easy" notation is known to have been utilized by at least one other compiler [21]—and probably by more than one—perhaps its greatest interest to us is as a harbinger of the extraordinary flood of notational innovations characteristic of the later American scene. As an instructional device, it must have proved useful and practical when applied to the simplest of music, but the mildly florid tunes in the *Introduction* itself (such as ISLE OF WIGHT and NORTHAMPTON) are sufficient to demonstrate its all too evident limitations. The shape-notes devised by William Little almost eight decades later were a more adequate solution to the problem.[22]

Table II

CONSPECTUS OF EDITIONS

Date	Ed.	No. Parts	No. Tunes	Collation	Locations
1721	1	1	20	unknown	none
1721	2	1	28	unknown	none
1723	3a	2	18	unknown	none
1723	3b	2	34	unknown	none
1723	4	1	36	unknown	none
1726	5	3	37	1 p.l., 9, [1] p.; 12 1.	MB, MWA, NjPT
1728	6	[3]	[37]	[1 p.l., 9, [1] p.; 12 1.]	none
1728	7	3	37	1 p.l., 9, [1] p.; 12 1.	CtY, MWA
1731	8	3	37	1 p.l., 9, [1] p.; 12 1.	MH, MHi, NhD
1736	9	3	37	1 p.l., 8, [2] p.; 12 1.	MSaE
1738	10	3	37	1 p.l., 7, [3] p.; 12 1.	CtY, DLC, MB, MH, NHi, NN, NhD
1744	11	3	37	1 p.l., 7, [3] p.; 12 1.	CtY, DLC, MWA, MeB, NHi, NjPT, RPJCB, ViU

21. Thomas Johnston brought out a collection of tunes in Tufts's notation in 1762, described in Britton and Lowens, "Unlocated Titles," 41. See also fn. 1 in Appendix A.

22. For further information about shape-notes, see Chapter 5.

Nevertheless, John Tufts should be remembered and honored for his sincere attempt to solve some of the basic riddles of elementary music education, riddles so difficult of solution that they are still very much with us today. His concern with music instruction for "Children, or People of the meanest Capacities" was without doubt unique in his time. Certainly, he should be considered the originator of music pedagogy in America, and if Lowell Mason is properly called "the father of singing among the children," then John Tufts should be known as the grandfather.

4

---- ➤➤ ⧏⧏ ----

ANDREW LAW
AND THE PIRATES

FOUR DAYS BEFORE Lord Cornwallis surrendered to Washington at Yorktown, the Connecticut Legislature received the following unusual petition:

To the honb^e. General Assembly of the State of Connecticut now sitting at Hartford the Memorial of Andrew Law of Cheshire in New Haven County humbly sheweth, that after much application to gain a competent Degree of Knowledge in the Art of singing to qualify himself for teaching of Psalmody; he in the year 1777 made a large Collection of the best & most approved Tunes, Copies of some of which he purchased of the original Compilers, others he took from Books of Psalmody printed in England which were never printed in America & after much pains & Expence he made such a Collection that he thot it might be useful to the public to engrave a new plate & strike of[f] a Number of Books—when he procured assistance to purchase the Engraving a plate, which together with making the Collection cost your Memorialist nearly £ 500.0—Lawful Money since which your Memorialist has struck of[f] a Number of Copies which have been very acceptable to the public, but by the rapid Depreciation of the Continental Currency the three last Years he has rec^d. very little Compensation for the great Sums he is in Advance & since the Medium of the Country has been established upon a more fix^d. & solid Basis, he has hopes of being reimbursed in part— but to his great Surprize he now finds that some person or persons unknown to your Memorialist who are acquainted with the Art of Engraving are making attempts to make a plate in Resemblance of that procured by your Memorialist & to strike of[f] books under the Name of your Memorialist thereby to defeat the Int[e]rest of your Memorialist in his plate & in the Sale of his books, your Memorialist conceives that the

works of Art ought to be protected in this Country & all proper enco[u]r-
agement given thereto as in other Countries.—He has no Doubt but that
your honors will give him all reasonable Enco[u]ragement which does
not interfere with the rights & priviliges of others—he prays your honors
to give him an exclusive patent for imprinting and vending the Tunes
following—for the Term of five years from this Date, he conceives such
an exclusive right, is not incompatible with the principles of a free State
& not invading the rights of any individual, your Memorialist will furnish
to the public as many Copies as they shall Demand & at as reasonable a
Rate as they can be afforded, and your Memorialist as in Duty bound
will pray dated at Hartford this 15th Day of October AD 1781—

Andrew Law [1]

In 1781, Americans were legally defenseless against the depre-
dations of literary pirates. So long as they were British subjects,
they were protected by the Copyright Law of 1710, the so-called
Statute of Anne, which provided authors with a 14-year exclusive
patent if the provisions of the statute were complied with, but
after independence, they could hardly look to an English law as
a bulwark against literary theft.

Although the Connecticut General Assembly had its hands full
with other matters at the moment, it was favorably impressed by
Law's appeal. The following bill in form was drawn up—apparently quite hastily—and approved by both houses before the end
of the month:

Upon the Memorial of Andrew Law of Cheshire in Newhaven County
shewing to this Assembly that he hath with great Trouble & Expence
prepared for the Press & procured to be engraved & imprinted a Collection of the best & most approved Tunes & Anthems for the Promotion
of Psalmody, containing the following Tunes, Viz. Aynhoc, Balldoc,
Blendon, Bunker Hill, Cheshire, Denbigh, Denmark, Easter, Elstow,
Falmouth, Farmington, Freedom, Greenwich, Judgment, Keen, Leeds,
Leicester, Loughborough, Middletown, Milford, Northhampton, Ode on
Spring, Providence, Psalm 21, 22, 25, 32, 46, 115, 122, 136, 148, Rugby,

---

1. A list of 42 tunes and 9 anthems, identical to that given in the bill, was
appended. The petition is preserved in the Connecticut Archives, Manuscript
(Colleges and Schools, 1661–1789), Series 1, Vol. II, Document 147, pp. a–b
(Hartford, Conn.). A facsimile reproduction appears in N. H. Allen, "Old
Time Music and Musicians," *Connecticut Quarterly*, III (1897), 66–67.

Salem, Southington, Springfield, Trumpet, Wallingford, Wallingbor-ough, Waybridge, Weathersfield, & Worcester & sundry Anthems begin-ning with the following words respectively viz. Arise, Shine Oh Zion &c. If the Lord himself &c. I said I will take heed &c. Oh Clap your hands &c. Oh Lord, our Governor &c. Oh Lord, God of Israel &c. O Sing unto the Lord &c. Praise the Lord O my Soul &c. The Beauty of Israel is slain &c. as by s^d. Collection printed & published under the s^d. Memorialist's Name may fully appear—Humbly praying this Assembly to grant the s^d. Memorialist an exclusive Patent for imprinting & vending the s^d. Tunes & Anthems for the Term of five years next ensuing, as p^r. Memorial on file—Resolved by this Assembly that the s^d. Memorialist have & [*sic*] free & full Liberty & License is hereby granted for the sole printing, publish-ing & vending the several Tunes & Anthems above-mentioned to the s^d. Memorialist, his Heirs, Executors, Administrators & Assigns for the Term of five Years next ensuing; strictly forbidding all the Subjects of this State, to reprint the same, & each & every of the s^d. Tunes or Anthems, in the like, or in any other Volume, or Form whatsoever; or to import, vend, buy, utter, or distribute any Copies of s^d. Tunes or Anthems or of any of them Reprinted beyond the limits of this State during the aforesaid Term of five Years, without the Consent or Approbation of the s^d. Andrew Law, his Heirs, Executors, Administrators & Assigns, under his or their Hands & Seals first had & obtained or they will answer the Contrary at their Peril—under the Penalty of £500 lawful money for each & every offense together with just Damages to be recovered against such offender by the s^d. Andrew Law his Heirs, Executors, Administrators & Assigns—the s^d. Law, his heirs, executors, administraters or assigns, printing & furnishing a sufficient number of Copies of the s^d. Tunes for the Use of the Inhabitants of this State at reasonable prices.[2]

Thus, as one of the first citizens of the five-year-old United States to be granted a legal copyright,[3] Andrew Law, a rising star in the American musical firmament, added an interesting footnote to our social history. At the same time, he won in spectacular fashion

2. *Ibid.*, Document 148, pp. a–b.

3. Oddly enough, Law was preceded in his quest for copyright protection by William Billings, who repeatedly petitioned the Massachusetts Legislature for exclusive rights to the fruit of his own creative work between 1770–78. The earliest instance of copyright on this side of the Atlantic took place in May, 1673, when the General Court of Massachusetts gave to John Usher the excessive right to print and sell the Massachusetts Bay Colony laws for seven years. See Evans No. 168.

the initial skirmish in what was to be his long and acrimonious personal war with a succession of real and imagined literary pirates. This war left in its wake a number of knotty bibliographical and musico-historical problems. This study will attempt solutions to some of them.

WHO was pirating what from Andrew Law in 1781? This intriguing question, rising naturally from Law's memorial, has never been satisfactorily answered. Quite obviously, the pirated work must have been one of the two collections of music compiled by Law which had been published before October, 1781. The earlier of the two was a beautifully engraved collection of 54 psalm-tunes entitled *A Select Number of Plain Tunes Adapted to Congregational Worship*. Designed to be bound in with the standard psalm-books as a tune-supplement, it could have appeared as early as 1775, but it probably did not come out before 1777.[4] The later collection—one of the most popular tune-books of the 18th century—was the celebrated *Select Harmony*, a 44-page edition of which was published in December, 1778.[5] Less than three

---

4. The caption title on all extant copies gives Law's name as "Andrew Law, A.B." As the degree was granted in September, 1775, earlier publication is very unlikely. Although 1767 and 1772 editions are listed in Evans (Nos. 10662 and 12427), the dates are those of the psalm-books with which the tune-supplement happened to be bound rather than those of the *Select Number* itself. A 1794 edition (Evans No. 27208) is probably another ghost.

Law himself gives 1777 as the year in which he first "made a large Collection of the best & most approved tunes;" it is therefore doubtful that the *Select Numbers* was published before that date.

5. Two copies of this hitherto overlooked edition are known: one at the Library of Congress and the other at the Connecticut Historical Society at Hartford. An advertisement on the title page, dated Cheshire, December 10, 1778, reads: "The times being such, that it is impossible to get plates cut for all the musick at first proposed, there will be an addition made as soon as they can be done; and what is now printed with types, with a further illustration of some things, will then be printed on paper of the same size and quality of that on which the music is now printed." The title page and prefatory matter, printed from type, are on a sizably smaller page than the 44 pages of engraved music which follow. The music is identical with that of the first 44 pages of the 100-page edition which was published a few months later. Curiously enough, the music in the Connecticut Historical Society's copy of the 1778 edition is printed on a distinctive, greenish-tinted paper; the first 44 pages of

months later, Law added 56 more pages of music, new introductory matter, and an elaborate engraved title page from the skilled burette of Joel Allen, who was also responsible for the engraving of the *Select Number*. In the light of Law's astonishment that someone should have had the temerity to make "a plate in Resemblance of that procured by your Memorialist," it is amusing to note that Joel Allen's elaborate design for the title page of this 1779 edition of the *Select Harmony* turns out to be an exact copy of that drawn by Henry Dawkins for James Lyon's famous *Urania* (Philadelphia, 1761). (See Illus. 4.)

Very few collections of music were published between September, 1775 and October, 1781, the period in which the piracy must have occurred. The war with England, the depreciating currency, the difficulty of obtaining paper, and the scarcity of qualified engravers made such ventures expensive and financially hazardous. Hence, it is not at all surprising that besides Law's two collections, only five others are known to have been issued. Four of the five can be absolved of any borrowings from Law's collections almost immediately: William Billings's *Singing Master's Assistant* (Boston, 1778; other editions, 1779, 1780, 1781) and *The Psalm Singer's Amusement* (Boston, 1781) contain only his own music; the Billings tune supplement *Music in Miniature* (Boston, 1779) contains a few tunes by others but is essentially another all-Billings compilation; Daniel Bayley's *Essex Harmony* (Newburyport, 1780) is merely a reprint of earlier editions of the same work issued in 1770, 1771, and 1772. The finger of suspicion points directly to the fifth work, the *New Collection of Psalm Tunes Adapted to Congregational Worship* (n.p., n.d.) by an unknown compiler, which probably dates from 1781. (See Illus. 5.)

If the *New Collection* was in fact the piracy which impelled Law to seek the protection of the Connecticut General Assembly,

---

a 100-page edition also owned by the Society is printed on this unusual paper too, with the additional 56 pages on normal white paper. The printer of the 1778 edition was undoubtedly William Law, Andrew's brother and Cheshire's only printer.

4. Title page, Law's *Select Harmony* (1779) engraved by Joel Allen; Lyon's *Urania* (1761) engraved by Henry Dawkins. Courtesy of the Library of Congress.

the work pirated must have been the *Select Number*. There are a number of striking resemblances between the two. Both are tune-supplements containing 16 pages of music. Both lack title page and imprint. There is some similarity in the engraving. The titles of both end with the identical phrase, "adapted to congregational worship." And—most convincing of all—23 of the 51 tunes in the *New Collection* are identical to those Law chose for the *Select Number*.

5. Page 1 of Andrew Law's first published collection of tunes. Courtesy of the Library of Congress; Page 1 of the anonymously compiled *New Collection*. Courtesy of the Clements Library, University of Michigan.

Who was responsible for bringing out the *New Collection*? Although the evidence favoring such an attribution is certainly not conclusive, there is some reason to believe that Law's imitator was John Norman, then of Boston, one of the few expert music engravers active at the time. Several authenticated examples of his work are known, among them the Billings *Psalm-Singer's Amusement* dating from 1781. Comparison between that work and the *New Collection* reveals certain resemblances in engraving technique which suggest the same artisan. Furthermore, a relationship between Norman and the *New Collection* can be inferred from the only contemporary reference to the tune-supplement I have been able to track down. At the end of an advertisement by Norman in the August, 1784 *Gentlemen and Ladies Town and Country Magazine* announcing the publication of the *Massachusetts Harmony* (another anonymous collection in which the engraving suggests that of the *New Collection*), "a New Collection of Psalm Tunes, Suitable to bind up with Psalm Books" is offered for sale. It is of course true that the phrase "New Collection of Psalm Tunes" hardly constitutes a distinctive title. Norman may have been referring to a newly issued tune-supplement rather than to the one here under discussion, but no such supplement is known and it does not seem reasonable to assume that his use of the exact wording of the *New Collection's* title was purely coincidental.

Although the physical resemblance between the *New Collection* and the *Select Number* cannot be denied, a closer look at the shared tunes reveals that this was not quite so plain a case of thievery as it appears to be at first glance. Norman may have imitated Law, but he did not have to go to the *Select Number* for more than two of the 23 tunes found in both tune-supplements. BLENDON was the only one of the 23 to which Law claimed an exclusive right. He seems to have published IRISH for the first time on this side of the Atlantic, and it could perhaps be considered his property for that reason. But the remaining 21 were all familiar old favorites which had appeared in print (some many times) long before Law's *Select Number* saw the light of day. They were in the public domain, so to speak. Norman was, of course, familiar with the *Select Number*—the presence of BLENDON and IRISH in the *New Collection* proves this beyond doubt —but the borrowing of two tunes from a total of 54 cannot be considered excessive depredation, in view of the common practices of the time.

It is difficult to escape the conclusion that Law was considerably overstating the case in his plea to the General Assembly. This tendency to dramatize may perhaps explain why he not only accused the "person or persons unknown to your Memorialist who are acquainted with the Art of Engraving" of making "a plate in Resemblance of that procured by your Memorialist" but also of striking off "books under the Name of your Memorialist." Law's name appears nowhere in any extant copy of the *New Collection*. If Law's assertion is not to be written off as fancy, there must have been another edition of the *New Collection* which has since disappeared, or else there was a completely different piracy issued between 1775 and 1781 which is now unknown. The possibility that one or the other was in existence cannot be ruled out entirely, but it certainly does not seem very likely. Unpalatable as such an assumption is, it is easier to believe that Law was exaggerating.

Although the General Assembly was clearly laboring under the impression that Law intended to bring out, or had already brought out, a collection containing the 51 copyrighted tunes and anthems, this does not seem to have been his intention, and despite a reported 1781 "Collection of the Best and Most Approved Tunes and Anthems for the Promotion of Psalmody," it is doubtful that such a tune-book ever appeared.[6] By the time of

6. See Evans No. 17201; also Nos. 16317 and 17572, entries for identical titles for the years 1779 and 1782. These would appear to be ghosts manufactured by Evans. A *Collection of the Best* lacking title page, supposedly located in the New York Public Library, is merely an incomplete copy of the 1779 *Select Harmony* incorrectly cataloged by someone unaware of the bibliographical complexities of Law's publications. For a discussion of this point,

the 1781 petition, Law had already published 43 of them: 10 in the *Select Number*, 13 in the 1778 *Select Harmony*, and 20 in the 1779 *Select Harmony*. If any tune-book at all can be said to have resulted from the granting of the patent, it was probably the 1782 *Select Harmony*, which contained 41 of the 51 tunes and anthems, including the eight previously unpublished. With the appearance of this edition of the *Select Harmony*, all of the licensed items could be found in one or another of Law's compilations, and under the terms of the Act, all were protected for the stipulated five years, provided that Law printed "a sufficient number of Copies of the s^d. Tunes for the Use of the Inhabitants of this State at reasonable prices." There was no provision in the Act that they must be gathered together in a single collection, even though the Legislature obviously thought that Law had done, or was about to do, this.

Was the patent effective? Within the state of Connecticut, it would seem so—or else Law's tunes were singularly unpopular there. I have been able to locate no other Connecticut printings of any of the 51 before 1786. Outside Connecticut the patent was somewhat less effective, as the second battle in Law's war against predators clearly demonstrates.

Two years and two months after the approval of the patent, Law revealed that the *Select Harmony* had also been pirated. Early in December, 1783, the first edition of a new tune-book, the *Rudiments of Music*, came from the presses of his brother William Law in Cheshire with the following statement on the verso of the title page:

In a former publication entitled Select Harmony, I endeavored to render every part of the scale of music as concise and plain as possible; but, by long experience I am convinced that emendations may be added, greatly to the benefit of learners.

I now offer the public this musical Treatis[e], and have the pleasure

see the author's "Copyright and Andrew Law," *Papers of the Bibliographical Soc. of America*, LIII (1959), 158–59.

SELECT HARMONY,

CONTAINING IN A PLAIN AND CONCISE MANNER, THE

R U L E S of *S I N G I N G*

CHIEFLY BY

ANDREW LAW, A. B.

TO WHICH ARE ADDED

A NUMBER OF PSALM TUNES, HYMNS AND ANTHEMS, FROM THE BEST AUTHORS,

WITH SOME NEVER BEFORE PUBLISHED.

Printed and Sold by DANIEL BAYLEY, at his houf in NEWBURY-PORT, where may be had a Collection of Tunes for Pſalm-Books——Alſo a Collection of Anthems and Hymn Tunes, Quarto.

6. Title page, Daniel Bayley's *Select Harmony* (1784). Courtesy of the American Antiquarian Society.

to think that my labours in this production will be secured to me by the laws of my country, and that it will not be pirated as the other was, by those who look, not at the public good, but at their own emolument.

The predator to whom Law was here referring was almost certainly Daniel Bayley of Newburyport.

In Bayley's piracy, Law's name *was* prominently featured and an effort to capitalize on his growing reputation as a singing-master appears to have been made. (See Illus. 6.) The title page reads as follows:

Select Harmony, containing in a plain and concise manner, the rules of singing chiefly by Andrew Law, A.B. To which are added a number of psalm tunes, hymns and anthems, from the best authors. With some never before published. Printed and Sold by Daniel Bayley, at his house in Newbury-port, where may be had a Collection of Tunes for Psalm-Books—Also a Collection of Anthems and Hymns Tunes, Quarto.[7]

There is, however, a rather disconcerting fly in this ointment—

7. Excepting a fragment in the library of the Moravian Music Foundation at Winston-Salem, the American Antiquarian Society in Worcester, Mass. holds the only known copy of this most interesting tune-book.

the preface to this edition of Bayley's *Select Harmony* happens to be dated February 23, 1784, almost three months after the *Rudiments* was published! It is obvious that unless Law happened to be clairvoyant, he could not possibly have been referring to this particular piracy in December of 1783. Nevertheless, there is good reason to believe that he was attacking the same book, but in an earlier edition.

Evidence of the existence of two editions can be found in a notice inserted by Bayley in the November 24, 1784, Newburyport, Mass. *Essex Journal:*

> Daniel Bayley informs the public that he is now printing, and has ready for sale at his house, near the church in Newbury-port, a singing book, entitled Select Harmony, containing in a plain and concise manner, the rules of singing, chiefly from Andrew Law, to which are added, a large number of psalm-tunes, hymns and anthems, from the best authors, with some never before published, containing one hundred eighty-eight pages of copper plate, and are well bound in leather, which he is now selling at seven shillings.
>
> N.B. *Some few errors which were in a former edition, are now corrected,* also his book of anthems and hymn tunes in large quarto.

The actual content of what Bayley calls the "former edition" in the postscript can be determined from a comparison of the discrepancies between the index of the 1784 edition and what is actually found in the tune-book. Five items are listed in this index which do not appear. Instead of the tunes ELENBORO, NEWCASTLE, and NORFOLK (pp. 35–40), there is the anthem I SAID I WILL TAKE HEED (pp. 33–40);[8] instead of the anthem ARISE, SHINE, O ZION (pp. 25–32), there are the tunes LANESBOROUGH, CHESTER, PLYMOUTH, MECHIAS, and SAPPHICK ODE; instead of the anthem THEY THAT PUT THEIR TRUST IN THE LORD (p. 3), there is the tune PSALM 115. These differences can be explained only if it is assumed that Bayley used the index of the earlier edition as copy for the

---

8. This anthem must have also appeared in the postulated earlier edition, but there it occupied only two or three pages (pp. 33–34 or 33–35). In the 1784 edition, it was extended to eight pages, displacing the three tunes in the process.

index of the later edition without correcting it to take into account the changes he had made on page 3 and pages 25–40. This was apparently a common procedure of the time which may be traced in other multi-editioned works, including some of the earlier ones by Bayley himself.

In view of Law's reference to a *Select Harmony* piracy in the 1783 *Rudiments*, the earlier Bayley edition can be tentatively dated 1783. This 1783 Bayley *Select Harmony*, containing the tunes and anthems listed in the index of the 1784 edition, was doubtless the tune-book Law had in mind—that is, unless one assumes yet another presently unknown piracy of the *Select Harmony* preceding the 1784 Bayley, something the writer hardly considers very likely.

This time, the piracy was publicly exposed and the pirate himself was named in the press. The following appeared in the *Essex Journal* on November 17, 1784:

> Andrew Law informs the public, that a book, entitled 'Select Harmony, chiefly by Andrew Law,' which is printed by Daniel Bayley of Newburyport is *not* chiefly, nor *any part* of it by him. The title is absolutely false. There are in that book ten or fifteen capital errors in a single page, and whoever purchases that book for Law's collection, will find it a very great imposition.

Bayley did not allow this attack on his integrity to pass unchallenged, and two weeks later, on December 1, 1784, he too took space in the *Essex Journal*, naively insisting that, regardless of what Law might say, his tune-book *was* "chiefly by Andrew Law:"

> I would inform the publick, in answer to Mr. A. Law's charge, that the rules for singing, laid down in my book, as to the scales, characters, and examples are very nearly the same with Mr. Law, excepting some few emendations—as to the music, out of 65 pieces in Mr. Law's book, I have 45 of them in mine, with the addition of 100 psalm and hymn tunes and anthems. As to the errors, let him who is without cast the first stone.

Bayley's fortuitous enumeration of "65 pieces in Mr. Law's book" enables us neatly to establish the 1779 *Select Harmony* as the work pirated—the 1782 edition contained only 59. As Bayley correctly states, there are 145 items in his 1784 *Select Harmony* (the 1783 edition contained 144), but his counting was not quite so accurate in regard to the number of Law's pieces appearing in his collection. He claimed a few too many—there were only 43 shared items in the 1784 piracy (42 in the 1783). Exactly half of these were among those to which Law had been given a copyright by the Connecticut General Assembly.

Although Bayley did pretty thoroughly raid Law's preserves, one should beware of the automatic assumption that he took all of the shared tunes from Law. In this case, the fallacy of such a view can be demonstrated conclusively. It so happens that no less than 16 of the shared tunes were reprinted by Bayley from the identical plates he had used in a considerably earlier tune-book, John Stickney's *Gentleman and Lady's Musical Companion* (Newburyport, 1774).[9] Plainly, Bayley's publication of the 16 anticipated Law's by some four or five years. Furthermore, three of Law's copyrighted anthems are among the pieces Bayley reprinted from the Stickney plates. Here the shoe would appear to be on the other foot—although Bayley cannot be accused of having stolen them from Law, Law can be accused of having stolen them from Bayley! To further complicate matters, Bayley, who might well be suspected of having appropriated Stickney's musical properties for his edition of the *Select Harmony*, was probably the legal owner of the copper plates, which had been engraved for him by John W. Gilman. A pretty problem in ethics, indeed!

It is, as a matter of fact, very likely that Law used Bayley's publications as sources for his own tune-books. It would have been strange if he hadn't. Bayley's were certainly among the best-

9. Bayley's *Select Harmony* is, in effect, merely a drastically revised edition of the Stickney work. No less than 122 of its 184 pages (pp. 1–2, 5–80, 89–128, 178–79, 182–83) are printed from the Stickney plates with altered pagination, signature letters, and a few minor corrections. Law's materials occupy 31 pages (pp. 3–4, 82, 129, 132, 141, 153–73, 176–77, 180–81). The remaining 31 pages contain other tunes and anthems apparently selected by Bayley, among them important first publications of music by James Lyon (who may have been associated with him in some way), Timothy Swan, and Jacob Kimball.

known music imprints issued on this side of the Atlantic at that time, and it is very difficult to believe that Law, one of the most literate of the American singing-masters, was not perfectly familiar with the most popular tune-books of his day. Of course, Bayley used Law's *Select Harmony* in compiling his own tune-book of the same name. He makes no bones about it, and his contemporaries were not shocked. Marc Pincherle, discussing France in the 17th and 18th century, noted that plagiarism troubled very few people at that time, quoting a note from the Paris *Avant-Coureur* of June 12, 1769 to the effect that "De Machi's violin duets, previously announced, will not be sold under that name, because they happen to be the same as those by Domenico Wateski, which have appeared before." [10] The situation was doubtless very much the same in America, and what strikes us today as reprehensible was then quite customary. That this was the fact of the matter can be seen by Bayley's amusingly naive public defense of his actions. It is significant that he was concerned only with the charge of misrepresentation and not with that of piracy. Odd as it may seem, it was Law's attitude rather than Bayley's act that was unusual.

It was not only such little men as Daniel Bayley of Newburyport who were guilty of the sort of "borrowing" that Andrew Law found so annoying. The big men, the major publishers, were apparently just as rapacious. In a letter dated September 13, 1792, addressed to the Rev. Jedidiah Morse, author of the celebrated *American Geography*, Law unmasked (in passing) yet another pirate:

Revd. and Dear Sir
I have never lit of [i.e., on] your Geography where I could have an opportunity of perusing it, [so] that I am not yet able to inform you whether it be correct in those parts where I have been acquainted. I think some of them would sell in Virginia, if they could get them; were

10. "On the Rights of the Interpreter in the Performance of 17th- and 18th-Century Music," *Musical Quarterly*, XLIV (1958), 149.

the books printed by some other person than Mr. Thomas, we might perhaps exchange some of ours for them; but I wish no connection with him, neither do I wish to promote the sale of books printed by him, so long as he is pillaging my books. . . .[11]

The "Mr. Thomas" mentioned with such evident distaste was none other than the illustrious Worcester printer Isaiah Thomas, in later years founder of the American Antiquarian Society and author of a memorable history of printing in the United States. In 1792, however, he was merely a successful businessman, the senior member of the Boston firm of Thomas & Andrews, rapidly growing book publishers.

What tune-book or tune-books did Law have in mind when he castigated Thomas as a "pillager" of his work? Thomas began publishing tune-books in 1786 with the extremely popular *Worcester Collection of Sacred Harmony*. By the date of Law's letter to Morse, he had added at least three more collections of music to his list, Abraham Wood's *Divine Songs* (Boston, 1789), Samuel Holyoke's *Harmonia Americana* (Boston, 1791), and Oliver Holden's *American Harmony* (Boston, 1792).[12] A quick check of the contents immediately clears the Wood, Holyoke, and Holden collections from suspicion—each contains (with insignificant exceptions) only music by its own compiler. The culpable work was unquestionably the eclectic *Worcester Collection* (see Illus. 7), which reached its fourth edition in December, 1792. Analysis of the 1786 (first) edition turns up the interesting fact that of its 143 items, no less than 54 had been previously published in one or another of Law's tune-books.

Over a period of some five years, Thomas took from Law 18 tunes and anthems covered by the Connecticut legislation of 1781. The 1786 edition contained 14 of Law's items; in the 1788 (second) edition, eight of these were dropped and two others were

---

11. Quoted through the courtesy of the New-York Historical Society, New York City, owners of the original.

12. Another tune-book, John Hubbard's *Harmonia Selecta*, was advertised as forthcoming in 1788 but was probably never issued. See Evans No. 21893.

LAUS DEO!

THE *WORCESTER*
COLLECTION of Sacred Harmony.
In THREE PARTS.
CONTAINING,

I. An INTRODUCTION to the GROUNDS of MUSICK: Or, RULES for LEARNERS.
II. A large Number of celebrated PSALM and HYMN TUNES, from the most approved ancient and modern Authors; together with several New ones, never before published: The whole suited to all Metres, usually sung in Churches.
III. Select ANTHEMS, FUGHES, and Favourites Pieces of MUSICK, with an Additional Number of Psalm and Hymn Tunes.

The WHOLE compiled
For the Use of SCHOOLS, and SINGING SOCIETIES.
And RECOMMENDED by many approved Teachers of Psalmody.

PRAISE ye the LORD: For it is good to SING Praises unto our GOD.   PSALM CXIVII.

Printed, Typographically, at *WORCESTER*, MASSACHUSETTS,
By ISAIAH THOMAS,
And Sold at his BOOK-STORE. Sold also by the BOOKSELLERS in Town and Country.   MDCCLXXXVI.

7. The first edition of Isaiah Thomas's *Worcester Collection* (1786). Courtesy of the American Antiquarian Society.

added; in the 1791 (third) edition, one was dropped, two more new ones were added, and two of the tunes eliminated in the 1788 edition were restored.[13]

In 1783, Law had obtained state copyrights in Massachusetts for two of his compilations, the *Collection of Hymn Tunes* and the first edition of the *Rudiments of Music*, and it is noteworthy that Thomas was apparently quite careful to avoid taking material from either of these works. Not a single one of the 18 copyrighted tunes he reprinted was to be found in either of the collections protected in Massachusetts. On the other hand, Thomas did make free with the *second edition* of the *Rudiments*, which was not copyrighted in Massachusetts, taking over no less than 24 of its 41 tunes. The "borrowing" is especially clear in the 1788 edition of the *Worcester Collection*, but all three editions contain Law's tunes. It is significant that all eight of the additional tunes bor-

13. The items dropped from the 1st edition had all appeared in Part III of the *Worcester Collection*, a separate section containing anthems and longer pieces. This Part III was not included in the 2nd and 3rd eds.—hence the falling off in the number of borrowings.

rowed from the second edition of the *Rudiments* for the 1788 *Worcester Collection* were probably published by Law for the first time anywhere, or at least in the United States.

It would certainly seem that Law had ample justification for feeling annoyed with Isaiah Thomas. His bitterness about Thomas's lack of scruples was echoed less than a year later, curiously enough, by the New Haven singing-master Daniel Read in a letter dated June 10, 1793, to the Massachusetts composer-compiler Jacob French:

Sir

Your favour of the 22d April I did not receive until the 7th inst. It is not only ungenerous but unjust to publish the works of any author without his consent. Irritateted [*sic*] beyond measure at the unprovoked Robbery committed upon the American Singing Book by the Editor of the Worcester Collection and having no redress but by retaliation there being then no law in existance to prevent such abuses I availed myself of that opportunity to publish some peices [*sic*] from the Worcester Collection to which I had no right. But since the Statute of the United States made for the purpose of securing to Authors the Copyright of their work, I do not mean to give any person cause to be offended in that way, on the other hand I think it my duty to prosecute any person who prints my music without my consent, as much as if he were a common Theif [*sic*] or Housebreaker. . . . I wish for an harmonious agreement with all professors of music and particularly with Authors and Publishers, and should be peculiarly happy to make acquaintance with you. There has an Anthem entituled [*sic*] *The farewell by French* been published here by one Asa[h]el Benham of Wallingford. I give you this information because I think it my duty to do as I would be done by. . . .[14]

As a comparison between Read's *American Singing Book* of 1785 and the *Worcester Collection* makes clear, Read had even more reason to be outraged than did Law. There was no possible ques-

14. Quoted by permission of the New Haven Colony Historical Society from Daniel Read's letter-book, in the Society's collections. For a discussion of this important but neglected source of information about early American music, see Chapter 8.

The tunes Read admits having lifted from the *Worcester Collection* may be found in his *American Musical Magazine* (New Haven, 1786–87). Here they are labelled—quite honestly—"taken from Thomas"!

tion of the validity of his claim to the tunes Thomas took from him—he had composed them all himself.

The *Worcester Collection*, thanks in part to Thomas's free-wheeling approach towards the property of others, contained the most popular tunes of the day. Its great success was considerably aided by additional features, however: it was bigger and cheaper than its rivals. Thomas was able to print more and charge less because his music was printed from type, thanks to a music font he had imported from England,[15] while his competitors continued to use the laboriously engraved, expensive copper plates from which music had been printed here for more than half a century. Thomas's enterprise paid off handsomely—although typographically printed music was ugly, difficult to read, and full of misprints, it was comparatively inexpensive. Thanks to the process, Thomas captured a good share of the tune-book market and revolutionized the trade.

In the light of the compiler's somewhat flexible ethics, the following extract from the preface of the second edition of the *Worcester Collection*, dated August, 1788, is not without its amusing side:

> It gave great pleasure to the Editor of the Worcester Collection of Sacred Harmony, that the first Edition of it was so generally approved. Owing to the small number of which that Edition consisted, it was soon out of print, and many persons who were desirous of purchasing could not obtain copies. Some persons in Boston taking advantage of the scarcity, printed a spurious edition from copperplates, and palmed it on the undiscerning for the real Worcester Collection of Sacred Harmony.

Thus the pirate shouts piracy.

The Boston imitation of the *Worcester Collection*, not hitherto identified, bears the following title page:

15. As Allen P. Britton has pointed out in his unpubl. diss. (University of Michigan, 1949) "Theoretical Introductions in American Tune-Books to 1800" (University Microfilms, No. 1505), pp. 667–71, Charles Evans was mistaken in his assertion that the *Worcester Collection* was "the first music book printed typographically in America" (Evans No. 19752). Britton lists five earlier music books printed from type.

Sacred Harmony or A Collection of Psalm Tunes, Ancient and Modern. Containing A Great Variety of the most approved Plain & Simple Airs, taken from the Massachusetts Harmony, Worcester Collection, Laws &c. To which is Added, several new Tunes, never before Published, Together with An Introduction to the Art of Singing, By R. Harrison, London. Boston Printed & Sold by C. Cambridge near the Boston Stone.[16]

It is characteristic of this publication, which as the title page states, owed its content to Law as well as to Thomas, that the highly ornamental border within which the legend is enclosed was copied in reverse from that in Ralph Harrison's *Sacred Harmony* (London, 1784). (See Illus. 8.)

On July 20, 1805, during the course of a visit to Dartmouth College, Law took the time to write the following letter to the "Messrs. G. and R. Webster, Booksellers," of Albany, New York:

Gentlemen,

Mr. John West of Boston was here yesterday and informed me, that he understood (tho' he could not be certain) that you had purchased a Copy Right of a Music book which is printed with different characters, similar to one for which I have a patent from Congress. I showed him the patent, and he advized me to write to you on the subject.

I wish you to write and inform me, if you have such Copy Right, and of whom you purchased it.

I had the plan fit for publication nineteen years ago, and showed it to a number of Gentlemen at that time among whom were Noah Webster, Esqr. of New Haven and Dr. Mason W. Cogswell of Hartford, who are ready to testify to the same. There was no type Foundery in the Country

---

16. The date of this rare tune-book, of which only three copies are known, has been a matter of some dispute. It was, however, published no later than 1788—a note in a contemporary hand on the Brown University copy states that the owner purchased it in that year.

The printer C. Cambridge was not, by the way, the first to borrow the preface to Harrison's *Sacred Harmony*. Portions of it may be found in Adgate's *Select Psalms and Hymns* (Philadelphia, 1787). Nor was he the last—it was also found in John Poor's *Collection of Psalms and Hymns* (Philadelphia, 1794) and in all editions of the celebrated *Easy Instructor* discussed in Chapter 6.

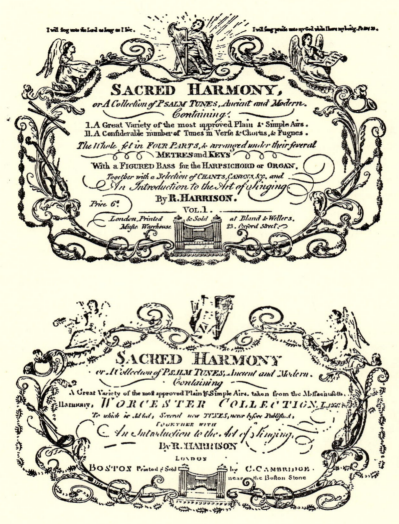

8. *Sacred Harmony* (1788?), an early piracy of both Law's *Select Harmony*; Thomas's *Worcester Collection*, shown with the title page of Ralph Harrison's *Sacred Harmony* (1784), the English tune-book from which the border was copied in reverse. Courtesy of the American Antiquarian Society and the Library of Congress.

at that time, and as soon as I could procure a type I published the plan.
Let me hear from you and you will oblige yours Respectfully
Andrew Law [17]

The "Messrs. G. and R. Webster, Booksellers" [18] were undoubtedly Charles R. and George Webster, twin brothers, who had obtained the copyright to a tune-book called *The Easy Instructor,
or A New Method of Teaching Sacred Harmony,* probably by
purchase from one of its authors, William Little. Whether the
Websters replied to Law's letter or not is not known. It certainly,
however, had no effect in stopping them from bringing out *The
Easy Instructor.* In their hands, this tune-book became one of the
most lucrative American musical properties of the early 19th
century.[19]

The patent referred to by Law was obtained on May 12, 1802,
for a new plan of printing music.[20] Law's "new plan" did not,
however, make its appearance in book form until more than a
year and a half later. On December 10, 1803, he entered for copyright in the District of Massachusetts the fourth edition of the
Art of Singing, "printed upon a new plan," and on December 24,
1803, he inserted the following notice in the Boston *Columbian
Centinel:*

Music. A New Plan of Printing Music, and a new Method of teaching
the Art of Singing, are exhibited in a Book, just Published, by Andrew
Law, and for Sale by him, and at the Book-store of John West, No. 75,
Cornhill. Price 75 cents single, and 7 dollars and 50 cents per dozen.

17. This most significant letter was copied by Law on the blank verso of a
broadside in which he announces the opening of a singing-school, apparently
in Salem, Mass.; the original has disappeared. The broadside is in the collections of the American Antiquarian Society—the letter is quoted by permission.
18. Curiously enough, the initials Law uses in addressing the Webster
brothers happen to be those of the New York firm G. and R. Waite, who appear to have been the last to publish *The Easy Instructor* before the copyright
was acquired by the Websters.
19. See Chapter 6.
20. Unfortunately, the original patent application (which ordinarily would
have been preserved) was destroyed in one of the many fires which ravaged
the U. S. Patent Office early in its career, and only a bare notice of the patent
grant is extant.

This book contains a Plan and Method which are different from any that have yet appeared. Four kinds of characters are used which denote the four singing syllables; and the learner will immediately learn the notes with great facility, and will read them with equal ease in every part, and in all the different changes of the keys. The method of teaching by these characters is explained in such a manner that will give a full view of the plan; and a variety of such practical lessons added as will soon enable even children to read music as easily as they read other books.

Upon this plan and method the knowledge of the Art will be easily obtained; music will be read in a short time and with great facility; and the performance of it will be ready and familiar. The natural consequence of this will be, that the cultivation of the art will become more general; and the practice of it will be rendered more pleasing and entertaining.

This advertisement describes only Part I of the *Art of Singing*, the *Musical Primer*—the remaining two parts had not yet been published. Part III did not come out until about a year later— the *Musical Magazine No. 1*, fourth edition, was not copyrighted until November 5, 1804—while Part II, the last to be issued, was announced as "in the Press" on September 10, 1805, in the Windsor, Vt. *Post-Boy.*

What are the facts behind Law's letter? Had he once again been victimized by an unscrupulous pirate? The answers to these questions are tied to the answer to another, more significant one: who was the inventor of shape-notes, Andrew Law or William Little? This was the real import of this skirmish with the enemy.

On June 15, 1798, the following title was registered for copyright in the Southern District of Pennsylvania:

The *Easy Instructor*, or a New Method of teaching *Sacred Harmony*, containing the Rudiments of *Music* on an improved Plan, wherein the Naming and Timing the notes, are familiarized to the weakest capacity. [21]

Although no printed book appears to have been available at that time, a manuscript almost certainly was. This manuscript had been

---

21. Quoted from the original printed slip which was deposited for copyright, now in the Music Division of the Library of Congress.

submitted to the Uranian Society of Philadelphia for its opinion, and exactly two months to the day after the title was registered for copyright, a committee appointed to examine the *Easy Instructor* brought in an enthusiastic recommendation.

Until just a few years ago, it had been believed that no actual edition of the *Easy Instructor* was published until November, 1802. This was almost six months after Law had obtained his "new plan" patent, and despite the registration of the *Easy Instructor* title and the recommendation by the Uranian Society's committee in 1798, it could appear that Law's patent might give him some claim to priority, at least in a legal sense. It is now established, however, that the *Easy Instructor* was in existence, in printed form, as early as August, 1801, nearly a year before the granting of Law's patent. The following notice was published in the August 22, 1801, *Philadelphia Repository and Weekly Register:*

PSALMODY

A work has just made its appearance in this city, entitled, *"The Easy Instructor: or, a New Method of Teaching Sacred Harmony. By William Little and William Smith."* This work contains a pretty large collection of Psalm Tunes and Anthems, a considerable number of which are original; but it chiefly claims attention on account of a new method laid down for facilitating the learner in acquiring the knowledge of the notes as designated by the four singing syllables, which is done by diversifying the shapes of the notes; as for example, the shape of *Fa* is a triangle, *Mi* a diamond, *La* an oblong square, and *Sol* the usual form. It is evident that their different characters, indicating at sight the names of the notes, will greatly aid the student of Sacred Harmony. A Certificate from a committee of the Uranian Society accompanies the work, in which they observe, that it "contains a well-digested system of principles and rules, and a judicious collection of tunes;" and that, "were it possible to acquire the sounds of the eight notes but by *imitation,* they verily believe they might be obtained by the help of this book, even without an instructor." The copyright is secured. [22]

That an actual printed book was in fact in existence is corrobo-

22. I am grateful to Dr. Donald W. Krummel of the Newberry Library for calling this notice to my attention.

rated by the records of the Secretary of State, where the following entry is found:

Decr. 22 1801. Received a copy of a work entitled "The easy instructor or a new method of teaching Sacred Harmony &c. &c. By William Little & William Smith in pursuance of an Act of Congress, entitled "An Act for the encouragement of learning &c. &c. &c.

It is thus plain that there can be no question about the priority of Little's legal claim to the shape-note idea. The title of his *Easy Instructor* was registered in 1798; the book itself was published around August, 1801; and a printed copy was deposited with the Secretary of State in December of the same year. The copyright was a perfectly valid one which anticipated Law's May, 1802 patent by almost six months.

But what about Law's claim that he "had the plan fit for publication nineteen years ago," that is, in 1786? In 1809, in the prefatory remarks to his *Art of Playing the Organ and Piano Forte or Characters Adapted to Instruments* (Philadelphia, n.d.), Law expanded somewhat on the statements made in the letter to the Websters:

The system which I have brought forward to public view, has not been the creature of accident, nor the offspring of a day. It has been a subject of reflection from the time I was at school learning the first rudiments of the art, and before I had ever seen a printed music book of any kind. I then had an idea of representing musical sounds by characters without lines, but did not form any regular system for the purpose till after I became a teacher of the art. In the year 1785 I attended more particularly to it, and in the beginning of 1786 I prepared it for publication, and showed it to many of my friends, numbers of whom are still living, and are ready to give their testimony to the truth of it. But the impossibility of procuring a type for the purpose, and the want of health, at that time prevented the publication.

I have since procured a type and obtained a patent which embraces four kinds of characters, and also seven.

There is no reason to doubt the accuracy of Law's assertion that as early as 1785, he had been playing with the idea of some inno-

vation in musical notation. His explanation of why the plan, prepared for publication in 1786, was not actually printed until 1803
does not ring true, however. It will be remembered that in 1786,
no one except Isaiah Thomas was printing music from type. Music
was printed from engraved plates. Why could Law's scheme not
have been engraved also? What was there about it that made type
mandatory? If it was the distinctive shape of the note-heads that
was making the difficulty, the feasibility of engraving is proved
by the early editions of the *Easy Instructor*, all printed from
engraved plates. If it was the representation of characters "without lines," the possibility of error in engraving would have been
no greater than in typesetting, and may have been less. It is
extremely difficult to accept Law's explanation to the effect that
the 17-year delay in the appearance of the "new plan" was due to
printing problems and ill health, especially since his brother was
a skilled printer who did much work for him, and his "want of
health" did not prevent him from bringing out quite a few other
musical works.

And there is no getting around the indubitable fact that when
Law's plan finally did appear in print in 1803, it resembled that
of the *Easy Instructor* in striking fashion. Of all the shapes available to represent note-heads, Law chose just the four that Little
had used before him in print—and there can be no question that
Little's work did precede Law's in print. Law did interchange the
shapes for *fa* and *la*, it is true, so that there is a superficial difference between the two. But the common use of oval, triangle,
square, and diamond cannot have been purely concidental. That
either Little knew Law's shapes or Law knew Little's seems to be
an inescapable conclusion. (See Illus. 9.)

DID Little take the shapes from Law? Although such a possibility
cannot be ruled out entirely, there is not much that can be said
in its favor and much can be said against it. Little appears to
have been a rather unsuccessful Philadelphia printer with some
interest in music. If he saw Law's manuscript "new plan" of 1786,

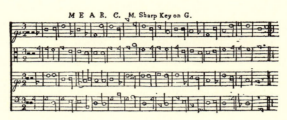

9. William Little's shape notation, from *The Easy Instructor* (1802); Andrew Law's shape notation, from *The Art of Singing*, 4th edition (1803). Courtesy of the Library of Congress.

it must have been before October 19, 1787, as the record of Law's travels shows that on that date he left Philadelphia and did not return again until January, 1799, well after the August 15, 1798, date upon which the Uranian Society recommended the *Easy Instructor*. One must then believe that more than 10 years elapsed before Little brought out his system, using exactly the shapes for it claimed by Law to have been previously invented by him.

One might well ask what could have prompted Little to keep just these shapes when any others would have done as well? And, as Law's system was unpublished, what could be gained from exact imitation? Disguise was an exceedingly simple matter, if one wanted to crib the shape-note idea, as many later imitators of the *Easy Instructor* knew: one had only to alter the shapes. It is exceedingly difficult to find anything resembling a logical motive for such an action, or to advance a logical reason why Little should have used Law's shapes.

The case against Law, on the other hand, while not conclusive, is certainly convincing. Law returned to Philadelphia after his long absence early in 1799 and opened a singing-school. He easily could have learned about the *Easy Instructor* through the subscription papers which were then being circulated in the city. According to the advertisement printed in the various editions of the tune-book, "upwards of three thousand" subscriptions were received before publication. Perhaps some of Law's own scholars brought the collection to his attention; perhaps one of the singing members of the Uranian Society. At any rate, it is not reasonable to believe that Law was completely ignorant of the existence of the *Easy Instructor*. Even had he escaped seeing the manuscript, the chances that he never saw the printed work are slim indeed. He must have known of the book's existence, as the periodical in which the 1801 notice of the *Easy Instructor* appeared was at the very moment printing a lengthy series of letters (both pro and con) about Law's abilities as a music teacher. Law probably followed the exchanges with interest, as he sent a letter to the editor of the *Repository* himself which was published less than a month after the appearance of the *Easy Instructor* review.

What probably happened was that Law realized, having seen the *Easy Instructor*, that the idea he had toyed with long ago and had for one reason or another subsequently neglected had been anticipated in some respects in print. He was stirred into activity. As soon as he could, he brought out a new edition of the *Art of Singing* on a "new plan." One of the elements of the "new plan" was the peculiar notation, the shapes for which he had borrowed from those in the *Easy Instructor*.

Why did not Law use new shapes? Perhaps because the old ones served a definite purpose. Over and over again, Law stressed the point that the essence of his "new plan" was the representation of musical sounds *without lines*, that is, through the elimination of the staff. The fact that someone had made a start in the right direction by identifying certain shapes with certain syllable names was all to the good so far as Law's "new plan" was concerned—it made it just that much easier to achieve his basic purpose. The transposition of shapes for *fa* and *la* was sufficient to avoid any legal complications.

One final point. The letter to the Websters was very circumspectly phrased. Law did not, contrary to first appearances, claim ignorance of the existence of the *Easy Instructor*—he merely claimed ignorance of the Websters' purchase of the copyright. Unless it is assumed that he was aware of the prior publication of the *Easy Instructor*, the paragraph about the age of his own plan is hardly necessary. It appears to be a bit too much of a good thing.

In the case of the shape-note innovation, circumstantial evidence thus points to Law, not Little, as the pirate.

As HE approached his 67th birthday, Law, now living in Newark, N.J., once again addressed a petition to the legislature—but this time of the United States:

> To the honourable the Senate and House of Representatives of the United States of America, in Congress assembled.
>
> The petition of the subscriber, Andrew Law, humbly showeth that your petitioner, on the 12th day of May, A.D. 1802, obtained, according to law, a patent for a new plan of printing music, then lately invented by your petitioner, vesting in him the exclusive right and property thereof, for the term of fourteen years thence next ensuing, which patent will of course expire on the 12th day of May, A.D. 1816. And your petitioner prays that his said patent may be renewed or extended by an act of Congress, for the term of twenty years from and after the expiration of the present patent; and in support of this prayer of your petitioner, he begs leave humbly to submit the following facts and reasons.
>
> First. Your petitioner states it to be a fact, which he can abundantly verify, that the expenses he has already incurred in procuring the type for printing music on his plan, have amounted to near fifteen hundred dollars, and that it will cost you [sic] petitioner from six to seven hundred dollars more to complete the type, and render it fit for advantageous use.
>
> Secondly. That the prejudices in favor of the old method of printing music, are so deeply rooted in the minds of most of the singers in the United States, that it will require many years yet to eradicate these prejudices, and to introduce your petitioner's plan so generally as to make it profitable to him.
>
> Thirdly. That there are a great many printers in the United States,

who are in possession of type for printing music upon the old plan; consequently their interest leads them to reject your petitioner's method; and these printers have many teachers of music under their influence, and these again have their friends and patrons, all uniting in favour of the old plan; and hence it must require many years before the invention of your petitioner can be introduced so generally, as to indemnify him for his labours and expenses.

Fourthly. These circumstances operating against the introduction of your petitioner's plan, the sales of his books have been slow and inconsiderable. Added to this, the difficulty and expense of printing music, with the present incomplete state of your petitioner's type, have been so great, that his profits on the books he has sold, have not been equal to the interest of the money expended for paper, printing and binding; consequently the inventer can calculate upon no remuneration for his labours and expenses, until he can complete his type and get a more general and rapid sale of his work.

Fifthly. Your petitioner states, that he has by actual experiment and much labour and attention, made many valuable improvements in the detail of his plan, both as respects the science of music and the making of types and the manner of setting them; all of which must remain unknown and be lost, unless your petitioner can procure an extension of his patent, and thus be enabled to mature and complete his system.—From all these considerations your petitioner is persuaded that a renewal of his patent for the space of twenty years will be necessary to afford him an opportunity, should his life be spared, of reaping some advantage from his past labours, and perfecting a system of music so desirable and important to the amateurs of that science, and to the friends of that delightful part of divine worship which consists in singing praises.

Your petitioner therefore prays the aid of Congress in the premises, and as in duty bound he will ever pray.

Andrew Law

Newark, New-Jersey, January 2d, 1816.[23]

Appended to the petition was the following endorsement, signed by 29 of Law's fellow residents of Newark:

We, the subscribers having been acquainted, some of us for a long time, with the Rev. Andrew Law, are fully persuaded that the foregoing statement is correct, and from our knowledge of his music, most heartily

23. "Petition of Andrew Law," State Papers, 14th Congress, 1st Session, House Document No. 37.

wish that his application to Congress for a renewal of his patent may be attended with success.

The petition was presented in the House on February 1 by Mr. Ward of New Jersey, and the matter was referred to a committee consisting of Mr. Ward and the Messrs. Gold and Archer. On March 20, Mr. Ward reported back to the House, and presented a bill to extend the patent, which was to be acted on by the House on the following day.

Things were apparently going well—but there was a sudden cessation of activity. Finally, the matter came up again on April 27. It was then ordered that "the committee of the whole be discharged from a further consideration of . . . the bill to extend the patent granted to Andrew Law for an improvement in the mode of printing music." [24] That finished the petition; it was never again considered.

Perhaps someone had checked Patent Office records. Just a few weeks before, on February 28, a patent covering the casting and using of shape-note types had been granted—to George Webster of Albany, New York, publisher of the *Easy Instructor*. Here was a truly ironical note, because although Little's shape-notes had anticipated Law's by some months, Law's development of a font of shape-note type had anticipated Webster's by some years.

Thus, for the last time, the motif of piracy entered Law's career.

24. *Journal of the House of Representatives of the United States, at the First Session of the Fourteenth Congress* (Washington, 1816), pp. 257, 513, 746–47. This tells the whole legislative story of Law's petition.

5

——— ≫≪ ———

BENJAMIN CARR'S
Federal Overture (1794)

ALTHOUGH NO ONE can reasonably claim that Benjamin Carr's *Federal Overture* (See Illus. 10) is a musical masterpiece, no one can reasonably deny that it is an important historical document. One provocative aspect of cultural dynamics on the American scene during the 1790s was an unusually close interaction between music and politics, with the theater serving as catalyst. The *Federal Overture* illustrates this interaction with great precision. Viewed against the backdrop of its own exciting era, the piece tells us a good deal about not only specifically musical matters, but more particularly about the manner in which citizens of the infant nation felt and acted in regard to the issues of their day. Its scarcity—only a single copy has been located—has kept it hidden from the eyes of those who might be interested in the story it has to tell.

From the music historian's viewpoint, Carr's patriotic potpourri is of more than ordinary moment because of a fortunate accident. One of the nine tunes included by Carr happened to be that of *Yankee Doodle*, and this happened to be the first time that the jaunty air appeared in print on this side of the Atlantic.

The origins of *Yankee Doodle* have remained unknown despite extraordinary interest in the ditty and much detective work by some extremely able musical sleuths. Perhaps the most distinguished scholar to concern himself about the matter was Oscar G.

10. Title page, Carr's *Federal Overture* (1794). Courtesy of the New York Public Library.

Sonneck, the first Chief of the Library of Congress's Music Division and one of the most persistent and imaginative students of American music history who ever lived. In a closely reasoned report published in 1909, Sonneck demonstrated with his customary thoroughness that none of the dozens of theories advanced to account for the beginnings of *Yankee Doodle* was tenable. He summed up the results of his researches by noting that "the origin of 'Yankee Doodle' remains as mysterious as ever, unless it be deemed a positive result to have eliminated definitely almost every theory thus far advanced and thus by the process of elimination to have paved the way for an eventual solution of the puzzle." [1] Sonneck never examined Carr's *Federal Overture* although he knew that it had been published; during his lifetime all copies were believed to have perished. It would have been interesting to know what he would have deduced from it. Despite the passage of nearly half a century and the discovery of not only Carr's piece but also another early printing known to Sonneck only by reputation,[2] the "eventual solution of the puzzle" seems no closer. *Yankee Doodle* remains an unanswered riddle.

The year 1794 was an astonishingly late date for the first American publication of *Yankee Doodle* in view of the fact that the tune must have been familiar here at least as early as 1767. At that time, the libretto of *The Disappointment*, "a new American comic opera of two acts" by Andrew Barton, was printed in New York. It contained 18 songs with the names of the airs to which the words were to be sung given. Air IV is *Yankee Doodle*.[3] A version of the tune in manuscript which probably antedates the reference to it in *The Disappointment* was reproduced in facsimile by Sonneck.[4]

Despite these and other evidences of the popularity and antiq-

---

1. O. G. Sonneck, *Report on "The Star-Spangled Banner," "Hail Columbia," "America," "Yankee Doodle"* (Washington, 1909), p. 156. Hereafter referred to as Sonneck.
2. Sonneck, p. 121.
3. Sonneck, p. 110.
4. Sonneck, pp. 230–31.

uity of the tune, the earliest printing of *Yankee Doodle* thus far
discovered dates from 1782. In that year, James Aird, a Glasgow
music seller and publisher, included it in the first volume of his
Selection of Scotch, English, Irish and Foreign Airs.[5] Before Carr
used it in the *Federal Overture*, the tune had also popped up in
several other English imprints, Samuel Arnold's ballad opera
Two to One (London, 1784)[6] and Charles Dibdin's *Musical Tour*
(Sheffield, 1788).[7] And although there was apparently no American printed version, newspapers here printed dozens (and perhaps hundreds) of topical poems during the 1780s and 1790s
bearing the legend, "Air—*Yankee Doodle.*"

Why was it that what was obviously a "favorite ditty" appeared
in print so infrequently and so late? Although there is no indubitable evidence to that effect, I would hazard the guess that the
reason lies with the words rather than the tune. There is some
indication that *Yankee Doodle* was one of those persistent melodies, known almost instinctively, which had some sort of affinity
for bawdy words. We have such tunes today also, and they too
are rarely found in print. Although the tune of *Yankee Doodle*
was clearly innocent of any evil, it seems possible that it would
have been excluded from polite society because of its propensity
for bringing to mind off-color texts. It is interesting to note—for
example—that *The Disappointment* was unusually coarse in its
language,[8] while broadside versions of *Yankee Doodle* are replete
with four-letter Anglo-Saxonisms.[9]

Also curious is the fact that virtually no two early versions of
the tune are alike; the melodic variation is strikingly wide. From
this we must infer that *Yankee Doodle* had already had a long
history in the oral tradition before it achieved publication. The

5. Sonneck, p. 120; reproduced in facsimile on pp. 222–23.
6. Sonneck, p. 120; reproduced in facsimile on pp. 218–19.
7. Sonneck, pp. 119–20; reproduced in facsimile on pp. 214–15.
8. O. G. Sonneck, *A Bibliography of Early Secular American Music (18th Century)*, rev. and enl. by William Treat Upton (Washington, 1945), p. 109. Hereafter referred to as Sonneck-Upton.
9. Such a broadside is reproduced in facsimile in S. Foster Damon, *Yankee Doodle* (Providence, 1959), p. 3.

implication is plain that we are here dealing with a genuine folk melody, the origins of which are lost in antiquity.

Yankee Doodle has overshadowed the other eight tunes in the *Federal Overture*, but these are nevertheless not without interest of their own. However, before delving too deeply into other facets of the Carr work, a sketch of the worlds in which it came into existence, particularly those of the theater and of politics, will bring the whole picture into sharper focus.

ON OCTOBER 16, 1778, less than four months after the British had evacuated Philadelphia, the Continental Congress, returning to that city, took the following action:

Whereas frequenting Play Houses and theatrical entertainments, has a fatal tendency to divert the minds of the people from a due attention to the means necessary for the defence of their country and preservation of their liberties: *Resolved*, that any person holding an office under the United States who shall act, promote, encourage or attend such plays, shall be deemed unworthy to hold such office, and shall be accordingly dismissed.[10]

Times were hard for actors. Some six months later, the Pennsylvania Legislature made matters even harder by passing a law prohibiting anyone from acting or being "in any way concerned [with] any play house, theatre, stage or scaffold for acting, showing or exhibiting any tragedy, comedy or tragi-comedy, farce, interlude or any other play or any part of a play whatsoever." [11]

The provisions of the law certainly appeared to be broad enough to interdict any attempt to mount theatrical entertainments, but the lawmakers had failed to reckon with the ingenuity of the hard-pressed thespians and the strong desire of many Philadelphians to see plays. During the hectic decade in which the antitheatrical law remained in effect, it was more honored in the breach than in the observance. For example, all through 1784 and

10. *Journal of the Continental Congress*, XII (1778), as quoted in Thomas Clark Pollock, *The Philadelphia Theatre in the Eighteenth Century* (Philadelphia, 1933), pp. 38–39. Hereafter referred to as Pollock.
11. Quoted in Pollock, p. 40.

running into July of 1785, "lectures" of one sort or another were offered by the Hallam-Henry troupe in the old theater in Southwark. That these were by no means actually lectures was made plain by Washington, who noted on May 22, 1784, that he had "purchased four Play Tickets" [12] while in Philadelphia. In 1786–87, the same company presented not only lectures, but also "concerts" and "Spectaculum Vitae." These were given in the "Opera-House in Southwark," someone apparently having noted that music and opera were not specifically mentioned in the law.[13] Typical camouflage was a presentation by the Hallam-Henry company, unnamed in the advertisement, of a "Moral and Instructive Tale called FILIAL PIETY: Exemplified in the HISTORY of the Prince of Denmark" [14]—quite obviously Shakespeare's *Hamlet*. During the 1788 season, they offered such entertainments as "a Lecture on the Disadvantages of Improper Education, Exemplified in the History of Tony Lumpkin" [15] (Goldsmith's *She Stoops to Conquer*) as well as other lectures on "the Pernicious Vice of Scandal" [16] (Sheridan's *School for Scandal*) and on "the Fate of Tyranny" [17] (Shakespeare's *Richard III*).

To evade the law in this manner was a pretty game, but by the winter of 1788–89, the liberal element in Philadelphia as well as the actors were getting pretty tired of it. In January of 1789, a Dramatic Association, numbering among its members some of the city's most distinguished citizens, was formed "for the Purpose of obtaining the Establishment of a Theatre in Philadelphia, under a liberal and properly regulated plan." [18] A few weeks later, the Association petitioned the Legislature to repeal the old law and backed up its appeal to reason with long lists of the names of citizens who were in agreement with its principles. Finally, on

12. Pollock, p. 135.
13. Pollock, p. 44.
14. Pollock, p. 44.
15. Pollock, p. 45.
16. Pollock, p. 142.
17. Pollock, p. 142.
18. Pollock, p. 46.

March 2, 1789, the Legislature declared rescinded "any act or part of an act which prohibits theatrical representations . . . within the city of Philadelphia and the neighborhood thereof," retaining for the executive and judicial heads of the state the power to suppress any "exceptionable" plays for the next three years.[19]

At long last the theater was free to expand in the City of Brotherly Love; a new era was about to begin.

WHEN THE Dramatic Association won its great victory in 1789, the only structure in Philadelphia suitable for theatrical presentations was a large frame building on South (then Cedar) Street, between Fourth and Fifth Streets, "of wood principally and painted red, without outward ornament, and in its appearance no ornament to the city." [20] The theater in Southwark (which it was most frequently called), or the "Theatre, Cedar-street," had been erected in 1766 and was old and uncomfortable. One contemporary described it as "an ugly ill-contrived affair outside and inside. The stage [was] lighted by plain oil lamps without glasses. The view from the boxes was intercepted by large square wooden pillars supporting the upper tier and the roof." [21] To make matters worse, the audience was likely to either freeze or broil, depending on the season. Three days after the Hallam-Henry troupe, now called the Old American Company, began its season in January, 1790, the managers declared the building closed while "Alterations and Improvements" were accomplished "to prevent the Complaints made of the Coldness of the Theatre." [22] In July, it was announced that "a Wind Sail is erected for the purpose of keeping the House Cool" [23]—the next summer, it was arranged to have fire engines playing water on the roof during performances.[24]

19. Pollock, p. 48.
20. William Dunlap, *A History of the American Theatre* (New York, 1832), p. 22. Hereafter referred to as Dunlap.
21. John F. Watson, *Annals of Philadelphia* (Philadelphia, 1830), p. 410.
22. *Pennsylvania Packet and General Advertiser*, Jan. 13, 1790.
23. *Ibid.*, July 1, 1790.
24. Pollock, p. 49.

Hallam and Henry were not quite so diligent about improving the quality of their presentations and adding new talent to their company, however. By 1791, there were frequent complaints not only about the old theater, but also about the plays and the acting. There was internal dissension as well. Thomas Wignell, an important member of the troupe, resigned at the end of the season. He immediately joined forces with Philadelphia's most prominent musician, Alexander Reinagle, and the two men became co-managers of the new theater proposed to be erected "in a central part of the city." [25] Shortly thereafter, Wignell went to England to recruit talent for a new company which was to play in the new theater. Hallam and Henry were quick to realize the threat to the Old American Company posed by the Wignell-Reinagle venture, and John Henry also went to England. There, he succeeded in rounding up a number of talented actors and actresses, most of whom made their American debuts in the fall of 1792.

Wignell's stay in the Old World was longer and more fruitful. When he finally returned to the United States in the summer of 1793, it was with a really exceptional company of 56. By that time, the new theater on the northwest corner of Fourth and Chestnut Streets, a copy of the Royal Theatre at Bath and without question the finest home of the drama in America, had been completed. The opening was delayed, however, by the most devastating epidemic of yellow fever ever chronicled in Philadelphia, from which the Wignell-Reinagle troupe took refuge in New Jersey until the danger was past. On February 17, 1794, the Chestnut Street Theatre opened with Samuel Arnold's pasticcio, *The Castle of Andalusia,* and Mrs. Cowley's afterpiece, *Who's the Dupe.* The long season of theater, opera, and dance which then followed was the most brilliant and spectacular Philadelphia had yet seen.

In triumph, the Wignell-Reinagle troupe then proceeded to Baltimore to open another new theater, which had been built in anticipation of their coming. It was at this unpropitious moment that the Old American Company, now led by Lewis Hallam and

25. Pollock, p. 50.

John Hodgkinson (one of the actors recruited by Henry in England in 1792), decided to reopen the old theatre in Southwark and challenge the Wignell-Reinagle forces.

ON SEPTEMBER 17, 1794, the following announcement appeared in the Philadelphia newspapers:

Theatre, Cedar-street.
OLD AMERICAN COMPANY

Messrs. Hallam and Hodgkinson respectfully acquaint the public in general, that their Theatre will open on Monday the 22d of September when Mrs. Melmouth, formerly of Drury Lane and Covent-Garden, and last from Dublin, will make her first appearance in this city.

The house has been fitted up and decorated at a very considerable expense, and no pains spared to produce such novelty, both of pieces and performers, as may render the Old American Company worthy a share of that patronage, which hitherto it has been their pride both to possess and merit.

Mons. Quenet, principal ballet-master, from Paris and Madame Gardie, will make their appearance a few days after the commencement in a grand Pantomime. Also Mr. & Mrs. Marriott, from the Theatre Edinburgh; Mr. Richards, from Dublin; Mr. Nelson, from the Theatre Richmond; Mr. Munto, from Goodman's Fields, and Mr. Carr, of the Ancient Concerts, London; who will make his first entry on any stage in a principal singing character.[26]

Thus was announced the last regular dramatic season at the old Southwark and the last Philadelphia season of the Old American Company, which had trod the boards there since 1754. Three days later, the details of the opening night were particularized:

Old American Company
Theatre—Cedar street,

will open Monday, September 22 (for a few weeks only,) with an occasional Prelude called the Old and New Houses. The characters by Messrs. Hodgkinson, King, Ryan, Martin, Mrs. Miller, &c. After which will be presented, the Tragedy of the GRECIAN DAUGHTER. Previous to

26. *Philadelphia Gazette and Universal Daily Advertiser.*

the Tragedy the Band will play a New Federal Overture, in which is introduced several popular airs; Marseilles hymn, Ça ira, O dear what can the matter be, Rose Tree, Carmagnole, Presidents' march, Yankee doodle, &c. composed by Mr. Carr. To which will be added the musical Farce of the ROMP. The doors will be opened at half after six, and the curtain drawn up precisely at half past 7 o'clock.

Messrs. Hallam and Hodgkinson, respectfully acquaint the citizens in general, that every expence has been cheerfully sustained, that might tend to make the Old American Company worthy a share of their patronage, during the short stay the nature of their engagements will permit them to make here.

Places in the Boxes may be had at the Box Office, from ten to one every day (Sundays excepted) and on days of performance from three to five P.M., where also tickets may be had, and at Mr. Bradford's Book Store, No. 8 South Front street, and Mr. Carr's music store.

Box one Dollar—Pitt three quarters—Gallery, half a dollar.[27]

So began the career of Benjamin Carr's *Federal Overture*.

DESPITE THE managers' implication that Benjamin Carr had just arrived from "the Ancient Concerts, London" the 26-year-old musician was already well known in Philadelphia at the time of his joining the Old American Company. As is evident from the later advertisement, he was the owner of a shop where he sold sheet music and musical instruments. The imprint "Carr & Co." was known in the city since July, 1793, when Benjamin and his father, "music printers and importers lately from London," opened a store at 136 High Street.[28] By June of 1794, Carr's father had left Philadelphia for Baltimore where he opened a similar music repository, the Philadelphia business remaining in Benjamin's sole hands. Furthermore, Benjamin had made four public appearances as a singer in concerts given "under the direction of Messrs. Reinagle, Gillingham, Menel and Carr, at Mr. Oeller's Hotel" in April, 1794,[29] and had demonstrated his skill as a composer with the "additional airs" he had contributed to

27. *Ibid.*, Sept. 20, 1794.
28. Sonneck-Upton, p. 577.
29. O. G. Sonneck, *Early Concert-Life in America, 1731–1800* (Leipzig, 1907), pp. 94–96.

the Wignell-Reinagle production of *The Spanish Barber* which played in the Chestnut Street Theatre on July 7 of that year. His debut as actor-singer was nothing more than a further evidence of his versatility and great energy.

Of Carr's life in England before his emigration to the United States virtually nothing is known. The Carr family was apparently a musical one, and his father was selling music in Middle Row, Holborn, London, around 1770.[30] Benjamin was born on September 12, 1768 and received his musical education from Samuel Arnold, celebrated editor of the works of Handel and opera composer. He is also known to have studied with Charles Wesley, musical nephew of John Wesley and reputedly an excellent organist.[31] Some time around 1790, the London music publisher John Bland brought out *Poor Richard*, a song composed by Benjamin to words by his younger brother John. The " favourite Ballad" was also published three times before 1800 in Philadelphia.[32] It is interesting to note that another Carr song, *The Little Sailor Boy*, was reprinted by Bland and Weller in London *after* it had been brought out by the composer in Philadelphia in 1798.

The claim made by the managers of the Old American Company that Carr was "of the Ancient Concerts, London" is usually taken as incontrovertible fact, but it does not seem to be supported by any evidence. The "Concerts of Antient Music" were established in 1776 by a group of music-loving noblemen who acted as board of directors. The chief rules of the concerts were that no music composed within the previous 20 years should be performed, and that the directors should select the programs. Joah Bates was the conductor of the concerts from their inception through 1793, and some of the finest singers and instrumentalists in England were participants. The records of the concerts are unusually complete—yearly program books were issued contain-

30. Charles Humphries and William C. Smith, *Music Publishing in the British Isles* (London, 1954), pp. 98–99.
31. Virginia Larkin Redway, "The Carrs, American Music Publishers," *Musical Quarterly*, XVIII (1932), 151.
32. Sonneck-Upton, p. 338.

ing full lists of artists and works performed. Carr's role—if he did indeed play any role—must have been a very minor one, as his name is nowhere mentioned in the program books. It is possible that he may have been one of the boy singers whose names were not specified, but if that was the case, his connections with the concerts could not have been very recent, as he was well past his 24th birthday in 1793, when he is presumed to have arrived in the United States.

Why did Carr leave London? We cannot know for certain, but it seems likely that the presence of Wignell and Henry in England had something to do with it. Perhaps James Hewitt, a friend of Carr's who arrived in New York late in 1792 and served as "leader of the band" for the Old American Company in that city (and who was probably indirectly responsible for the composition of the *Federal Overture*), was also impelled to emigrate for the same reasons.

However, let us return to Philadelphia, where Carr's *Federal Overture* was about to be unveiled.

IT WILL BE RECALLED that the main offering of the Old American Company's opening bill was a piece called *The Grecian Daughter*. This turgid tragedy by Arthur Murphy, an 18th-century Irish actor who penned biographies of Fielding and Garrick and translated Sallust and Tacitus from the Latin as well as wrote drama, means nothing to us today, but in the early 1790s it was a great favorite with partisans of the French Revolution. Here is a description of a New York performance which took place on November 25, 1793, written by an onlooker:

> One of the side boxes was filled by French officers from the ships of war in the harbour. The opposite box was filled with American officers. All were in their uniforms as dressed for the rejoicing day. French officers and soldier-sailors (we find the expression in a note made at the time), and many of the New-York militia, artillery, infantry, and dragoons, mingled with the crowd in the pit. The house was early filled. As soon as the musicians appeared, there was a general call for "*ça ira.*" The

band struck up. The French in the pit joined first, and then the whole audience. Next followed the Marseillois Hymn. The audience stood up. The French took off their hats and sung in a full and solemn chorus. The Americans applauded by gestures and clapping of hands. We can recall the figure and voice of one Frenchman, who, standing on a bench in the pit, sung this solemn patriotic song with a clear loud voice, while his fine manly frame seemed to swell with the enthusiasm of the moment. The hymn ended, shouts of "Vivent les François," "Vivent les Americains," were reiterated until the curtain drew up, and all was silent.

When the Grecian Daughter saves her father, and strikes the tyrant to earth, the applause usually bestowed on this catastrophe was drowned by the enthusiastic shouts of the excited spectators. Before or since we have never witnessed or felt such enthusiasm.[33]

The occasion of the New York performance of *The Grecian Daughter* described above was the 10th anniversary of the departure of the British troops during the Revolutionary War. The occasion of the Philadelphia performance of the same play on September 22, 1794, at which the *Federal Overture* was first played was the third anniversary of the birth of the French Republic. A description of events of New York on the same day reveals at least one of the reasons why Carr's piece was being offered:

A dinner was given by the Consul and other citizens of the French Republic, to a large number of respectable inhabitants, at the new assembly room in William street, on which were raised flags of the two Republics united. At half past three the company consisting of upwards of two hundred, sat down to a grand patriotic feast prepared by Citizen Gautier. The room was handsomely ornamented, and a fine band of music performed a number of national airs during the repast, amongst which were the Marseilles Hymn, Carmagnole, Ca Ira, Washington's March, Yankee Doodle, &c. &c. The Minister of the French Republic, who arrived in town on Saturday was present, also his Excellency the Governor, the Mayor, Brigadier General Alner, the Colonels of the different regiments of militia in this city, the Grand Sachem, and several other officers of the Democratic Society, and a number of other citizens civil and military.[34]

Note the names of the tunes performed by the "fine band of

33. Dunlap, p. 106.
34. *Dunlap & Claypoole's American Daily Advertiser*, Sept. 26, 1794.

music" at this celebration; all were included in the *Federal Overture.*

At first glance, it may appear rather odd that a piece of music called a *Federal Overture* should contain what were obviously the *anti*-Federalist songs—*Ça Ira, Carmagnole,* and the *Marseilles Hymn* could certainly so be characterized—as well as such Federalist favorites as *Washington's March* and *Yankee Doodle.* Except for *O Dear What Can the Matter Be,* which conceivably could have been an oblique reference to the unsettled state of the times, the other tunes chosen by Carr do not seem to have had any political implications.

The puzzle evaporates, however, when we consider the purpose for which Carr designed the overture. It is eminently clear that the piece was intended to evoke admiration which crossed party lines, to appeal to Federalist and anti-Federalist alike. The choice of title, which may well have been that of Hallam and Hodgkinson rather than Carr, becomes more comprehensible when we recollect that the anti-Federalists were formally known as the Federal Republicans.

The content of the *Federal Overture* gives us no clue to Carr's political philosophy, which may have been either Federalist or anti-Federalist. From what we know of his background, one might hazard the guess that it was the former. Why did he write the *Federal Overture?* Circumstances seem to point toward the fact that it was a commissioned work, requested by the managers of the Old American Company in order to minimize the possibility of certain events taking place in Philadelphia (and later in New York) which had transpired during the New York season some six months earlier.

THE INCIDENT referred to above happened on March 4, 1794. The Old American Company was presenting at the John Street Theatre "an opera (a new piece never before performed, written by a lady of this city) called Tammany, or the Indian Chief," [35] a

35. New York *Daily Advertiser,* Mar. 3, 1794.

work famous in the annals of American music. The author of the libretto was Mrs. Ann Julia Hatton, poetasting wife of a New York musical instrument maker, and the composer of the music was James Hewitt, a fine musician who was the leader of the band for the Old Americans during their New York season and a personal friend of Benjamin Carr.

At the moment, political feeling was running particularly high —which was in itself one of the reasons why *Tammany* was mounted at all. Unfortunately, none of Hewitt's music has been preserved, so that we cannot properly evaluate the work as an opera, but Mrs. Hatton's book proves to be nothing much more than a "melange of bombast" [36] obviously written to cater to the sentiments of the members of the Tammany Society, under whose auspices it was offered. Tammanyites were then extremely anti-Federal and pro-French, and the theater in John Street they considered an ideal place for demonstrations of their political ardor. But despite the fact that *Tammany* itself was vociferously favored by those in the gallery with hot blood, the Old Americans nevertheless succeeded in getting themselves into trouble with the Tammanyites for political reasons—a not inconsiderable achievement. A few days after the presentation of *Tammany*, a letter dated the night of the performance signed "A Calm Observer" appeared in the public press. The "Calm Observer" painted a vivid picture of what had occurred:

The *junto* were kept aloof, and to make up for their absence, (and determined to have *some* fun) the prelude was commenced upon an *individual*, poor Hewit[t], the leader of the band, and a very respectable inoffensive character. They quarrelled with him, because as a foreigner, he did not know the music called for, nor would they wait till he could recollect himself, and make up the tune from the rest of the band, which was afterwards done. Perplexed as the leader of a band always is, by the variety of calls from every busy creature who is fond of the sweet sound of his own voice at a theatre, how *pleasant* a situation would his

36. O. G. Sonneck discusses the opera at length on pp. 57–63 of his *Miscellaneous Studies in the History of Music* (New York, 1921). The quotation is from Dunlap, p. 108.

be if every call not instantly complied with was thus resented. But it was no matter, something was necessary for a beginning, "a word and a blow" did the business, and afforded excellent sport.

After much altercation on the score of *music*, the opera (the music of which could not proceed without Mr. Hewitt) was permitted to make its appearance.[37]

It is plain that Hewitt, who had been too slow in producing the expected patriotic tunes to satisfy the more excited members of the Tammany Society in attendance, had actually been physically attacked. It is, moreover, quite possible that despite the fact that he had written the music for *Tammany*, Hewitt was no anti-Federalist—and those in the gallery may well have been aware of it. Certainly, the political bias of the "Calm Observer" is plain, and his excuses for Hewitt's actions seem a bit disingenuous. After all, Hewitt had been in New York since the fall of 1792 and even had he wished to, he could not possibly have avoided familiarity with such tunes as *Ça Ira, Carmagnole*, and the *Marseillaise*, all of which were sung everywhere on the slightest provocation. Perhaps Hewitt was a Federalist—at any rate, that would seem to be the import of another letter to the editor printed two days after that by the "Calm Observer:"

> If Mr. Calm Observer feels himself insulted or injured by the blow given on Monday night last at the Theatre, to a very respectable, inoffensive, fiddler, whose respectability consist[s] in being respected by beings whose political principles are infamous as his own: His inoffensiveness in his cowardice[,] may have the satisfaction he merits, by calling at No. 43 Broadway, where he will find the man
> WHO GAVE THE BLOW [38]

IN VIEW of these hectic proceedings and the political fever of the time, it can hardly be considered eccentric if the managers of the Old American Company, caught in the middle and certainly more interested in trying to earn an honest dollar than in slighting any of the political factions, should have tried to make some provision

37. New York *Diary, or Evening Register,* Mar. 6, 1794.
38. *Ibid.,* Mar. 8, 1794.

to prevent any recurrence of this sort of scandalous brawl. There was probably no need for further action during the remainder of the season in New York. No doubt Hewitt was exceedingly prompt in responding to requests for patriotic tunes after his March 4 experience. But in Philadelphia, where Jacobin clubs were active, their members parading and dancing in the streets singing *Ça Ira* and the *Carmagnole* with red mobcaps on their heads, where worried John Adams wrote that "ten thousand men were in the streets day after day, threatening to drag Washington out of his house, and effect a revolution in the government," [39] matters were likely to be a bit sticky. And the theater was not noted for gentility. A cynical French observer, describing affairs at the beautiful new Chestnut Street theatre, remarked that "the performance is boisterous, and the interludes are even indecent. It is not unusual to hear such words as Goddamn, Bastard, Rascal, Son of a Bitch. Women turn their backs to the performance during the interludes. The actors are well enough dressed; the style of the plays, which are English and in the English taste, is extremely coarse and full of pleasantries highly repugnant to the French taste." [40] Hallam and Hodgkinson probably called upon Carr and asked him (perhaps upon the recommendation of Hewitt) to put together such a piece as the *Federal Overture* for their use. At the same time, they seem to have persuaded Carr to join the Old American Company and to take a flyer at a dramatic career.

CARR's patriotic potpourri, first performed on September 20, 1794, "previous to the Tragedy" at the old Southwark theater (see Illus. 11), apparently served its purpose well. Both Jacobins and Federalists seemed to be well pleased with the piece and it was repeated by the band on September 24, 26, 29, October 1, and 3.

39. Quoted in Struthers Burt, *Philadelphia, Holy Experiment* (Garden City, 1946), p. 321.
40. *Moreau de St. Méry's American Journey* (1793–1798), trans. Kenneth and Anna M. Roberts (Garden City, 1947), p. 347.

The probability is that it continued to be heard at subsequent performances although no statement to that effect appeared in the press. There is record of only one untoward incident during the Old American Company's short Philadelphia season. On October 24, the audience got pretty well out of hand and according to one newspaper, half the instruments in the orchestra were broken by missiles from the gallery.[41] This time, however, the demonstration appears to have been theatrical rather than political. The evening's offering was a tragedy entitled *Barbarossa*, which was having its premiere. It is significant that its first performance was also its last.

The *Federal Overture* was so successful that Carr decided to publish it, and on November 21, 1794, he advertised that the work, "as performed at the Theatre, Cedar street," was for sale at his music store in an arrangement for piano. (See Illus. 12.)[42] In this connection, the legend on the title page of the only surviving copy is somewhat puzzling. There, it is stated that the piece was "as performed at the Theatres in Philadelphia and New York" and also that it was "Printed and Sold at B. Carrs Musical Repositorys in Philadelphia and New York." [43] Were there then two editions published? It seems doubtful—what probably happened was that Carr knew that the *Federal Overture* was to be performed in New York when the Old American Company opened there in December, and had already made some arrangement to open the "Musical Magazine Repository at No. 131 William St." [44] which actually did open before January 9, 1795, and which was taken over by James Hewitt in August, 1797.

After closing their Philadelphia season on December 4, 1794, before an audience which included President Washington, the Old Americans proceeded to New York. There they began a longer season with a presentation of *Love in a Village*, a pasticcio

---

41. *General Advertiser and Political, Commercial, Agricultural, and Literary Journal*, Oct. 25, 1794.
42. *Dunlap & Claypoole's American Daily Advertiser*, Nov. 21, 1794.
43. See title page of this edition.
44. Sonneck-Upton, p. 581.

OLD AMERICAN COMPANY.
Theatre—Cedar Street.
Will open MONDAY, September 22.
(For a few weeks only,) with an occasional
Prelude, *called,* The
OLD & NEW HOUSES.
The characters by Meffrs. Hodgkinfon, King,
Ryan, Martin, Mrs. Miller &c.
After which will be prefented, the Tragedy of the
GRECIAN DAUGHTER.
Previous to the Tragedy the band will play
a New Federal Overture, in which is in-
troduced feveral popular airs ; Marfeilles
hymn, Ca i·a, O dear what can the matter
be, Rofe Tree, Carmagnole, Prefident's
March, Yankee doodle &c. Compofed by
Mr. CARR.
To which will be added the mufical Farce of
The
R O M P.
The doors will be opened at half after fix,
and the curtain drawn up precifely at half
paft feven o'clock.
₊ Meffrs HALLAM & HODGKIN-
SON, refpectfully acquaint the Citizens in
general, that every expence has been chearful-
ly fuftained, that might tend to make the
Old American Company, worthy a fhare of
their patronage, during the fhort ftay the
nature of their engagements will permit them
to make here.
PLACES in the Boxes may be had at
the Box Office, from ten to one every day
(Sundays excepted) and on days of perform-
ance from three to five P. M. where alfo
Tickets may be had, and at Mr. Bradford's
Book Store, No. 8, South Front ftreet, and
Mr. Carr's Mufic Store.
BOX, one Dollar—PITT three quarters—
GALLERY, half a dollar.

11. An advertisement for the opening night of the Old American Company's Philadelphia season in *Dunlap & Claypoole's American Daily
Advertiser* for September 20, 1794.

MUSIC.

B. CARR,

R ESPECTFULLY informs the patrons of mufic,
he has received per fall veffels, and has for fale
at his Mufical Repofitory, No. 122 Market ftreet,
an elegant and extenfive affortment of Grand Patent
Piano Fortes, portable grand and fquare grand do.
and fmall Piano Fortes, of the very firft quality at
various prices; Violins, patent and common German Flutes, Fifes, Guitars, Clarinets, Oboes, Baf-
foons, Trumpets, Horns, &c.

Beft Roman Strings, and every other article of
mufical line—A large affortment of mufic for every
inftrument—The moft Favorite NEW SONGS,
" The Federal Overture," as performed at the theatre, Cedar ftreet, for the Piano Forte ; feveral valuable periodical works, &c. &c.

Nov 21   dtf

---

12. Announcement of the publication of Carr's *Federal Overture* in
Dunlap & Claypoole's American Daily Advertiser for
November 21, 1794.

in which Carr had made his Philadelphia debut as a singing
actor. The New York performance on December 15 also included
the *Federal Overture*, which was as successful in Gotham as it
had been in the City of Brotherly Love. We are fortunate in having a detailed critique of the evening's entertainment by the
anonymous author of a "Theatrical Register" in the *New-York
Magazine*:

The orchestra was a pleasing spectacle; but when the band struck up,
it excited in us as delightful sensations as ever we remember to have experienced on a similar occasion. Let us here pay a due tribute of praise
to Mr. Carr's overture, which, besides its intrinsic merit, has the advantage of being eminently calculated to attract an *universal* admiration.

Previous to the commencement of the opera [*Love in a Village*], Mr.
Hodgkinson addressed the audience in his new capacity as manager.
We shall only remark upon that part of his address which had for its
object the good order and tranquillity of the house; by suppressing the
indecencies which have been customary with the gallery, and the results
which a few of that part of the audience have thought themselves privileged liberally to bestow upon every other part of the house, and more
especially upon the gentlemen who compose the orchestra. We hope our

fellow-citizens will aid the managers in this attempt, and show that they are determined there shall be no privileged order in the play-house more than in the state. It is the interest of the manager's that every part of their audience should be pleased; therefor popular tunes and favorite overtures will be performed at stated times, (as we understand from the managers address) and Mr. Carr's overture was composed for this purpose. But a few riotous people must not expect the arrangements of the theatre, the peace, pleasure and feelings of the whole audience, to be sacrificed to their senseless whims and brutal love of indecency. Now, fellow citizens, is the time, by supporting the managers, to begin this very necessary reform—a reform, without which every subsequent attempt at theatrical improvement will be vain.[45]

As in Philadelphia, Carr's *Federal Overture* was publicized for the first few weeks of the season and was then no longer mentioned in the newspapers. Probably it continued to be played nonetheless. Carr continued with the company until the end of the season as an actor-singer (although on rather infrequent occasions, it must be admitted), and also provided incidental music for a performance of *Hamlet* and additional accompaniments for ballad operas such as Dibdin's *Deserter* as well as ballet scores for dancing master William Francis (such as *The Caledonian Frolic*), who was one of the troupe's prime attractions. At the same time, he gave several New York concerts independently of the Old Americans and opened a music store. Carr's formal relationship with the Company and his career as an actor terminated in the early summer of 1795. He then plunged with great energy into composing, publishing, and teaching, activities in which he carved for himself a prominent niche in the annals of early American music.

THE *Federal Overture* begins with an introduction based on part of *Yankee Doodle* and then, after a transitional passage, launches into the *Marseilles March*, the first of nine numbered tunes, all given titles in the score. The framework of the piece, the details of its construction, its balance and craftsmanship, all demonstrate

45. *New-York Magazine; or, Literary Repository*, V (1794), 716.

that Carr was a skilled and imaginative artisan. Curiously enough, he seems to have been responsible for the first American appearances in print of most of the tunes used in the *Federal Overture*.

The *Marseillaise*, composed during the night of April 24, 1792, by Claude Joseph Rouget de Lisle, achieved almost instantaneous popularity not only in France, but in England and the United States as well. As early as December of 1793, Carr had advertised an edition of "the Marseillois hymn in French and English." [46] Its inclusion in the *Federal Overture* represented its second American publication by Carr.

Carr was also the first in the United States to publish *Ça Ira*, number two in the *Federal Overture*, which was then regarded as the official song of the French Revolution. One of the oddities of history is that the phrase "ça ira"—roughly translated, "it will pass"—is attributed on fairly good authority to Benjamin Franklin. According to a source contemporary with the French Revolution, when the news of the American Army's disastrous retreat through New Jersey and the misery of Valley Forge reached France in 1777–78, many friends of the struggling states began to believe that all was indeed lost. Not Franklin, however, who is quoted as having said: "Cela est fâcheux, mais ça ira, ça ira." Old diplomats and courtiers, amazed at his confidence, passed about his words and they were picked up by the newspapers. Apparently they were remembered by the people, and during the dark days of the French Revolution were repeated over and over again. [47] A popular singer of the day put the words into verses designed to fit the tune of *Carillon National*, a favorite contredanse by an obscure theater violinist named Bécourt, and *Ça Ira* was launched on its spectacular career. Carr's edition came out, possibly as early as July, 1793, with the *President's March*, number seven in the *Federal Overture*. [48]

46. Sonneck-Upton, p. 251.
47. The story is given in the Paris *Moniteur Universel*, Sept. 21, 1792, and is quoted, along with other pertinent material, in John Bach McMaster, *A History of the People of the United States* (New York, 1891), II, 89–91.
48. Sonneck-Upton, p. 342.

Numbers three, four, and five, *O Dear What Can the Matter Be* (familiar to toddlers today as a nursery rhyme), *The Irish Washerwoman* (also well known as a fiddle tune), and *Rose Tree* (a popular song from William Shield's *Poor Soldier*, Washington's favorite opera, now forgotten), were all seemingly apolitical and were probably utilized in the medley for purely musical reasons. The first two were also original contributions to the American published repertory made by Carr, but the third was familiar here as early as 1789 when Alexander Reinagle included it in his *Collection of Favorite Songs*.[49]

Credit for the first American publication of *La Carmagnole*, number six in the *Federal Overture*, goes to James Hewitt, who advertised an edition as "just published" on March 29, 1794. Carr was close on his heels—his sheet-music edition was for sale in June.[50] The *President's March*, immortalized a few years later as the air to Joseph Hopkinson's *Hail Columbia* text, was introduced by Carr (who also published the first edition of *Hail Columbia* itself in 1798).[51] *Yankee Doodle*, number eight, was discussed earlier.

The last number, *Viva Tutti*, a popular air which Donald W. Krummel [52] has traced back to a 1772 opera by Pietro Guglielmi entitled *Il Carnovale di Venezia*, was perhaps intended by Carr to symbolize a note of reconciliation, friendship, and good fellowship, since it was probably best known as the tune for a set of words beginning, "Here's a health to all good lasses."

ALTHOUGH the *Federal Overture* was plainly well received in 1794 and 1795, Carr's career as a singing actor with the Old American Company created much more of a public stir. His stage debut

49. Sonneck-Upton, p. 362.
50. Sonneck-Upton, p. 56.
51. Sonneck-Upton, pp. 171–73.
52. *"Viva tutti:* the Musical Journeys of an Eighteenth-Century Part-Song," *Bulletin of the New York Public Library,* LXVII (1963), 57–64. In the original version of this study, I was forced to confess myself completely baffled by the origins and implications of this number. Dr. Krummel has cleared up the little mystery in his very entertaining article.

took place not on the opening night of the season but on September 24, two days later. On hand to witness his performance as
Young Meadows in the pasticcio *Love in a Village* was "The
Bystander," theatrical observer for a popular Philadelphia newspaper, who noted that

The Opera gives an opportunity of displaying the musical talents of
a new candidate on the boards. The bill of Fare informs the public that
it is his first attempt on any Stage. Mr. Carr undoubtedly possesses great
merit, and notwithstanding an evident perturbation of spirit, he performed Young Meadows with universal applause; no doubt he will soon
repeat his attempt, and he may assure himself that he will meet a cordial
and unaminous reception. The Bystander recommends him to study
a little more of the *Suaviter in Modo* in moving his arms, which may
have proceeded from the embarrassment natural on a first appearance.[53]

In Philadelphia, Carr's roles appear to have been few and far
between; it is not known whether he added another to his repertory before he arrived in New York where he also made his debut
in the same part. Once again, a critic who left us a characterization
of Carr's art was at the performance:

Mr. Carr made on this occasion his first appearance on our stage; and we
confess, to us a very prepossessing first appearance. Good sense and
modesty, united to a perfect knowledge of his profession as a musician,
and a pleasing and comprehensive voice, are not the only qualifications
which this young gentleman possesses for the stage; he speaks with propriety, and we doubt not but practice will make him a good actor, in
addition to his being an excellent singer.[54]

The note of disparagement, stressing his musical rather than
his dramatic abilities, was sounded again by one of Carr's contemporaries:

His deportment was correct, but timid, and he never acquired or de-
served reputation as an actor. His voice was mellow, and knowledge of
music without the graces of action, made him more acceptable to the
scientific than to the vulgar auditor. . . . An overture was performed,
composed by him, and much approved: the orchestra had been en-

53. *Gazette of the United States,* Sept. 25, 1794.
54. *New-York Magazine; or, Literary Depository,* V (1794), 717.

larged, and the best band collected that ever had been heard in the New-York theatre.[55]

Perhaps Carr's decision to abandon any thought of a career on the boards was sound.

Carr maintained an active interest in theatrical matters for some years after he had parted ways with the Old American Company, however, writing accompaniments, arrangements, and occasional songs for operas by other men and composing several operas of his own, of which *The Archers* was the biggest success. By the beginning of the 19th century, the direction of his musical efforts had altered. The 18th-century Carr was particularly interested in publishing, composing, and singing; the 19th-century Carr seems to have devoted most of his time to teaching, playing the organ, and church music. He gave up his Philadelphia musical repository in 1800, and although he was associated with George Schetky in the music publishing business from 1806 on, there is no strong evidence that the connection was much more than nominal. A Roman Catholic, Carr took charge of the music at St. Augustine's Church from 1801 until his death 30 years later, and devoted much effort to the improvement of choir training and the provision of better music for the church. He helped found the Musical Fund Society of Philadelphia and served as one of the first conductors at its concerts.

THE *Federal Overture* is so unfamiliar, even to scholars, that the medley is still listed as unlocated in such standard reference books as the latest editions of *Grove's Dictionary* and Scholes's *Oxford Companion to Music*. Its existence became known to a few specialists when Elliott Shapiro, former Vice-President of the music publishing concern of Shapiro, Bernstein & Co. and owner of one of the most magnificent collections of American sheet music ever assembled, purchased the imprint from another great collector, the late J. Francis Driscoll, probably some time in the 1930s. How,

55. Dunlap, p. 13.

where, or when Mr. Driscoll obtained this *unicum* is not known, but one of the provisions of the sale to Mr. Shapiro was the stipulation that no reproduction of the work be allowed. As a consequence only those few scholars who were privileged to study the work at Mr. Shapiro's home were familiar with its content.

Upon Mr. Shapiro's untimely death in 1956, his entire collection, including the unique *Federal Overture*, passed into the hands of Harry Dichter, Mr. Shapiro's associate in the compilation of the definitive *Early American Sheet Music* (New York, 1941). Through Mr. Dichter's efforts, the Shapiro collection passed intact into the hands of yet another ardent private collector, Mr. Franklin Klasse of New York, and a facsimile of the *Federal Overture* was published. The original of this exceptionally interesting American music imprint is now in the Music Division of the New York Public Library, which subsequently acquired the entire Shapiro collection from Mr. Klasse.

6

—————— ⤜⤜⤜ ⤛⤛⤛ ——————

The Easy Instructor (1798-1831):
A HISTORY AND BIBLIOGRAPHY
OF THE FIRST SHAPE-NOTE
TUNE-BOOK

A CRUCIAL PROBLEM faced by our earliest music educators—and
one whose difficulties puzzle us still—was how to teach successfully the core skill of reading music at sight. The approach
through notational reform, now considered hopelessly quixotic,
came in for a good deal of attention in 18th- and early 19th-
century America. Indeed, the first music textbook published on
this side of the Atlantic, John Tufts's *Introduction to the Singing
of Psalm-Tunes* (Boston, 1721) presented an innovation which
was no doubt of some value in a situation where the art of reading orthodox notation had virtually disappeared. The nub of the
problem was to devise a system in which pitch, time, and solmization were combined into a single, easily assimilated notation. The
Tufts solution, apparently not wholly original,[1] was to abandon
ordinary notes entirely and to substitute upon the staff the initial
letters of the four solmization syllables (*fa, sol, la, mi*) then in
universal use in Great Britain. Time values were indicated with
punctuation marks. This was quite adequate for the traditional
psalm-tunes Tufts included in his clearly written and unpretentious

1. See Chapter 3.

little pamphlet, but the system was unwieldy and ill-adapted to music of greater complexity. It failed to win many imitators, although the *Introduction* itself proved to be something of a best-seller, going through 11 editions.

Among the ingenious notations which followed in the wake of the Tufts experiment, none was more remarkable than the "shape-note" system which made its first public appearance in the pages of a quite extraordinary tune-book, *The Easy Instructor*, "by" William Little and William Smith. The shape-note idea was the kind of inspired solution to a knotty problem which seems perfectly obvious once it has been suggested. It consisted merely of using a differently shaped note-head to represent each of the four syllables. Thus, a triangular note-head represented *fa*, a round note-head *sol*, a square note-head *la*, and a diamond note-head *mi*. In all other respects, the notation was completely ortho-dox. (See Illus. 13.)

13. Lewis Edson's BRIDGEWATER (1782) and Daniel Read's RUSSIA (1786), as published in William Little and William Smith, *The Easy Instructor*, Edition F (Albany, 1809?). Courtesy, Library of Congress.

The clear advantages of the shape-note system are almost immediately apparent. Providing an individual shape for each syllable enables anyone, after a modicum of attention to the matter, to name the proper syllables of any piece of music instantaneously. One of the genuine difficulties in ordinary solmization lies in the fact that keys change and hence *do* (or *fa* in the *fasola* system) does not remain in the same place. The student must make continual mental computations. With shape-notes, this is completely avoided. A somewhat subtler advantage is that the shapes are continually before the singer whether he happens to be singing words or syllables. Thus, the true function of any solmization system—that of aiding in the automatic identification of scale degrees—is emphasized and capitalized upon through shape-notes in a fashion impossible in any system which permits abandonment of the process of syllabification when words are sung. Comparison of the shape-note system with that of Tonic Sol-Fa, so successful in the British Isles, highlights the superiority of the *Easy Instructor* idea. The symbols of Tonic Sol-Fa are not posited upon a staff, and hence the pictorial suggestion of tonal direction provided by staff notation is lost. Failure to use the staff demands a complicated method of octave identification, and failure to use regular notes demands a similarly complicated method of representing time values. Furthermore, Tonic Sol-Fa is quite independent of orthodox notation, whereas the shape-notes utilize the standard notation and add to it a graphic, quickly comprehended key to relative scale degrees.

No one who has witnessed the astonishing sight-singing virtuosity exhibited by the shape-note singers of the rural South today, trained with what is basically the *Easy Instructor* method, can possibly doubt the effectiveness of the device. Had this pedagogical tool been accepted by "the father of singing among the children," Lowell Mason, and others who shaped the patterns of American music education, we might have been more successful in developing skilled music readers and enthusiastic amateur choral singers in the public school. The reasons for the rejection of shape-notes—Thomas Hastings, one of their most vociferous early detractors, called them "dunce notes" [2]—had nothing to do with the system's merits or demerits. The shape-notes from their very inception were closely associated with a remarkable indigenous music which began its development in Connecticut in the 1780s and shortly afterward blanketed New England and the Middle Atlantic states.[3] The "reformers" who quickly arose in earnest protest against this first flowering of American musical expression, all too conscious of the European musical tradition and possessed of an inferiority complex regarding peculiarly American cultural manifestations, eventually saw to the elimination of this music from American life, at least in the North. In the meantime, the shape-note system and the music itself became completely identified. Shape-notes came to be regarded in urban centers as the musical notation of the country people, the naive, simple people who sang for their own enjoyment songs in a strange, almost primitive native idiom. Leaders of fine city choirs, busy with Pucitta and Neukomm as well as Handel and Haydn, would have nothing to do with such music nor with such notation. Inevitably, the city choir leaders became the first music teachers in the public schools. Shape-notes were never admitted to the classroom. As a result, the child who learns music in our schools today must do so without the aid that they might give.[4]

THE earliest reference to *The Easy Instructor* and to the shape-note system is to be found in a "title page" deposited for copyright in the Southern District of Pennsylvania on June 15, 1798 (see Illus. 14):

2. *Musical Magazine*, I (1835), 87.

3. For a brief analysis of this music, see Allen P. Britton, "The Musical Idiom in Early American Tune Books," *Jour. of the Amer. Musicol. Soc.*, III (1950), 186.

4. This entire subject is dealt with in the unpubl. diss. (University of Michigan, 1949) by Allen P. Britton, "Theoretical Introductions in American Tune Books to 1800" (University Microfilms, No. 1505), pp. 313–32. For the results of a recent study supporting the value of the shape-note idea, see George H. Kyme, "An Experiment in Teaching Children to Read Music with Shape-Notes," *Jour. of Research in Mus. Ed.*, VIII (1960), 3–8.

THE *Easy Instructor*, or a New Method of teaching *Sacred Harmony*, containing the Rudiments of *Music* on an improved Plan, wherein the Naming and Timing the notes, are familiarized to the weakeſt capacity.

Likewiſe, an Eſſay on Compoſition, with directions to enable any perſon with a tolerable voice, to take the air of any piece of Muſic at ſight, and perform it by word, without ſinging it by note. Alſo, the Tranſpoſition of Mi, rendering all the keys in muſic as eaſy as the natural key, whereby the errors in Compoſitiori and the preſs may be known. Together with a choice collection of Pſalm Tunes, and Anthems, from the moſt celebrated Authors in Europe, with a number compoſed in Europe and America, entirely new; ſuited to all the metres ſung in the different Churches in the United States.

Publiſhed for the uſe of Singing Societies in general, but more particularly for thoſe who have not the advantage of an Inſtructor.

By EDWARD STAMMERS,
WILLIAM LITTLE.

Copy right secured according to Act of Congress.

14. "Title page," *The Easy Instructor*, deposited for copyright June 15, 1798.

The *Easy Instructor*, or a New Method of teaching *Sacred Harmony*, containing the Rudiments of *Music* on an improved Plan, wherein the Naming and Timing the notes, are familiarized to the weakest capacity.

Likewise, an Essay on Composition, with directions to enable any person with a tolerable voice, to take the air of any piece of Music at sight, and perform it by word, without singing it by note. Also, the Transposition of Mi, rendering all the keys in music as easy as the natural key, whereby the errors in Composition and the press may be known. Together with a choice collection of Psalm Tunes, and Anthems, from the most celebrated Authors in Europe, with a number composed in Europe and America, entirely new; suited to all the metres sung in the different Churches in the United States.

Published for the use of Singing Societies in general, but more particularly for those who have not the advantage of an Instructor.

By EDWARD STAMMERS,
WILLIAM LITTLE.
Copy right secured according to Act of Congress.[5]

Surprisingly, the name of Edward Stammers appears where one might expect to find that of William Smith. Who was Stammers? His name appears in every known edition of *The Easy Instructor* (together with that of a Richard T. Leech) in connection with a

5. From the original at the Library of Congress.

report of a committee of the Uranian Society of Philadelphia printed therein. The report reads as follows:

PHILADELPHIA, August 15, 1798.

The Committee appointed by the URANIAN SOCIETY of PHILADELPHIA, to examine a Singing Book, entitled, "THE EASY INSTRUCTOR," BY WILLIAM LITTLE,

REPORT . . . . . . That having carefully examined the same, they find it contains a well digested system of principles and rules, and a judicious collection of tunes: And from the improvement of having only four significant characters, indicating, at sight, the names of the notes, and a sliding rule for timing the same, this book is considered easier to be learned than any we have seen.

Were it possible to acquire the sound of the eight notes but by imitation, they verily believe they might be obtained by the help of this book, even without an instructor.

The Committee are of opinion the Author merits the patronage and encouragement of all friends of Church Music:

Which is submitted to,
> EDWARD STAMMERS,
> RICHARD T. LEECH.[6]

Two aspects of this report present special difficulties when considered together: (1) Little is given as sole author in the body of the report; (2) the names of Stammers and Leech are preceded by the phrase "which is submitted to." [7] A number of questions arise. Since the "title page" was deposited for copyright two months before the report, why is not Stammers credited as co-author in both? Did Stammers actually assist Little in compiling the book, or had he perhaps contracted in some way to sponsor its publica-

6. Ed. A, pp. [3]–4. What the "sliding rule" might have been remains a matter of conjecture. No further reference to it occurs in the introductory musical instructions. The title of Benjamin Dearborn's *The Vocal Instructor,* copyrighted in Massachusetts in 1797 but apparently never published, mentions "a sliding music scale, never before publish'd in which a moveable index points out the names and distances of the notes in all their variations." See Evans No. 32021.

7. The complete phrase appears before the names of Stammers and Leech only in Eds. A*a*-D*a*. In Eds. D*b*-I, the phrase reads, "which is submitted," thus making it appear that the two men *submitted* the report. In Eds. J-BB, the whole phrase is omitted, and Stammers and Leech seem to be the *signers* of the recommendation.

tion in return for credit as coauthor? What is the meaning of the strange closing phrase, i.e., did Stammers and Leech *submit* or *receive* the report? Since Little is given as sole author in the report, how is it that the name of William Smith is found as co-author on the title pages of all known printed editions? (A further difficulty arises in connection with the 1802 New York copyright to be discussed below, which, like the report, gives Little as sole author.) None of these questions can now be answered with certainty although some general conclusions regarding the Stammers-Little-Smith relationship will presently be deduced.

The "choice collection of Psalm Tunes, and Anthems, from the most celebrated Authors *in Europe* [italics supplied], with a number composed in Europe and America, entirely new" of the 1798 "title page" clearly does not describe any of the known early editions of the tune-book, all of which contain almost exclusively American music in the distinctive native idiom. This description of an *Easy Instructor* unknown in print presupposes a compiler familiar with the European tradition, which Stammers certainly must have been. As a member of a prominent singing society and the compiler of a posthumously published tune-book, the *Philadelphia Chorister* (Philadelphia: J. McCulloch, 1803),[8] Stammers was obviously quite capable of having edited *The Easy Instructor*. Whether he actually did so must remain an unanswered question; what little evidence is now available points to the probability that he was responsible only for instructions and music in the 1798 manuscript, which, so far as is known, never achieved publication—at least under the title *The Easy Instructor*. As to the invention of the shape-note system itself, something even more difficult to establish, here probability favors Little as

8. Stammers is listed as a baker in the Philadelphia directories of 1798 through 1802. In 1803 appears, "Stammers, widow of Edward, baker." As the directories were invariably published in the October preceding the dated year, Stammers apparently died prior to October, 1802. It is possible that his *Philadelphia Chorister* is actually the original manuscript of *The Easy Instructor* in print, since it corresponds fairly well with the description of content in the 1798 copyright of the latter work. The only *Philadelphia Chorister* located to date is at the New-York Historical Society.

originator.

William Little's very obscurity as a practicing musician lends
some credence to such a theory. The phrase in the 1798 copyright
deposit, "whereby errors in . . . the press may be known," and
the typographical nature of the shape-note concept give rise to
the suspicion that someone engaged in the printing trades was
in some way associated with the venture. If this supposition is
correct, the William Little who was an obscure printer in Philadelphia during 1802 and 1803 [9] may well have been Stammers's
associate. The assumption that Little was a printer interested in
music (he was interested enough to do a little composing, for
four of his tunes appear in the earliest known edition) rather
than a professional musician may help to explain why another
collaborator, William Smith, became necessary upon the death of
Stammers, and also the peculiarly distant relationship between
Little and the tune-book of which he was supposedly one of the
compilers.

Although it is clear from the Uranian Society committee report
that a manuscript utilizing shape-notes must have been in existence in 1798 before William Smith entered the picture, it is extremely doubtful that the work was published in that year or that
it was ever published at all in the form in which it received the
recommendation. The existence of a copyright entry is by no
means proof that a title actually achieved publication. As it was
only necessary at that time to file the *title* of a book to receive
copyright protection, not an actual copy of the book itself, early
copyright records are filled with ghost titles of books which were
never printed. This appears to have been the case with the original manuscript of *The Easy Instructor* seen by the committee of
the Uranian Society. The unique 1798 "title page" preserved at

9. H. Glenn Brown and Maude O. Brown, *A Directory of the Book-Arts and
Book Trade in Philadelphia to 1820* (New York, 1950), p. 76. A William Little
—perhaps the same individual—was also active in New York as a printer dur-
ing 1808 and 1809; see George L. McKay, *A Register of Artists, Engravers,
Booksellers, Bookbinders, Printers & Publishers in New York City, 1633–1820*
(New York, 1942), p. 44.

the Library of Congress was apparently imprinted for the specific purpose of entering the title in the copyright records, and examination proves that it bears no possible physical relationship to any printed copy of the book known today.

The only supposed record of a 1798 edition of *The Easy Instructor* appears in a thoroughly self-contradictory entry in Evans's *American Bibliography*, No. 34004:

LITTLE, WILLIAM. The Easy Instructor; or, a new method of teaching sacred harmony. Containing, I. The rudiments of music on an improved plan, wherein the naming and timing of the notes are familiarized to the weakest capacity. II. A choice collection of psalm tunes and anthems, from the most celebrated authors, with a number composed in Europe and America, entirely new; suited to all the metres sung in the different churches in the United States. Published for the use of singing societies in general, but more particularly for those who have not the advantage of an instructor. By William Little and William Smith. [Philadelphia, 1798. Pp. 74. Obl. 12mo.]

Evans evidently transcribed the title page from one of the undated Albany editions published between 1809 and 1816 (Editions F-O*b*). The imprint appears to have been supplied on the basis of the known 1798 Pennsylvania copyright and the dated report of the Uranian Society committee—which Evans erroneously associates with the advertisement signed by Little and Smith to be found in all known editions (see fn. 12). The 74-page collation seems inexplicable, but the nature of the entry strongly suggests that it is an attempted reconstruction of a book not actually examined.[10] This supposition is strengthened by the fact that Evans locates no copy of this purported edition. Why he failed to use the title as given in the 1798 Pennsylvania copyright, with which he was familiar, remains a mystery. Thus, it must be assumed that

10. The Massachusetts Historical Society copy of Ed. R. may perhaps be the source of the Evans entry. The following, written in a 19th-century hand, appears on the flyleaf: "This Book is probably the 4ᵈ Ed. of the Easy Instructor has 127 pages & index makes 128 pages—& issued abt 1818. The First Ed. had 74 pages, 2ᵈ Ed. 104 pages & 3ᵈ Ed. has 112 pages. The Preface by Little & Smith dated 'Phil. Aug. 15, 1798' is the same in Each Ed. But the Music & Tunes are quite different in Each Ed. W. Latham."

no 1798 edition was actually published until more convincing evidence of its existence is uncovered.

BECAUSE very little factual information is available, any account of *The Easy Instructor* between 1798 and 1801, when the genuine first edition seems to have appeared, must be largely speculative. The gap of three years between manuscript and book may be accounted for by the typographical novelty of the project and the not inconsiderable difficulty of preparing suitable plates. During this period Stammers apparently died, and Little entered into collaboration with one of the most tantalizingly mysterious figures in the history of American music, William Smith. Certainly, he is not to be confused with the comparatively prominent Rev. William Smith who published *The Churchman's Choral Companion* (New York, 1809). While the author has not as yet managed to pierce Smith's disguise, he has been able to uncover one very faint and perhaps fruitless clue to his identity. In the manuscript letter-books of Daniel Read, one of the most distinguished practitioners of the American idiom, are five letters written between 1794 and 1802 addressed to an otherwise unknown New York singing master called William H. Smith.[11] The content of the letters does not preclude the possibility that this was Little's associate. Unfortunately, New York directories and other contemporary sources such as newspapers disclose no William Smith or William H. Smith engaged in musical activities during this period. In 1803 and 1806 our Smith was evidently a resident of Hopewell, New Jersey, as this is the place given in the dated prefaces of a tune-book published unilaterally by him, *The Easy Instructor, Part II* (discussed in detail below).

Whoever Smith might have been, he apparently differed sharply from Stammers in musical taste. The 1798 copyright describes a tune-book with a European orientation, whereas the music in the earliest known edition, presumably compiled by Smith, is almost

11. See Chapter 8; also *Notes,* IX (1952), 247.

entirely American. Since both Smith and Little were composers in the American idiom (Smith is represented by one work in Editions A*a* and A*b* and Little by four), the change in orientation seems understandable enough. Both men must have originally worked well together, for by 1801 they had gathered "upwards" of 3,000 subscriptions for *The Easy Instructor*, a number presaging its future success.[12]

The first edition (Edition A*a*) apparently was published in Philadelphia shortly before August 22, 1801, as the following notice printed in the *Philadelphia Repository and Weekly Register* of that date makes clear:

PSALMODY

A work has just made its appearance in this city, entitled, "*The Easy Instructor: or, A New Method of Teaching Sacred Harmony. By William Little and William Smith.*" This work contains a pretty large collection of Psalm Tunes and Anthems, a considerable number of which are original; but it chiefly claims attention on account of a new method laid down for facilitating the learner in acquiring the knowledge of the notes as designated by the four singing syllables, which is done by diversfying the shapes of the notes; as for example, the shape of *Fa* is a triangle, *Mi* a diamond, *Law* an oblong square, and *Sol* the usual form. It is evident that their different characters, indicating at sight the names of the notes, will greatly aid the student of Sacred Harmony. A certificate from a committee of the Uranian Society accompanies the work, in which they observe, that it "contains a well-digested system of principles and rules, and a judicious collection of tunes;" and that, "were it possible to acquire the sounds of the eight notes but by *imitation*, they verily believe they might be obtained by the help of this book, even without an instructor." The copyright is secured.

On December 22, 1801, the records of the Secretary of State reveal that a copy of a work entitled "The easy instructor or a new method of teaching Sacred Harmony &c. &c. By William Little & William Smith" was received on deposit.

12. Eds. A*a* and A*b*, p. [3]. In later editions the August 15, 1798, date is typographically set so that it appears to pertain to the advertisement rather than to the recommendation printed immediately below it. That the date pertains to the recommendation is clear in Eds. A*a* and A*b*.

FOR REASONS that are not at all clear, the scene of *Easy Instructor*
activity shifted from Philadelphia to New York shortly after the
first edition was published. There, the firm of G. & R. Waite
(which was apparently more interested in selling patent medi-
cines and lottery tickets than book publishing, to judge from its
advertisements) announced on November 25, 1802, in the New
York *Chronicle Express*, "This day is published . . . THE EASY
INSTRUCTOR; or A New Method of Teaching Sacred Harmony
by William Little & William Smith. . . ." [13] A few weeks *after*
this edition was published, on December 10, 1802, Little entered
the title of the book in the District of New York for copyright.
Apparently for the specific purpose of befuddling later generations of scholars, Little signed himself sole author in the New
York records.[14] The peculiarity of the copyright situation makes
it evident that Smith was a junior partner in the venture, and
that Little's was the controlling interest. The 1802 copyright also
makes it amply clear that Little wished to retain undivided control of *The Easy Instructor* and perhaps that he had become
somewhat suspicious of Smith's intentions.

No copy bearing an 1802 date or a G. & R. Waite imprint has
been located, but Edition A*b* (see the check-list in Appendix B),
a later variant of the Philadelphia edition, is presumed on circumstantial evidence to be the New York edition. Editions A*a* (one
copy located) and A*b* (three copies located) are the *only* known
editions which possibly could have been referred to in the G. & R.
Waite advertisement. Furthermore, one small bit of evidence turns
the possibility into probability. The preface to Smith's *Easy Instructor, Part II* (see below), dated 1803, begins as follows: "The
Publisher of this work meeting with great encouragement in the
first edition of the '*Easy Instructor*,' is induced to publish a second edition, and having added the flats and sharps, so that the

---

13. The complete advertisement is quoted in Frank J. Metcalf, "*The Easy
Instructor:* a Bibliographical Study," *Musical Quarterly*, XXIII (1937), 91.
14. The 1802 New York copyright entry is also quoted in its entirety in
Metcalf, p. 90.

singer may take his choice, either to sing by characters or by line and space, he hopes to meet the approbation and patronage of the friends to Vocal Music." The music Edition A*a* is *without* "flats and sharps" (i.e., key signatures) except for three numbers; Edition A*b* lacks key signatures in all but two numbers. Unless Smith had published an earlier edition of *Part II*, an extremely unlikely event, it must be presumed that he is referring to either Edition A*a* or A*b*—or both, since the differences between the two are minimal, and he may have considered them both "the first edition." In any event, Edition A*b* is plainly the younger, and if Edition A*a* is considered the edition noted in the *Philadelphia Repository*, then Edition A*b* must be the New York edition put out by G. & R. Waite.

The sole identifiable remnant of the 1798 manuscript appearing in Editions A*a* and A*b* would appear to be the preface, which consists basically of the first six paragraphs and a portion of the seventh of the preface of Ralph Harrison's *Sacred Harmony* (London, 1784). This same preface had been utilized by Andrew Adgate in his *Select Psalms and Hymns* (Philadelphia: Young and McCulloch, 1787). As Adgate was one of the founders of the Uranian Academy of Philadelphia, of which the Uranian Society was a direct outgrowth,[15] the possible connection between the preface and Stammers, an official of the Uranian Society, is obvious.

Of the 105 compositions included in Editions A*a* and A*b*, only five are of European origin; even these were old American favorites which had appeared in almost every New England tune-book from the time that Daniel Bayley of Newburyport commenced to reprint the works of the English singing-masters William Tans'ur and Aaron Williams in the 1760s. The American compositions, among them 41 claimed as "never before published," are excellent examples of the characteristic native idiom of the time. Thus, perhaps we can assume that between 1798 and 1801, the European musical bias of Stammers had been transformed into the thor-

15. See O. G. Sonneck, *Early Concert-Life in America, 1731–1800* (Leipzig, 1907), pp. 103–20.

oughly American one of Smith, with Little serving as a bridge between the two musicians. From a strictly musical point of view, the interest of *The Easy Instructor* is considerably enhanced because of this change in orientation; from the point of view of the future acceptance of the shape-note idea by the eventual arbiters of musical progress in America, the change was disastrous. In this manner, the individual tastes of a single obscure musician, William Smith, may have changed the whole future course of American music history.

In the year after *The Easy Instructor* appeared in print, Smith, apparently without help from Little, brought out another tune-book making use of the shape-note system:

THE Easy Instructor OR A *New method of teaching Sacred Harmony.* PART II. Containing the Rudiments of Music on an improved plan.— With a choice collection of Psalm Tunes, a number of which are entirely new. *By William Smith & Co.*

The omission of any reference to "European music" on the title page and the absence of any in the collection itself bear out the idea that Smith's preference was for American music in the native idiom. Where the book was published is not known, but a physical resemblance between the title pages of *Part II* and Editions A*a* and A*b* arouses the suspicion that the printer who was responsible for the latter also may have brought out this imprint. No copyright record of *Part II* has been located, and the strong probability is that no application was made, as it does not appear to have been authorized by Little. Little was the sole owner of the 1802 New York copyright, and Smith may have overstepped the bounds of propriety, if not of legality, with the curious author ascription on the title page of *Part II* where the senior partner is reduced to the unenviable status of an "& Co." There seems to be little doubt that the appearance of *Part II*, with its nonchalant disregard of Little, did not help build amicable relations between the two. Indeed, indications are that it caused a complete break, for when a second edition of *Part II* was published in 1806, "& Co." was no longer on the title page, and Smith appears as sole author.

A DISAGREEMENT about *Part II* may well have precipitated the next phase in the history of *The Easy Instructor*. If Little was in fact a printer by trade, the book must have been at best a peripheral interest, and the rupture of his partnership with Smith deprived him of a collaborator. Perhaps annoyance decided him to sell out on the best possible terms. Perhaps he considered the copyright, already violated by Smith, no longer of any particular value. At any rate, some time between 1803 and 1805—no record of the transaction has been found—he apparently sold or reassigned the copyright to a trio of Albany, New York, printers, possibly suggested to him by G. & R. Waite, who maintained a branch of their firm in that city. Thereafter, neither of the co-authors of Editions A*a* and A*b* seems to have been in any way connected with the book, and another person assumed the responsibility for its ever-changing musical content. All introductory material remained unaltered throughout all editions.

In Albany *The Easy Instructor* really hit its stride, thanks to the astuteness of an editor who successfully followed the musical fashions of the moment. A veritable flood of editions, the first in 1805 and the last in 1831, poured from the presses. Tens of thousands of copies were sold, and the tune-book became celebrated throughout the country, extending its influence far beyond its Albany base. If Little was then still alive, he must have regretted his decision to dispose of the copyright, which suddenly had become an extremely lucrative property.

One of the most intriguing of the many historical riddles in connection with *The Easy Instructor* is the identity of its Albany editor, who certainly deserves a small niche in America's musical hall of fame. Who chose the music and decided what changes should be made from edition to edition? The little evidence available points to Daniel Steele (1772–1828), one of the three figures who obtained the 1802 copyright from Little. There is no reason to believe that either of the other two, Charles R. Webster (1762–1832) or his twin brother George Webster (1762–1821), was sufficiently interested or skilled in music to undertake such a difficult editorial task. Both were prominent printers in the community, and there is no indication in their well-documented life histories that they participated in any musical activities; their only connection with music seems to have been through their publishing, which they are known to have commenced as early as 1800. On the other hand, Steele, although a lesser figure in Albany local history and consequently a more obscure one, may have been the singing-master who advertised as follows in the Albany *Argus* of December 16, 1817:

SINGING SCHOOL

Mr. Steele will commence school this evening for the purpose of instructing youth in the Rudiments of vocal Music, at the Session Room of the Presbyterian Church in Beaver Street. Those who are desirous of attending, can become members by applying at the room.

Although no definite evidence that Steele functioned as a practicing musician earlier than 1817 has been found, there are indications that this may have been a part-time career engaged in over a long period of time, simultaneously with his bookselling and printing activities. The tune-books he advertised for sale as early as 1801 strengthen the impression that he was more than casually interested in music. The fact that creative revision of *The Easy Instructor* virtually ceased at the close of his life is suggestive; until more information comes to light, it should probably be assumed that the Albany editions published prior to 1828 are the product of Steele's imagination and labor.

Apparently, the transaction between Little and the Albany group did not include the transfer of the original plates, as a new set engraved by Henry W. Snyder, an Albany craftsman, was used for the earliest group of Albany editions (Editions B, C, D*a*, D*b*, and E), the first of which was issued in 1805 and the last in 1808.

Snyder's work was more skillful than that of the anonymous original engraver (who may perhaps have been Little himself), but it is still quite crude compared to the productions of other engravers active during the same period. Although the music editor radically revised the contents, omitting 25 tunes from the first edition and adding 22 others, he did not change its emphasis upon music in the native idiom.

BEGINNING with the first undated Albany *Easy Instructor* (Edition F), the engraved music plates characteristic of prior editions were abandoned. This and subsequent editions were printed from a type font designed specifically for the shape-note system.[16] The originator of this font was undoubtedly either William Wood or Obadiah R. Van Benthuysen, whose names are found in the colophon of Edition F. The probability is that Van Benthuysen deserves the major share of the credit, as Wood disappears from the history of *The Easy Instructor* after the appearance of this single edition, while Van Benthuysen continued his association with the book throughout its existence, first as its typographer and later as its printer. In 1810, Van Benthuysen formed a brief partnership with George Newton (see Editions G and H), who died on November 20, 1811. Thereafter he continued in business independently (see Editions I and J) until 1813, when he joined forces with Robert Packard (see Edition K and all following Albany editions). The firm of Packard and Van Benthuysen was to become illustrious in the annals of the Albany printing trade,

16. One might naturally assume that this was the first such type font in existence, but facts are otherwise. About two years after the appearance of Ed. A*a*, Andrew Law, one of the most prominent singing-masters of the day, brought out the fourth edition of his *Art of Singing* (Cambridge: W. Hilliard, 1803) "printed upon a new plan." This particular edition and later publications of Law's were printed typographically with shape-notes identical to those in *The Easy Instructor;* however, Law interchanged the characters for *fa* and *la* and entirely abandoned the use of staff lines. While Law cannot be credited with the invention of the shape-note system, he no doubt was first to make typographical use of the characters. See Chapter 4 for a fuller discussion of this point.

continuing in existence throughout the 19th century and well into the 20th, finally closing its books in 1922.[17]

Typographical editions of *The Easy Instructor* were brought out at the rate of one or two each year from 1808 to 1822. Thereafter, as the demand for the book tapered off, they were issued at bi-yearly intervals with one exception. The printing record of *The Easy Instructor* demonstrates that it probably reached the peak of its popularity between 1813 and 1817. Editorial changes, presumably made by Steele to keep the collection up to the moment, followed a clear-cut pattern. In each new edition, a greater or lesser number of old American favorites was deleted and new and fashionable European tunes were added (see Appendix B, Table VIII). At irregular intervals, extra eight-page signatures containing almost exclusively European music were also added, thus progressively enlarging the number of pages from 104 in the first typographical edition to 136 in the last. At the same time, the uniquely native flavor of the early editions was gradually watered down to the point where the character of its music was practically indistinguishable from that of the "reform" collections. Indeed, except for title, instructions, and notation, there is but little resemblance between the early and late editions of *The Easy Instructor*.

BEFORE the last of the engraved editions came out in 1808, other publishers, particularly in Pennsylvania, had become aware of the phenomenal success of *The Easy Instructor* and imitations began to appear in print. Ironically, one of the first of these brings the story back to Philadelphia, where the history of *The Easy Instructor* had its inception in 1798. The John Jenkins Husband[18] edition

17. See John Clyde Oswald, *Printing in the Americas* (New York, 1937), p. 226, and Clarence S. Brigham, *History and Bibliography of American Newspapers, 1690–1820* (Worcester, 1947), I, 587.

18. An English musician who apparently arrived in the United States in 1806 or 1807. He has a stronger claim to immortality if the tune "Revive Us Again" (better known in secular circles as "Hallelujah, I'm a Bum"), attributed to him in Lester Hostetler, *Handbook to the Mennonite Hymnary* (Newton, Kans., 1949), pp. 253–54, is actually his composition.

appropriation of the distinctive shapes as well (see Illus. 15). As the *Leichter Unterricht* was designed to appeal to the German-speaking Pennsylvania population which would not ordinarily be reached by such a book as *The Easy Instructor*, its compiler chose primarily music from the continental European tradition, although he did include some of the favorite native American tunes set to German texts. Wyeth's comprehensive *Repository of Sacred Music* (Harrisburg, 1810; also 1811, 1812, 1814, 1816, 1818, 1823, 1826, 1834), on the other hand, duplicated the character of *The Easy Instructor* almost exactly, but masqueraded its indebtedness to the earlier tune-book under a totally different title. There appears to be strong evidence that nearly half its 156 tunes were taken directly from various editions of *The Easy Instructor*, as in many cases Wyeth reprinted without change distinctive typographical errors and mistakes in composer ascription found only in the Little and Smith work. One of the most significant music publications of the early 19th century was Wyeth's *Repository of Sacred Music, Part Second* (Harrisburg, 1813; also 1820). This proved to be the first really influential anthology of what the late George Pullen Jackson dubbed spiritual folk-song, and *Part Second* was a major source drawn upon for materials by later compilers such as Ananias Davisson, James M. Boyd, Joseph Funk, Allen D. Carden, William Walker, and many others.[20] It undoubtedly set the pattern for the distinctive combination of Yankee psalm- and fuging-tunes and secular folk melodies which constitutes the Southern folk-hymnody tradition out of which such magnificent tune-books as Walker's *Southern Harmony* and the White and King *Sacred Harp* grew. *Part Second* was perhaps more important than *The Easy Instructor* itself in the eventual dissemination of the shape-note idea to the South. Still another of Wyeth's shape-note publications was Johannes Rothbaust's bilingual *Die Franklin Harmonie, und leichter Unterricht* (Harrisburg, 1821; Vol. II, 1821), reprinted by a different publisher as a second, revised edition

20. For a study of the important role played by this tune-book in the development of the Southern tradition, see Chapter 7.

under the English title *The Franklin Harmony and Easy Instructor* (Chambersburg: H. Ruby, *ca.* 1830). This curious production, with its frank indebtedness to *The Easy Instructor* flaunted on its title page, exhibits a most interesting crossblend of German and Anglo-Saxon music traditions in its contents.

THE FIRM NAME Websters & Skinner, found in the second engraved Albany edition of *The Easy Instructor* (Edition C), came into existence on May 19, 1806, when Elisha W. Skinner, the brothers Webster's nephew, joined them in their business. In the fall of 1811, Elisha's two brothers, Hezekiah and Daniel, were taken into partnership and the firm then became known as Websters & Skinners. Despite mutations in the firm's name, the *Easy Instructor* copyright seems to have remained the sole property of the two Websters and Daniel Steele. Understandably enough, the three men were not anxious to surrender their lucrative property to the public domain when the copyright on the work was due to expire on December 10, 1816. One of the three, apparently George Webster, hit upon a clever idea to prolong their control of the shape-note idea regardless of the expiration of the copyright, which could only be renewed, according to the law, by the original owner. On February 28, 1816, a patent covering the casting and use of the shape-note types was granted to George Webster, obviously as agent for the Albany trio. Most unfortunately, the original patent application, which ordinarily would have been preserved, was destroyed in one of the many fires which ravaged the United States Patent Office early in its career, and only a bare notice of the patent grant is extant. Were the details of the application itself available, considerable information about the early history of *The Easy Instructor* might have been gathered from it. Notice of the patent grant is found on the title page of the 120-page Edition P, published shortly after the expiration of the copyright, where the familiar phrase "Proprietors of the Copy-Right" is omitted and in its place appears the legend: "The Music Types used in printing this Book are secured to the Proprietors by

Patent Right." This notice is unquestionably the genesis of the term "patent-notes," frequently used in later years as a synonym for shape-notes.

With the expiration of the copyright, the proprietors apparently decided to license other publishers to cast and use their patented shape-notes and to reprint *The Easy Instructor* itself. The first to obtain such a license seems to have been William Williams of Utica, New York, whose name is found in the list of authorized agents printed on the title page of Edition P. Williams, who was also the publisher of Thomas Hastings and Solomon Warriner's influential *Musica Sacra* (Utica, 1816; many later editions),[21] brought out editions of *The Easy Instructor* in 1818 and 1820 (Editions S and W), using the 120-page Edition P as prototype. His only editorial change was to delete a single long American tune and to substitute for it three shorter European ones, thus giving his editions, both of which are identical in content, a total of 127 compositions as compared with the 125 of his model. Working with the unfamiliar shape-notes apparently proved somewhat troublesome to him, as his editions are poorly executed and are replete with typographical errors in both music and text. Only one other printer, J. Pace of Cincinnati, is known to have brought out an authorized *Easy Instructor*. The Pace imprint, published in 1819 (Edition U), used the first of the Williams editions as the source of its music rather than the 120-page Albany edition, in some instances duplicating textual errors found there only. The Cincinnati edition omits the last 13 tunes in the Utica edition.

That the Albany group failed to sell additional licenses is not surprising. Part of their plan, possibly conceived at the same time application for a patent was made, may well have been to cut the ground out from under the feet of their self-manufactured competitors by issuing revised editions while selling licenses to reprint the old. Thus, on the one hand, they hoped to reap a profit from

21. See John C. Williams, *An Oneida County Printer, William Williams, Printer, Publisher, Editor* (New York, 1906).

the sale of permissions, while on the other, they maintained command of the market by continuing to adjust the content of their own editions to conform to the changing musical tastes of the moment. On the latter account, all Albany editions published after Edition P are designated "revised and enlarged." These, the last of which appeared in 1831, bring to a close the history of *The Easy Instructor.*

7

JOHN WYETH'S *Repository of Sacred Music* *Part Second* (1813): A NORTHERN PRECURSOR OF SOUTHERN FOLK-HYMNODY

THE AMERICAN FOLK-HYMN (or spiritual folk-song, as it was christened by the late George Pullen Jackson) is basically a secular folk-tune which happens to be sung to a religious text. In many cases the text is also folk-derived, but not infrequently it is drawn from the body of orthodox hymns found in the hymnals of earlier days. The music, however, is almost invariably of folk origin, and its antecedents can be generally traced to the family of Anglo-Celtic folk-music, either vocal or instrumental.

The practice of singing religious texts to secular folk-tunes is more closely linked with the early history of American music than is usually realized. As early as the 1730s, folk-hymnody appears to have flourished, prospering under the impetus of the "Great Awakening," when Jonathan Edwards, George Whitefield, and other inflammatory preachers seared the religious conscience of New England. It is highly probable that folk-harmony was an omnipresent phenomenon during the second half of the 18th century, although it is difficult to cite concrete written evidence to that effect. Certainly, the fact that the *composed* singing-school music of early America (beginning in the 1770s and mushrooming at a tremendous rate in the next three decades) was stylistically so closely akin to the folk-music of the British Isles, and hence to the folk-hymn, strongly suggests that such was the actual state of affairs. Furthermore, it is reasonable to assume that the highly characteristic style of composition practiced by Daniel Read, the Lewis Edsons, Jacob French, Oliver Brownson, Timothy Swan, Justin Morgan, and many others active in Connecticut and central Massachusetts during the 1780s and 1790s was based on the music they heard around them; the semi-folk idiom they cultivated was in all likelihood based on the music ingrained in their consciousness—Anglo-Celtic folk-music and its religious offshoot, American folk-hymnody.

Despite their popularity and widespread diffusion among the populace as a whole during the 18th century, folk-hymns do not seem to have achieved the permanence of print much before the beginning of the 19th. Folk-texts alone, as well as secular folk-tunes, had been published, but the peculiar combination of sacred text and lay tune only on very rare occasions.[1] It was not until after the second great wave of religious revivals swept the country around 1800 that the history of folk-hymnody in print actually began. The first compendia of folk-hymns were Northern collections, but very soon afterwards such collections began to appear in the South and the West of the time—Virginia, Tennessee, Kentucky, the Missouri Territory, Ohio, the Western Reserve. The transit of folk-hymnody from the North to the South seems to have taken place during the second decade of the 19th century, roughly coinciding with the retreat of the quasi-folk composed American music of the singing-schools from urban to rural surroundings. During the crucial decade, these two related types of music joined hands, so to speak, and ever since then the Yankee fuging-tune and psalm-tune are found side by side with the folk-

1. A few authentic folk-hymns can be found in the tune-books of the late 1790s. See for example, Amos Pilsbury's *The United States' Sacred Harmony* (Boston, 1799), which contains (among others) the first known printing of KEDRON, one of the loveliest and most popular of all folk-hymns. It is interesting to note that Pilsbury himself was a Southerner active in Charleston, South Carolina.

hymn. In this form (later to be known *in toto* as the Southern folk-hymnody (tradition) they become a prominent feature of Southern musico-religious life throughout the 19th century. Even today, the tradition is not yet extinct, although it must be said that it appears to be moribund. This essay attempts to point out the importance of a Northern tune-book, John Wyeth's *Repository of Sacred Music, Part Second* (see Illus. 16), in the origins of Southern folk-hymnody and in its subsequent development, as exemplified in Southern tune-books of the period.

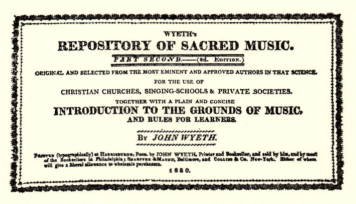

16. Title page, John Wyeth's *Repository of Sacred Music, Part Second,* 2nd edition. Courtesy of the Library of Congress.

THE Southern history of the printed folk-hymn begins in 1815 or 1816 with the publication of Ananias Davisson's *Kentucky Harmony* at Harrisonburg, Virginia (see Illus. 17). Like contemporary Northern tune-books, it was brought out in the typical oblong format and contained a selection of various tunes and the customary introduction to the grounds and rules of music. The *Kentucky Harmony* was peculiarly distinctive in that its contents included a large number of authentic folk-hymns. It was an extremely popular book in the South; edition followed edition, and it left its mark on Southern folk-hymnody for decades to come. The extent of its influence can be gauged from George Pullen

Jackson's classic study, *White Spirituals in the Southern Uplands* (Chapel Hill, N. C., 1933), which devotes many pages to tracing borrowings from its pages by later Southern compilers such as Carden, Boyd, Funk, Carrell, Moore, Walker, White, and King. The collections assembled by these men, as well as their individual teaching efforts and enthusiasm for the music they disseminated, were to a large degree responsible for the growth of the singing tradition throughout the South.

KENTUCKY HARMONY.

OR

A CHOICE COLLECTION OF PSALM TUNES HYMNS AND ANTHEMS:

IN THREE PARTS.

TAKEN FROM THE MOST EMINENT AUTHORS, AND WELL ADAPTED TO CHRISTIAN CHURCHES, SINGING SCHOOLS, OR PRIVATE SOCIETIES,

SELECTED, BY

ANANIAS DAVISSON.

FOURTH EDITION.

PRINTED, and sold by the *AUTHOR*, in Harrisonburg Virginia ; and by one of the principal Booksellers in each of the following places, *viz.* Staunton. Lexington and Abington Va. Knoxville, E. Tennessee, Nashville, W. Tennessee, Louisville Kentucky, and St. Louis Missouri.

N. B. All description of Music printing can be done at this office, upon as reasonable terms as any in the United States.

1821.

17. Title page, Ananias Davisson's *Kentucky Harmony*, 4th edition. Courtesy of the Library of Congress.

It can therefore be seen that an inquiry into the antecedents of these Southern tune-books (and of Davisson's *Kentucky Harmony* as the first of the Southern species, in particular) is of some genuine consequence despite the obscurity of the names of their compilers. As has been strongly hinted, the idea of printing folk-hymns was not original with Davisson; several men had preceded him in that field. Although Jeremiah Ingalls of New Hampshire has been generally credited with being the first to issue a collection which includes folk-hymns, primacy probably belongs to Samuel Holyoke, a more prominent New England compiler and singing-master. One of the lesser known of his half-dozen tune-

books, *The Christian Harmonist* (Salem, 1804), which was specifically designed for the use of Baptist churches, contains a large
number of folk-texts mostly selected from Joshua Smith's *Divine
Hymns, or Spiritual Songs* (Norwich, N. H., 1784) set to a variety
of folk-like tunes, many of which had never been previously
printed. From a study of the content of the tune-book, it would
appear that Holyoke here attempted to compose in the folk idiom,
and it is quite possible that some of the tunes were notated directly
from the oral tradition. The collection was not widely used, however, and it does not seem to have been known outside of north-
eastern Massachusetts and southeastern Vermont and New Hampshire. A similar fate greeted Ingalls's *Christian Harmony* (Exeter,
N. H., 1805), which in all probability did not circulate much
beyond the small orbit of the compiler's personal activity. There
is some possibility that Ingalls was familiar with the Holyoke
work, as he utilized many of the same texts, a few of the same
tune names, and perhaps modelled the title of his book after
Holyoke's.

Neither of these tune-books, however, appears to have been
known to Davisson at the time he compiled the *Kentucky Harmony*. Despite a similarity in character, there is virtually no dupli-
cation of musical content, and both Northern books must be
eliminated as significant precursors of the *Kentucky Harmony*.

THE progenitor of the Davisson collection is a third Northern
tune-book, very little known even among specialists in early American music history, John Wyeth's *Repository of Sacred Music, Part
Second* (Harrisburg, Pa., 1813; 2nd edition, 1820, differing from
the first only in minor details), which was published at least two
(and possibly three) years before the *Kentucky Harmony* came
from the presses. According to Wyeth, some 25,000 copies were
eventually sold, a quite respectable figure in view of the fact that
the population of Harrisburg in 1820 was only a little over 3,000.
As the town was directly on the main line of emigration to the
South and West, most of the copies of *Part Second* appear to have

travelled in that direction rather than towards New England.

By 1813, when *Part Second* appeared, Wyeth was already known as a tune-book compiler because of several collections, the most popular of which was his *Repository of Sacred Music* (Harrisburg, Pa., 1810; six subsequent editions, the last of which appeared as late as 1834). The *Repository* was quite different in character from *Part Second* despite the similar name. Indeed, it was unquestionably one of the best-selling tune-books of the entire decade. It was primarily an eclectic collection of the best-liked American psalm- and fuging-tunes of the day, quite similar in character and content to many others of earlier years. Its immediate prototype seems to have been the famous *Easy Instructor*[2] compiled by William Little and William Smith. From this tune-book, Wyeth borrowed the characteristic shape-note method of notation, which was eventually to become standard in the South, where it was almost universally adopted. No new tunes are to be found in the pages of the *Repository*.

Superficially, there appears to be little difference between the *Repository of Sacred Music* and the *Repository of Sacred Music, Part Second;* their formats are identical, and both make use of the Little and Smith shape-notes. In content, however, they are completely dissimilar. *Part Second* was something new in the tune-book field, an attempt to supply the musical needs of the vast market created by the revivals and camp-meetings prevalent in Pennsylvania at the time. As such, it was a thoroughly distinctive collection, quite independent of the first *Repository*. Wyeth may have deliberately cultivated the confusion that arose between the two (*Part Second* is frequently mistaken, even today, for a second edition of the less important *Repository*) in an attempt to cash in on the popularity of the first *Repository*. That he was certainly aware of it is evident from the preface to *Part Second*, where he writes that "while introducing this second part, he by no means wishes it to be understood that the first is to be

2. See Chapter 6.

laid aside." *Part Second* might well be better known today had Wyeth given it a title as distinctive as its content.

AN INITIAL CLUE to the close relationship between Davisson's *Kentucky Harmony* and Wyeth's *Repository of Sacred Music, Part Second* can be found in the preface to the Southern collection. There Davisson lists the names of compilers with whose works he was familiar: Little, Smith, Wyeth, Billings, Holyoke,[3] Atwell,[4] and Peck,[5] in the order named. To these should be added (from an analysis of the content of the *Kentucky Harmony*) Daniel Read and Nehemiah Shumway.[6] Except for Wyeth's *Part Second*, none of the many tune-books compiled by the men cited contains any appreciable number of folk-hymns, and a comparative analysis of the Davisson and Wyeth books conclusively demonstrates that *Part Second* was the salient folk-hymnodic influence in the content of the *Kentucky Harmony*.

Wyeth claims that 58 of the 149 tunes included in *Part Second,* more than one-third of the total number, are there published for the first time. The correctness of this assertion is of vital importance, because if it could be demonstrated that many of these were in actuality taken from earlier printed sources, the special role played by *Part Second* in the establishment of Southern folk-hymnody might be legitimately questioned. After a long search, however, I have been able to discover prior publication of only five[7] of these 58 tunes called "new"—certainly not a sufficient number to invalidate the general accuracy of the claim. When it is realized that no less than 44 of these 58 new tunes are quite definitely folk-hymns, *Part Second* begins to assume considerable

3. As has been previously stated, the Holyoke collection with which Davisson was familiar was probably not *The Christian Harmonist*.

4. Probably Thomas H. Atwill, compiler of *The New York and Vermont Collection*. A Richard Atwell is known as a composer, but no tune-book of his compilation has been discovered.

5. Daniel L. Peck, compiler of *The Musical Medley* (Dedham, Mass., 1808) and *A Valuable Selection of Sacred Music* (Philadelphia, 1810).

6. Compiler of *The American Harmony* (Philadelphia, 1793; also 1801).

7. For identification, see the notes to Table III.

significance.

Because this particular body of 44 folk-hymns began its printed existence on the pages of *Part Second,* the establishment of relationships between the Wyeth book and other later collections is a comparatively simple and clearcut task. Table III shows the extent of the eventual dissemination of the folk-hymns first published by Wyeth (which include some of the finest and best known in the entire tradition) through a comparison of the new music in *Part Second* with the content of six important and representative later Southern tune-books:

Table III

THE "NEW" TUNES IN WYETH'S *Repository of Sacred Music,* *Part Second* AS REPRINTED IN LATER SOUTHERN TUNE-BOOKS

Key

WR2   John Wyeth, *Repository of Sacred Music, Part Second* (1813)

DKH   Ananias Davisson, *Kentucky Harmony* (*ca.* 1815)

BVR   James M. Boyd, *The Virginia Sacred Musical Repository* (1818)

CMH   Allen D. Carden, *The Missouri Harmony* (1820)

FGM   Joseph Funk, *Genuine Church Music* (1832)

WSH   William Walker, *The Southern Harmony* (1835)

WKH   B. F. White and E. J. King, *The Sacred Harp* (1844)

Note: First editions of these rather scarce tune-books were not, unfortunately, uniformly available for purposes of comparison. Three of the above (*BVR, CMH,* and *FGM*) contain no composer attributions. Presence of an identical tune in any of these is indicated with an "X." Asterisked tunes are folk-hymns.

Tune name	WR2	DKH	BVR	CMH	FGM	WSH	WKH
°Adoration	?	Davisson[a]		X[a]			
°Animation	?						
Babylonian Captivity	Dare	Dare		X			
Band of Love[b]	?				X		
Bellevue	Dare			X			
Bridgetown	Dare						
°Christmas Hymn	?						
°Communion	Robison[c]			X[d]			?[d]
°Concert	?						

Tune name	WR₂	DKH	BVR	CMH	FGM	WSH	WKH
°Consolation (I)	?	Dean	X	X	X	Dean	Dean
°Consolation (II)	?					?	?e
°Davis	?			X		?	
°Dependence	Findlay						
°Dismission	Dare						
°Fairton	Dare						
Fall of Babylon	?						
Fidelia	Lewer			X			
°Fiducia	Robison	Robertson	X		X	Robison	
°Forster	?		X	X			
°Glasgow	Dare	Davisson	X	X		Dare	Dare
Gospel Trump	Dare						
°Hallelujah	?			X			
°Happiness	?						
°Heavenly Union	?						
°Kedronf	Dare	Davissong	X			Dare	Dare
°Landaff	Findlay		X				
Libertyh	?	Wyeth		X		?	?
Marcus Hook	Dare						
°Messiah	?						
°Middle Paxton	Austin						
°Millville	Dare						
°Minister's Farewelli	?					?	?
°Moralityj	?		X	X		?	?
Mount Hope	Dare						
°New Canaan	?	Davissonk		Xk			
°New Monmouth	?	Billings		X	X		
Ninety-Fifth	Chapin	Chapin		X		Colton	Colton
°Ninety-Third	Chapin	Chapin		X		Chapin	Chapin
°Perseverance	?						
°Power	White						
Providencel	C. Curtis						
°Redeeming Grace	?					?	
Redemption Anthem	?	Stephen-sonm				A. Ben-ham, Sr.	
°Restoration	?						
°Roadstown	Dare						
°Rockbridge	Chapin	Chapin		X	X	Chapin	
°Rockingham	Chapin	Chapin		X	X	Chapinn	
°Solicitude	?						
°Solitude	M'Kyeso		X				
°Spring Hill	?				X	?d	
°Sterling	?		X				
°Sublimity	?						
°Transport	?		X			?	
Triumph	?						

Tune name	*WR2*	*DKH*	*BVR*	*CMH*	*FGM*	*WSH*	*WKH*
*Twenty-fourth	Chapin	Chapin[p]	X	X	X	Chapin[p]	Chapin[p]
*Unitia	Chapin		X		X		
*Vernon	Chapin		X	X	X	Chapin	Chapin
*Willington[q]	?						
Wilmington	Dare						

a. Called "Condescension."

b. Previously published, called "Washington," in Andrew Law's *Select Harmony* (Philadelphia, *ca.* 1811).

c. In the second edition, the composer's name is given as "Robinson."

d. Variant.

e. Called "Consolation (New)."

f. Previously published in Amos Pilsbury's *The United States' Sacred Harmony* (Boston, 1799).

g. Variant, called "Garland."

h. Previously published in Stephen Jenks's *The Musical Harmonist* (New Haven, 1800).

i. Appears only in the 1st edition of *WR2*.

j. Previously published (with secular text) in A. Aimwell's (A. Adgate's) *The Philadelphia Songster* (Philadelphia, 1789), and frequently elsewhere, including England and Scotland, under the title "Alknomook," or "The Indian Chief." A very popular tune at the beginning of the 19th century, well known as "the death song of the Cherokee Indians."

k. Called "Reflection."

l. Not in *WR2* index; apparently substituted in the 2nd edition for "Minister's Farewell."

m. Truncated version.

n. *WKH* also includes a variant version, with the same name, claimed by Lowell Mason.

o. A misprint in the *WR2* index. Should read "M. Kyes."

p. Called "Primrose."

q. Previously published in James Lyon's *Urania* (Philadelphia, 1761) and elsewhere.

A relationship between *Part Second* and the *Kentucky Harmony* is immediately evident. Davisson borrowed 15 tunes from Wyeth and, curiously enough, three of these are claimed as his own compositions. Two of these three tunes, Adoration and New Canaan, are disguised under new names as Condescension and Reflection; the third, Dare's Glasgow, appears with the same tune name but is reprinted in a different key. The similarity in title between James M. Boyd's *The Virginia Sacred Musical Repository* and the Wyeth collection would in itself lead to the suspicion that Boyd knew *Part Second*. This is confirmed through the 13 tunes he borrowed from Wyeth, a selection quite different from that made by Davisson. In the preface to *The Missouri Harmony,* Allen D. Carden "acknowledges himself indebted to Mr. 'Wyeth's Repository, part second' for many of the rules and remarks contained in this introduction"; he was also indebted to Wyeth for 19 tunes. Funk borrowed 11 for his *Genuine Church Music,* despite his professed abhorrence for such "ephemera"; Walker 20 for *The Southern Harmony;* White and King 11 for *The Sacred Harp.* Only the last collection to appear in point of time, the 1844 *Sacred Harp,* does not show conclusive evidence of heavy borrowings specifically from *Part Second.* By that late date, however, it is quite likely that the Wyeth book was no longer a major factor in Southern folk-hymnody, having been supplanted by others, among them the very tune-books it had supplied with distinctive melodic materals.

Many of the folk-hymns which emerged in print for the first time in *Part Second* are to be found in modern anthologies of American folk-hymnody, generally rediscovered in later sources than the Wyeth collection. Table IV shows the extent to which the 44 Wyeth folk-hymns appear in five major collections of this sort.

Particularly noteworthy as an indication of the importance of the Wyeth body of folk-hymnody is the comparison with the list of the most popular tunes in the Southern tradition that appears in Jackson's *White Spirituals in the Southern Uplands.* The Jackson list is based on an analysis of 15 Southern tune-books. Of his 80 tunes, 65 fall in the folk-hymn category, and it is significant that 12 of these first appeared in *Part Second.*

IN VIEW of the undeniably important role played by *Part Second* in the beginnings of Southern folk-hymnody, some information about the men who were connected with it and something of the provenance of the collection itself might be useful. Oddly enough, John Wyeth (1770–1858) does not seem to have been a musician,

Table IV

FOLK-HYMNS FIRST PUBLISHED IN *Part Second*

Key

JWS George Pullen Jackson, *White Spirituals in the Southern Uplands* (1933)

JSF George Pullen Jackson, *Spiritual Folk-Songs of Early America* (1937)

BFH Annabel Morris Buchanan, *Folk Hymns of America* (1938)

JDE George Pullen Jackson, *Down-East Spirituals* (1943)

JAS George Pullen Jackson, *Another Sheaf of White Spirituals* (1952)

Note: The numbers are those of the folk-hymns as they appear in the various collections. Entries under JWS pertain to the list of the 80 most popular tunes in the Southern tradition as found there.

Tune name	JWS	JSF	BFH	JDE	JAS
Adoration		30			
Animation					85
Christmas Hymn			40		
Communion	57	24			
Concert					210
Consolation (I)			3	135	
Consolation (II)				131	
Davis			18		
Dependence					
Dismission					
Fairton					
Fiducia	15			183	
Forster				66	
Glasgow	56				
Hallelujah		101			
Happiness					
Heavenly Union			38	9	
Kedron	71	57			
Landaff				199	
Messiah					
Middle Paxton					
Millville					
Minister's Farewell	48			18	13
Morality	79			138	
New Canaan	26	122			

Tune name	JWS	JSF	BFH	JDE	JAS
New Monmouth					
Ninety-Third	25		29	146	
Preserverance					
Power					
Redeeming Grace			14		
Restoration					
Roadstown			30		
Rockbridge	38				204
Rockingham	29			150	
Solicitude					
Solitude				209	
Spring Hill			7	158	
Sterling					
Sublimity					
Transport				48	
Twenty-Fourth	5			165	
Unitia					
Vernon	49			19	
Willington					

and there is no evidence that he was even particularly interested in music other than from a purely business point of view. Wyeth (whose exciting youthful days included a stay in the island of San Domingo, from whence he escaped in a series of hairbreadth adventures) was a book publisher of some prominence and the editor and printer of *The Oracle of Dauphin*, a weekly Harrisburg newspaper, at the time he began to engage in the publication of tune-books. In all probability, he was attracted to this field because of the financial success of several earlier collections such as the Little and Smith *Easy Instructor*, Adgate's *Philadelphia Harmony*, the anonymous *Village Harmony*, and Isaiah Thomas's *Worcester Collection*. His 1810 *Repository of Sacred Music* was clearly modelled after these tune-books, from all of which he borrowed materials. Wyeth's function as "compiler" seems to have been similar to that of Isaiah Thomas (also a non-musician), who consulted with local musicians of his acquaintance in gauging popular taste and then attempted to cater to it.[8] Wyeth succeeded in hitting the jack pot with the 1810 *Repository*, which is said to have sold 120,000 copies. Its popularity was probably the principal factor in persuading him to continue publishing tune-books.

The idea of *Part Second* no doubt originated in Wyeth's mind as a potentially profitable business venture. The collection was designed to attract Methodist and Baptist groups, who were the singers of folk-hymnody at the time. This was a large and expanding market; the revivalistic fervor and religious enthusiasm then sweeping the country were making many converts, the ranks of the folk-hymn singers were rapidly increasing, and no collection of the sort envisioned by Wyeth was available to them. Wyeth himself had no personal religious inclination in that direction, as he was an extremely active Unitarian.[9]

The fact that Wyeth himself was no musician poses a collateral problem: whose were the *musical* brains behind *Part Second?* It appears highly probable that the person responsible for the organization of the tune-book and its general editorial supervision was the Rev. Elkanah Kelsay Dare (1782–1826), Methodist clergyman, Freemason, and musician, who at one time served as the dean of boys at Wilmington College, Wilmington, Del., an institution long since defunct. Dare was the author of a theoretical work on music, quoted at some length in the introduction to *Part Second*, which apparently never achieved publication.[10] He is represented

---

8. Frank J. Metcalf's attribution to Wyeth of the well-known hymn-tune NETTLETON (first published without composer attribution as HALLELUJAH in *Part Second*) is questionable. This claim is found in *Stories of Hymn Tunes* (New York, 1928).

9. Other examples of Wyeth's adventurous opportunism in tune-book publication are known. He attempted to tap the German-speaking Pennsylvania market with two most interesting collections, Joseph Doll's *Der leichter Unterricht* (Harrisburg, 1810) and Johannes Rothbaust's *Die Franklin Harmonie* (Harrisburg, 1821), both of which exhibit a most remarkable cross blend of all sorts of different cultural trends in American music, and both of which derive from *The Easy Instructor*. See Chapter 6, pp. 133ff.

10. See page 3 of *Part Second*, where Wyeth writes: "The following observations on Music, are extracted, by permission, from the Manusript [sic]

as a composer in the Wyeth collection by 13 tunes (all published for the first time), the largest number credited to any single individual in *Part Second*. It is logical to assume that Dare was perhaps charged with the responsibility of notating and arranging the 30 unattributed tunes newly published in the tune-book, but this should not preclude the possibility that one of the others associated with Wyeth may have performed this task. So far as it has been ascertained, *Part Second* is the only tune-book to which Dare personally contributed; all the tunes attributed to him in later collections can be traced to this original source. If Dare was the main musical figure behind *Part Second*, he must be considered most important in the foundation of the Southern singing tradition, and hence is undoubtedly entitled to at least a footnote in the history of American music.

Another little known but nevertheless important name that comes to light for the first time in *Part Second* is that of "Chapin," to whom seven tunes were attributed. Several of these (as well as some of Dare's tunes) are to be found in the Jackson list of the most popular tunes in the Southern tradition cited earlier. But despite the fact that music by "Chapin" is found in many Southern compilations, the identity of the composer remains something of a minor mystery. In all probability, he was one Lucius Chapin (1760–1842), a Massachusettsian who enlisted as a fifer in the Revolutionary War and went into the Shenandoah Valley of Virginia as a practiced singing-master as early as 1787.[11]

---

work of E. K. Dare, A. B. late of Wilmington college, which we hope, ere long to see published entire." Perhaps Dare submitted the manuscript to Wyeth for publication and thus came to his attention as a musician. If the book was published it seems to have completely disappeared; I have been able to locate no other mention of it.

11. See Charles Hamm, "The Chapins and Sacred Music in the South and West," *Jour. of Research in Mus. Ed.*, VIII (1960), 91–98. Both "L. Chapin" and "A. Chapin" are frequently cited in Southern tune-books, the latter being Lucius's brother Amzi Chapin (1768–1835), also a singing-master. Hamm points out that Amzi joined Lucius in Virginia in 1791, and feels that Ananias Davisson probably received his instruction in music from one or both of the Chapins. He also demonstrates that the confusion about the identity of the Chapin who composed the folk-hymns is perhaps a bit more complex than was

Interestingly enough, a Chapin appears to have been associated with Davisson as well as with Wyeth, and several Chapin tunes were published for the first time in the *Kentucky Harmony*. This Chapin may well have been the person responsible for introducing *Part Second* to the Southern compiler.

Still another name found in *Part Second* establishing a connection between Wyeth and Davisson is that of White, who probably was the same "White" with whom Davisson collaborated in the composition of a few tunes first published in *The Supplement to the Kentucky Harmony* (Harrisonburg, Va., 1820). An Austin is known to have contributed to Stephen Jenks's *Delights of Harmony, or Norfolk Compiler* (Dedham, Mass., 1805), and M. Kyes to Asahel Benham's *Social Harmony* (Wallingford, Conn. 1798). Of the others to whom new tunes are attributed in *Part Second* (Robison or Robertson,[12] Findlay, Lewer, and C. Curtis), nothing at all is known.

SOME attempt also has been made to trace the backgrounds of *Part Second* from the tunes found in its pages that were borrowed from earlier printed sources. These are 91 in number, and Table V shows the composers to whom they are attributed.

Discounting the 38 tunes that appear without composer attribution (most of which are, nevertheless, clearly of American origin), 33 of the remaining 51 are by Americans. Of the 91 old tunes, 28 are fuging-tunes; from these some of the exact tunebooks used by Wyeth in compiling *Part Second* can be identified. His sources include Daniel Read's *Columbian Harmonist* (Boston,

---

previously suspected, since no fewer than seven Chapins (six of them from the Lucius-Amzi Chapin family) were involved in music at the time. Confusion has been worse confounded, thanks to Joe S. James, editor of the "historical" edition of the White and King *Sacred Harp* published in Atlanta under the title *The Original Sacred Harp* as late as 1929. Mr. James manages to get Chapin mixed up with that well-known composer of American folk-hymns, F. F. Chopin! This is forgivable in a work that can be considered at best one of "folk musicology," but what is one to say about John Jacob Niles's *Shape-Note Study Book* (New York, 1950), where "Chapin" becomes Amzi Chopin?

12. Alternative spellings from the 1st and 2nd editions of *Part Second*.

Table V

TUNES IN *Part Second* BORROWED FROM EARLIER COLLECTIONS

Note: *American composers are asterisked.*

Composer	Number of tunes	Composer	Number of tunes
Anonymous	38	*Hibbert	1
Madan	10	*Holyoke	1
*Billings	9	*Ingalls	1
*Kimball	3	Kirby	1
*Holden	3	Lane	1
*Brown	2	*Morgan	1
*Bull	2	*Peck	1
*Selby	2	Pleyel	1
Tans'ur	2	Premmer	1
Arne	1	*Read	1
*Doolittle	1	Shrubsole	1
*French	1	*Shumway	1
*Gillet	1	Smith	1
*Hall	1	*Wood	1
Handel	1		

1807; 3rd edition), the Little and Smith *Easy Instructor* (Albany; an edition published between 1809 and 1811), Isaiah Thomas's *Worcester Collection* (Boston; one of the editions edited by Oliver Holden between 1797 and 1803—either the 6th, 7th, or 8th), Ebenezer Child's *Sacred Musician* (Boston, 1804), Thomas H. Atwill's *New York and Vermont Collection* (both the 1st edition, Lansingburgh, N.Y., 1802, and the 2nd edition, Albany, 1804), and the anonymous *Village Harmony* (Exeter, N. H.; either the 5th edition of 1800, the 6th of 1803, or the 7th of 1806). Others were unquestionably utilized, but it is impossible to establish their identity conclusively.

Even in such a strikingly homegrown collection of American music as is *Part Second*, the growing English influence that was driving the native music out of the urban centers is evident. Ten tunes attributed to Martin Madan, the English compiler of *The Lock Hospital Collection* (probably reprinted from other American sources, however) were included by Wyeth. This was actually a greater number than he printed by William Billings, a forecast of the coming victory of European church song and its American advocates.

Our folk-hymnody is, of course, significant as a written record of the exact state of the American singing tradition in the first half of the 19th century, but completely aside from its historical interest, it is a body of music of great individuality, genuine merit, and melodic charm. It is possibly the most valuable musical heritage that has come down to us from early American times. We are becoming increasingly aware of this, and we owe a debt of gratitude to George Pullen Jackson who, almost unaided by other scholars, brought this music to light. Tune-books still remain unworked mines of early American music; they still are worth digging in. John Wyeth's *Repository of Sacred Music, Part Second* is only one of hundreds containing (as well as folk-hymns) thousands of compositions by early American composers in a unique and little understood harmonic and melodic idiom. They have been unaccountably neglected, despite the fact that as primary sources of the first magnitude, they are essential to a full understanding and an accurate reconstruction of 18th- and early 19th-century American musical life. The "end-openers" or "long-boys" (as they have been graphically nicknamed) are repositories of a vital and interesting music; they are also the raw materials for pages of an as yet unwritten history of American music.

MEN

8

DANIEL READ'S WORLD:
THE LETTERS OF AN
EARLY AMERICAN COMPOSER

Two LEDGERS CONTAINING nearly 1,000 letter-drafts written by Daniel Read [1] have come to light among the memorabilia left to the New Haven Colony Historical Society in 1855 by his eldest son, George Frederick Handel Read. No modern scholar seems to have been aware of their existence with the exception of the late Frank J. Metcalf. Unaccountably, he failed to recognize their broad significance despite his intimate knowledge of the period. The Read letter-books, full of authentic detail, paint a most graphic picture of the life and times of a typical New England composer-compiler. They shed new light on certain little known aspects of America's musical history and are consequently of great value to the student of our cultural and musical growth.

Read's tunes and collections of tunes made him one of the most prominent musical figures of the post-Colonial era. Today he is forgotten. Perhaps it is time for a re-evaluation of his music as well as that of his entire age. Aside from the inherent worth of his own compositions, Read should be remembered for several reasons: his key role in the development of the unique melodic-harmonic idiom characteristic of American composed music in the

---

1. Born Attleboro, Mass., November 16, 1757; died New Haven, Conn., December 4, 1836.

decades after the Revolution, and the importance of his music and compilations (even greater than those of his famed contemporary William Billings) in establishing the high popularity of the American fuging-tune. Between the years of 1785 and 1810 Read was one of the most active composer-compilers in the country, and his tune-books[2] achieved a wide sale. During the last 26 years of his life he was associated with only one published compilation, *The New Haven Collection* (Dedham, 1818), which he prepared for the press but did not compile.

Like many other musicians of his own and later days, Read did not earn his living exclusively through music. The sale of his tune-books brought in some money, but most of his income was derived from a typical New England general store where he stocked the customarily wide variety of merchandise. For a number of years he also made ivory and horn combs, a trade for which he evinced no great affection. For some reason, when he is mentioned at all in the standard music histories, this latter occupation (perhaps his least important and least lucrative activity in a life-

2. *The American Singing Book* (New Haven, 5 located editions, 1785, 1786, 1792, 1793, 1795; 1 unlocated edition, 1796)
The American Musical Magazine, with Amos Doolittle (New Haven, 12 numbers published, May, 1786 to September, 1787)
Supplement to The American Singing Book (New Haven, 1787)
An Introduction to Psalmody (New Haven, 1790, no copy known)
The Columbian Harmonist No. 1 (New Haven, 1793)
The Columbian Harmonist No. 2 (New Haven, 1794; with additions, 1798; with further additions, 1801)
The Columbian Harmonist No. 3 (New Haven, 1795)
The Columbian Harmonist, Nos. 1, 2 and 3 combined (New Haven, 1795)
Additional Music to *The Columbian Harmonist No. 2* (New Haven, 1801)
The Columbian Harmonist, 2nd edition (Dedham, Mass., 1804)
The Columbian Harmonist, 3rd edition (Boston, 1807)
The Columbian Harmonist, 4th edition (Boston, 1810)

Despite the use of the old title, the 2nd (1804) editions is to all intents and purposes a completely new collection. A 3rd edition "by Daniel Read" dated 1806 is also known. This somewhat mystifying circumstance which has puzzled bibliographers for some time is clarified by Read's correspondence. The 1806 3rd edition of *The Columbian Harmonist,* which is basically identical with the 2nd, was not authorized or compiled by Read, nor was he aware of its existence as late as December, 1807. It was probably a pirated edition put out by its publisher, Herman Mann of Dedham.

time of 79 years) is almost invariably cited. The inference that he was a rude country bumpkin, often implied, is totally unwarranted. It is true that Read had little formal education, but he was nevertheless a man of intelligence, sensitivity, and culture, if not of deep erudition.

It was apparently Read's practice to write out a preliminary draft of his letters in a ledger he kept for that purpose. After making necessary emendations and corrections, he would copy the final draft on notepaper for the recipient. In all probability, the letter-books represent a complete file of his business and personal correspondence during some of the most interesting years of his life. Through these ledgers, much pertinent detail has been preserved that did not find its way into the letters as they were actually sent. An insight into Read's psychology and personality is gained from the numerous additions, deletions, afterthoughts, substitutions of word and phrase, and alternative drafts clearly evident in the letter-books. They are obviously of even greater value to the historian than the letters themselves would be.

The earlier book contains drafts of 963 letters, varying in length from a single line to several closely-written pages. The initial entry is dated January 9, 1793; the last, December 26, 1807. All are serially numbered (beginning with No. 1) with the exception of 20.[3] All bear dates and the names of the correspondents; a large number contain town addresses; a few, street addresses. All are in Read's hand except for several unimportant drafts, probably copied from the originals by Read's eldest son. The later book contains only 25 letter-drafts, but among them may be found several of the most revealing in the entire correspondence. The first item here is dated July 18, 1829; the last, December 12, 1832. They are not serially numbered, nor do they include addresses. The last pages are taken up with various miscellanea pertaining to *Musica Ecclesia or Devotional Harmony*,[4] an unpublished tune-

3. Seventeen bear duplicate numbers and three have no numbers. In a few cases, identical letters were sent to several recipients; these are not considered separate letters.

4. The original manuscript, executed in a remarkably clear and meticulous

book that Read completed in 1832, his 75th year.

As WOULD BE expected, Read's correspondence mirrors his varied daily activities, and not all of it pertains to music or musical matters. The proportion of letters dealing with music is astonishingly high, however; well over half are of interest to the music historian. It should by no means be assumed that the remainder are devoid of significant values. These vividly recreate Read's world. Among them may be found discussions of such diverse topics as politics,

The inhabitance [sic] of this Town, except "certain lewd fellows of the baser sort," are almost universally Federalists. Many moderate men however when they saw that Mr. Jefferson was actually *the President* and had seen his inaugural speech were inclined to support his administration and to hope that those measures which had been predicted by the Federalists would not be pursued. But when they saw the collector of this Port, a man of superior abilities and integrity, removed from office, to make room for one utterly incapable of performing the duties of his appointment, and for no other reason but because the former was a Federalist and the latter was not, they were filled with indignation! [5]

religion,

. . . Shall I then be guilty of heresy if I presume with humility to enquire into the truth of a doctrine commonly believed among Christians viz the divinity of Jesus Christ? [6]

education,

Understanding that you are in the practice of taking young men under your Care & Tuition I have an inclination to offer you a son of mine. He is in the 15th year of his age has been 2 quarters with the Rev. Z. Ely

---

hand, is also in the collections of the New Haven Colony Historical Society.

5. From Letter No. 547 to Warren Dutton of Boston, dated July 30, 1801. See Henry Adams's interesting discussion of this very incident in his *History of the United States of America during the Administration of Thomas Jefferson* (New York, 1930).

6. From Letter No. 131 to his brother, Peter Read, dated Feb. 16, 1795. Daniel was only momentarily touched by the "Unitarian heresy." This letter is atypical of his religious thinking.

of Lebanon studying Lattin. I wish to have him fit to enter College next September if he is capable of it without any extraordinary exertions.[7]

Yale University,

I beleive [sic] the reputation of this Colleige [sic] is very good; there are commonly Studients [sic] more or less from different States viz Massachusetts, Rhodisland, New York and not unfrequently from the Carolinas and Georgia. It has been the common practice for as many of the Studients [sic] as can be accomodated [sic] with rooms in College to eat in the College Hall.[8]

and many other subjects of wide sociological import. The family correspondence is unusually charming. For example, a series of letters to his son George, then boarding out with a tutor in a different town:

I send you a Catechism Book and hope you will try to learn it. Begin at the first Commandment and learn as far as you can and I will tell Sherman to do the Same and he that has learned the most when you come shall be entitled to receive two Oranges and the other one but if both have learnt it through from the first Commandment to the end, then both shall have two Oranges a peice [sic].[9]

. . . First then, when you are called to Breakfast or Dinner, loiter about until the Blessing is begun and then come rattling in and be ready to sit down as soon as any one at Table. Never wait to be helped but, if you cannot decently be the first, always be the second to help yourself that you may be sure to get the best piece, and if you do not see a piece handy to your liking, run your knife or fork or spoon to the bottom of the dish and poke and turn the whole upside down 'till you can find a peice to suit. . . . I hope your own good sense will direct you how to apply the above.[10]

To delve deeply into the letters primarily of interest to the social historian is, however, not the purpose of this brief study and must be left to a later time.

7. From Letter No. 625 to the Rev. Edward Porter, dated Sept. 28, 1802, regarding his son George.
8. From Letter No. 33 to Joseph Forman, Esq. of Stotsborough, dated May 30, 1793.
9. From Letter No. 378 to George F. H. Read, dated Feb. 20, 1799.
10. From Letter No. 621 to George F. H. Read, dated Aug. 2, 1802.

OF THE 539 letter-drafts directly concerned with one or another aspect of music, 335 are addressed to various booksellers, printers, engravers, bookbinders, and papermakers with whom Read had dealings in connection with the publication and sale of his tune-books. This segment of the correspondence is particularly note-worthy for the wealth of authentic bibliographical information it contains regarding Read's collections, both located and unlocated. Clear proof of the existence of certain editions never before sus-pected is apparent in several instances. No edition of *The Ameri-can Singing Book* after 1795 has been recorded, but one was nevertheless definitely issued in 1796:

I send you a Book for Copy having made some little alterations with regard to the Title page, Preface & Index as you will see. You will be careful to have the work Correct and well executed. Mr. Andrews who prints the Copper plates says 100 Copies shall be ready by the 1st Aug. and I shall endeavor to send them immediately forward.[11]

About a fortnight ago I sent you paper for the Introductions to the American Singing Book. I now Send the plate work for 100 Books and wish you to bind them and send them back as soon as you can. You will observe that the two last sheets of the book marked with the letters G H to have been regular should have been K L but the pages I beleive [sic] are regularly numbered. It may be well to mention this to your book-binder to prevent any mistake in Colating [sic].[12]

The great bibliographer Charles Evans, attempting to reconstruct the complex printing history of *The Columbian Harmonist No. 2* in his *American Bibliography* without benefit of the Read corre-spondence, erroneously dated its first appearance as 1795. The correct date should be 1794, as is clear from a letter to the Con-necticut singing-master Nathan Thayer dated January 1, 1795, where Read writes that he is sending him copies of the collection. In the 1807 and 1810 editions, Read himself cites 1794 as the date of first publication. Evans is also in error in listing T. and S.

11. From Letter No. 211 to Moses H. Woodward of Middletown, dated July 14, 1796.
12. From Letter No. 220 to Moses H. Woodward of Middletown, dated Aug. 2, 1796.

Green of New London as printers of the pre-1795 issues. According to the letter-books, credit should be given to Samuel Andrews of Cheshire. No bibliographer has cataloged any editions of *The Columbian Harmonist No. 2* after 1795, yet at least two appeared, one in 1798 and another in 1801:

I now send you four Dozen Columbian Harmonist No. 2. I have added a few pages of music and improved the binding with increasing the price. . . . If you think an advertisement published in a New London Paper mentioning the above particulars would tend to promote the Sale you may cause it to be done at my expense.[13]

I have added another half sheet of music to No. 2 Coln. Harmonist and now send you in sheets 400 Books. . . . In consequence of the Additional Music and the advanced price of Paper it has become necessary to anvance [sic] the price of the Books a little.[14]

The additional music mentioned in this letter was also sold as a separate publication:

I send 2 dozn of the Additional music to sell seperately [sic] at 25 Cents a piece.[15]

The frequent reference to *An Introduction of Psalmody* in the correspondence is of some bibliographical value, as no copies are known to exist today. The astute bibliographer can probably reconstruct its size and appearance from a study of these references, even though Read himself admitted that

Those Introductions to Psalmody are but little known. I will offer them for Sale & thank you to give them away ocasionally [sic] to Singing Masters and other Purchasers of Music Books where you apprehend it will have a tendancy [sic] to open a way for the Sale of them.[16]

Of course, this is a mere sampling of the copious bibliographical data to be found in the letter-books. Anyone concerned with the

13. From Letter No. 351 to Thomas C. Green of New London, dated Oct. 30, 1798.
14. From Letter No. 556 to Cornelius Davis of New York, dated Sept. 30, 1801.
15. *Ibid.*
16. From Letter No. 298 to Cornelius Davis of New York, dated July 18, 1797.

backgrounds of early music publishing will find the extensive correspondence with members of the bookselling and printing trades a treasure-house of the most valuable primary source materials. For example, the correspondence with the New York bookseller Cornelius Davis alone, extending over a period of nine years and including 91 letters, is a history in miniature of the book trade at the turn of the 18th century. Most fortunately, Read was constitutionally meticulous in regard to detail, and he invariably included exact figures. From these it is possible to establish such facts as the size of the various editions of his collections, their costs, the number of copies sold, the profit factor, and the extent of their diffusion.

THE STUDENT of American music history will be particularly interested in the 151 letters to various composers, compilers, and singing-masters of lesser or greater renown. Early in 1793, Read was busily engaged in assembling materials for the forthcoming *Columbian Harmonist No. 1.* A group of 14 letters addressed to composers whose tunes he was to include in the collection supplies valuable information about these men. There is a virtually complete dearth of information regarding such figures as Adams, Atwell, Camp, Caswell, Coan, and the Munson and Peck families, all of whom played some role in the development of the native American idiom. In some cases, even their first names have been previously unknown. These letters also give some insight into Read's own grasp of musical problems and his method of working with his contributors. The following is fairly typical:

[I] have been looking over the tune therein enclosed. I think it is a very good one but at the same time I think there are some passages which might be altered for the better. But I would rather chuse [sic] that those alterations should be made by the Author than by myself that the music may be all in his own Stile [sic]. Permit me therefore instead of altering the music to point out some few general passages which in this kind of Vocal music are in my ear disagreeable and request you if on looking over Ordination again you find any of those passages to rectify them according to your own mind.

Some of those disallowed passages are,

1st For two or more perfect concords such as unisons 5th or 8ths to be taken either ascending or descending

2d For discords viz 2ds 4ths or 7ths to be taken between the bass and any upper part in the accented part of a bar except when one of the parts is Stationary and the other moves from a concord to a discord and is again immediately followed by a discord

3d For the Counter to be heard above the treble

I do not pretend to say that my music is altogether exempt from such passages but the above are some of my general Rules.[17]

At the time that Read began to keep his first letter-book, he was seriously considering an idea to expand the sale and circulation of his tune-books throughout the country. One Richard Atwell, apparently a pupil of his, figured heavily in his plans:

I expect that Richard Atwell will be at Attleborough in May or June and I think it probable he will go to the Southward towards fall with Books to teach music. By information I have had from the Southern States A young man capable of teaching music may do exceeding well that way. One Ives who studied music with me about 18 months ago and has gone to Virginia has I have been informed cleared by one School only, 300 dollars in Six months. If you know of any you can recommend as capable of that business I wish you to mention them to Atwell as he will doubtless be glad of company if he should go.[18]

Read outlined his proposals in a letter to Atwell:

In short it is my wish that the American Singing Book, Columbian Harmonist, Child's Instructor be left with suitable persons in all the Capital Towns throughout the United States and that the favour and friendship of the Teachers of music in every part be obtained as far as is possible. . . . It is not my idea to enter into the execution of this Business for the sale of a few dozens or a few Hundreds of Books only; but I have no doubt but we may extend it to thousands and perhaps to tens of thousands within a year or two.[19]

This ambitious scheme did not come to fruition as Atwell backed

17. From Letter No. 27 to Julius Caswell of Kent, dated Apr. 23, 1793.
18. From Letter No. 16 to his brother, William Read of Attleboro, dated Mar. 12, 1793.
19. From Letter No. 5 to Richard Atwell of Huntington, dated Jan. 22, 1793.

out of the arrangement after several months of negotiations and Read was unsuccessful in finding anyone to take his place.

An unexpected facet of the Read correspondence is its pertinence to music conditions in the South in the early 1790s. It may appear somewhat surprising that so many references to music in Virginia may be found in the letters of a New England composer-compiler, but Read had already developed some channels for the distribution of his collections in that state and in South Carolina by 1793, and he clearly considered that part of the country a promising market. His tune-books appear to have been popular in the vicinity of Richmond and were undoubtedly known in other sections as well. At least two contributors of *The Columbian Harmonist No. 1,* Joel and Reuben Munson, were singing-masters active in Richmond. Another Southern correspondent, Amzi Chapin, was in later years to become an influential figure in the development of spiritual folk-song. The letter-books thus conclusively establish a link between the North and the South more than a decade before it had previously been considered an actuality. They also demonstrate that music *à la* New England was being composed in the South as early as 1793.

A MOST interesting series of letters is that addressed to Joel Read [20] regarding the compilation of the 2nd edition of *The Columbian Harmonist.* Daniel broached the subject as follows:

Would it be worth your while to join me in the publication of a Singing book to consist of the best part of the Columbian Harmonist with a few of the most popular tunes you & I can pick up with the leave of the Authors to publish. In looking over my account with my printer a few weeks ago I found that I had had printed in about 2 years & 2 months more than 5500 Columbian Harmonist No 2 not more than 2 or 300 of which are now unsold. But my plates are so much worn that they will scarcely answer for another season and Mr. Doolittle cannot be de-

20. Daniel's older brother. Joel later published a tune-book of his own, *The New England Selection* (Boston, 1808 and 1812) and compiled a supplement to the 2nd edition of *The Columbian Harmonist.* He also composed music.

pended on to engrave new ones. I have tho't of tipographical [sic] printing, but those printers are out of the circle of my correspondance [sic]. A
few new and Popular tunes might give a new spring to the sale in some
places while to retain a part of the old ones together with the title of
Columbian Harmonist I think would be the most likely way to insure [sic]
its success to the westward. Perhaps an Eddition [sic] of 2 or 3000 might
answer.[21]

Joel arranged with Herman Mann of Dedham to print the work
typographically. In 21 letters, some of them of considerable length,
Daniel discusses in great detail the merits and demerits of individual tunes previously published in *The Columbian Harmonist*
and evaluates others as candidates for inclusion in the new book:

Holyoke's *Champlain* I am unwilling to print without his consent. Holden's *Ordination* Anthem I am not in possession of, nor do I seem to
recollect it. Is it popular? Is it good? Connecticut Harmony I do not
recollect to have seen. *Symphony,* (if you mean a tune of that name of
the metre of the new 50th) I have. *Exhortation* I do not recollect. Of
Dominion, Calvary, Montague, Morning Triumph & Vespers I am doubtful whether the pages cannot be better filled; but if you know them to
be popular I shall not object; very few if any observations concerning
them have reached my ears.

The new tunes of which I have doubts are, 1st Belknaps Redemtion
[sic], the page it fills appears to me like waste paper. 2d Amenia and
Florence by Fitch; I am partly pleased with them and partly not and
feel a degree of uncertainty about their success. 3d Shelburn, Protection,
and Sardis, dont appear to me to be the best tunes that ever was but still
they may be popular and better than many others. Desired Rest and
Orient Clouds and Messiah I believe to be excellent tunes.[22]

Read was not happy about the results of his first experience with
music printed from type:

Some obvious blunders of the printer have excited my notice viz such
as printing all the pages wrong side up—working it in quarter sheets—
misarranging some of the tunes—breaking them to pieces—leaving out
the name of one tune or more in the index— and inserting wrong pages

21. From Letter No. 751 to Joel Read, dated Mar. 12, 1804.
22. Paragraph one is from Letter No. 769 dated Aug. 14, 1804; paragraph
two from Letter No. 780 dated Oct. 7, 1804, both to Joel Read.

for others, but what is quite unpardonable is that some of the tunes appear to be taken from Copies very different from those I furnished or requested you to furnish. I have not had time to serch [sic] much for typografical [sic] errors, I have however discouvered [sic] about a dozen which are not in the Errata.[23]

A similarly extensive correspondence regarding the 3rd (1807) edition of *The Columbian Harmonist* may be found in the 15 letters addressed to Ezra Read,[24] who served a similar function in regard to this edition as did Joel with the 2nd edition.

You will observe that my governing principles in the choice of tunes is like that of the Vicar of Wakefield in the choice of a wife, not so much for any glossy outside, or superficial appearance as for those intrinsic properties which induce me to believe they will *wear well*. At the same time remembering that as the Collection is for the use of the public, the public opinion is always to be respected. On this ground I ask for your opinion.[25]

One of the letters to Ezra contains a rather detailed notice of *The Sacred Minstrel No. 1* (Boston, 1806) by Uri K. Hill, father of Ureli Corelli Hill, the organizer and first conductor of the New York Philharmonic Society. This is a most unusual find at such an early date:

I have read the introduction to the Minstril [sic] and given the music a slight inspection. I think the Introduction very plain and well adapted for the use of learners. The *Essay on Modulation* is, from the nature of the subject not altogether so simple, yet very intelligible and calculated to be useful. . . . With regard to the character of the music you may reasonably suppose I am not prepared to deside [sic]. From the complexion of it however I may venture to say that I am of the opinion that it is of that kind which will not be so well received by the great body of singers in this country as that which has been published by Mr. Jencks [*recte*, Jenks] and for the same reason, perhaps, that the writings of John Bunyan are more read than those of Dr. Johnson, and Morgans

23. From Letter No. 816 to Joel Read, dated Apr. 8, 1805.
24. A nephew, also apparently musical. Daniel, in an earlier letter, suggested that he buy a font of music type being offered for sale by Manning & Loring of Boston, and set himself up in the music printing trade in New Haven.
25. From Letter No. 894 to Ezra Read, dated Nov. 28, 1806.

Judgement Anthem is so much more admired than that Anthem of Anthems as it has been called, *O give thanks* &c by Dr Arnold. It is however, I believe, best that in a worshiping assembly, the prayers, the sermon, the psalms and the music, should be in a language understood by the worshipers generally. [26]

A FIGURE prominent in the musical life of the period with whom Read corresponded and had business dealings was Oliver Holden, then famed as teacher, composer, and compiler. At the time, Holden was considered perhaps the leading musician in all New England by his contemporaries, and even today his name is still vaguely familiar, primarily because of the continued life of his fine hymn-tune CORONATION, which can be found in the pages of almost every modern American hymnal. The two men were apparently on cordial, although somewhat formal terms:

I called at your Store the 7th day of April But had not the pleasure of seeing you at home.—I have on hand, subject to your order a number of your Books viz 7 Union Harmony Vol. 1 5 Do Vol. 2 5 Do Vol. 1 & 2 and 17 American Harmony. Will you Sir be kind enough to inform me if an Organ can be procured in Boston at a price not exceeding 150 Dollars which shall in some measure answer the following description viz, Two, or two & half, Stops, the usual number of Keys, or from double C to C in Alt with all the intervening tones and Semitones, to be played with the fingers and to blow with the foot or hand at pleasure, Decent mohogony [sic] Case not exceeding 7½ feet in height. Or if one cannot be procured to answer the above description for the above sum how near answerable to the description can one be built for that sum, or, how much must I pay for one equal to the above description.—I have observed that in your Union Harmony you have republished a number of Tunes of which in my American Singing Book I had called myself the Author. Will you give me leave to republish some of those in your Collections of which you have stiled [sic] yourself the Author? [27]

Read's early music, especially that in *The American Singing Book* which was published before any federal copyright protection existed, was unmercifully pirated by other compilers. As it was extremely popular, Read understandably felt quite cheated

26. From Letter No. 896 to Ezra Read, dated Jan. 6, 1807.
27. From Letter No. 535 to Oliver Holden, dated May 20, 1801.

and consistently refused anyone permission to republish any tunes he composed after 1793. As he wittily put it,

The man who publishes a book of his own Tunes is like one who sends his property to sea in a number of Vessels. Those which are approved by the public may be considered as property arrived in port, those which are not as property lost at sea. Now Sir what would you say to the man who should lay his hands on your property in port and tell you you were welcom [sic] to that which was lost at sea? [28]

A fine letter to Jacob French, one of the most gifted of the early American composer-compilers, touches on this problem:

Your favour of the 22nd April I did not receive until the 7th inst. It is not only ungenerous but unjust to publish the works of any author without his consent. Irritateted [sic] beyond measure at the unprovoked Robbery committed upon the American Singing Book by the Editor of the Worcester Collection and having no redress but by retaliation there being then no law in existence to prevent such abuses I availed myself of that opportunity to publish some peices from the Worcester Collection to which I had no right. But since the Statute of the United States made for the purpose of securing to Authors the Copyright of their work, I do not mean to give any person cause to be offended in that way, on the other hand I think it my duty to prosecute any person who prints my music without my consent, as much as if he were a common Theif [sic] or Housebreaker. Your proposal to exchange music is doubtless a good one and provided we can accomodate each other I shall have no objection, but I have never had the pleasure of seeing *The New American Melody* and consequently know nothing about the Music contained in it and besides, the Law requires an agreement in writing signed in the presence of two credible Witnesses. There are some Tunes I have seen which I should like to print provided I publish any more music particularly one called All Saints I do not know but you are the proprietor of it. I wish it was convenient for you to take a tour this way and call on me, and tis very probable we could form a contract agreeable to your mind and if it is a matter of much consequence to you I make no doubt but you will be willing to take that Trouble. I wish for an harmonious agreement with all professors of music and particularly with Authors and publishers, and should be particularly happy to make acquaintance with you.

28. From Letter No. 140 to Thomas Bassel of Lansingburgh, dated Mar. 20, 1795.

There has an Anthem entituled *The farewell by French* been published here by one Asael [*recte*, Asahel] Benham of Wallingford. I give you this information because I think it my duty to do as I would be done by.[29]

The tunes Read admits lifting from Isaiah Thomas's extraordinarily successful *Worcester Collection* (Worcester, 1786, seven later editions) may be found by the curious reader in *The American Musical Magazine* (New Haven, 1786–87). Naively but quite honestly, Read labelled them as "taken from Thomas"!

AMONG the most fascinating letters in the whole correspondence, and far and away the most important musical letters sent by Read to non-musicians of his acquaintance, are six extremely lengthy communications addressed to the Rev. Samuel Merwin, his pastor, and the Rev. Absolom Peters, secretary of the American Home Missionary Society. These are concerned with Read's last collection, the unpublished *Musica Ecclesia*, and they embody a complete presentation of his musical philosophy during the era when Lowell Mason and Thomas Hastings were the colossi of the American scene. Read basically agreed with their point of view, and the letters of his last years are a thoroughgoing repudiation of the native American idiom he had been instrumental in developing in his youthful days. When they were penned, Read had long since ceased to write original music. The crude but eloquent American product had been supplanted by second-rate English importations and insipid "arrangements" from the classic masters. It was fashionable to sneer at American music, and Read succumbed to the overwhelming social pressures inherent in the situation. In today's historical perspective, the newer music appears to have marked a deterioration rather than an advance in popular taste, but to Read, the tune-books of the supporters of "scientific music" represented progress and an improvement over his own collections. In capsule form, Read's life is a history of the change in the musical climate which took place in America over a period of more than half a century. The musical correspondence in the

29. From Letter No. 38 to Jacob French of Uxbridge, dated June 10, 1793.

later letter-book is an accurate reflection of a different era in American music.

In February, 1829, in a long letter to the Rev. Merwin, Read explained the philosophy behind *Musica Ecclesia* and outlined the reasons impelling him to undertake the work. He asked Merwin's advice in several matters, and gave him permission to discuss the problems raised with other ministers. Merwin apparently showed Read's letter to a Rev. Luther Hart of Plymouth, evidently an enthusiastic supporter of the new and fashionable "scientific" music. In turn, Hart wrote a letter to Merwin in which he seems to have expressed the strongest doubts about Read's skill as a musician and his ability to execute the proposed work in such a manner as to "bear the critical inspection of the *few* scientific musicians in our country." [30] This was forwarded to Read by Merwin. The 71-year-old Read was deeply hurt by Hart's letter. It moved him to write a magnificent reply in which he defends his integrity and skill with poignant eloquence. There are two alternative drafts of this important letter in the letter-book. Both are equally revealing, as a few excerpts show:

[Mr. Hart's ideas] probably originated in a preconcieved [sic] opinion that my talents are inadequate to the undertaking. This Idea seems to run through the whole of the letter—he is fearful I shall do more evil than good. He probably thinks my knowledge in the abstruse science of harmony is deficient, and therefore if I make a book at all, it will abound with errors and unnecessary alterations, that I shall aim to please my own uncultivated taste without being guided at all by settled principles. On this subject, perhaps I ought to be silent. It is unimportant as it respects myself, what opinion Mr. H. or any other gentleman has respecting my knowledge of music; I have no ambition to appear knowing on that or any other subject. . . . But as it respects the work which I have undertaken I think it important that the truth should be known both by my friends & by myself. If I have made a mistake and undertaken a work which I am incapable of executing, the sooner I know it

30. From Letter E to the Rev. Samuel Merwin, dated May 2, 1829, not sent. Alternative draft of Letter F. This is apparently Read's direct quotation from Rev. Hart's letter.

and relinquish the work the better. On the other hand if I am capable of finishing the work in such a manner as to merit the approbation of the critic . . . it is important that those whose patronage I seek should have some well grounded confidence in my abilities. With this view of the subject I ask to be indulged in making a few remarks and my prayer is that I may be enabled to do it with humility. . . . It is probable that Mr Hart has formed his opinion of my skill in the science of music from the books which I published 25 to 40 years ago. He may say, "I have examined Mr. R's Books and I find nothing in them which warrants the conclusion that he is a 'scientific musician.' If he makes another book it may not be any better than those he has already made." This reasoning . . . might have been so twenty years ago: But since the publication of my last book about 20 years ago, since my first acquaintance with Professor Fisher, in whose lamented death the constellation of scientific musicians, has lost one of its brightest stars,—since studying the writings of such men as D'Alambert [*recte*, d'Alembert], Calcutt [*recte*, Calcott], Jones, Kollman [*recte*, Kollmann], Gieb, and Hastings, —since carefully examining the system of harmony practically exhibited in Handel's *Messiah*, Hayd'n's [sic] *Creation* and other similar works, since having an opportunity of trying and comparing different progressions of harmony, both allowed and forbidden, on the Organ, I say, since these things have taken place, my ideas on the subject of music have been considerably altered; I will not say improved. . . . There is something in those two words altering tunes which is very disagreeable in the ears of some good men who are lovers of the good old tunes; but not so with Messrs Hastings and Mason, both of whom have made many alterations in the old tunes if indeed correcting errors in old copies can be called altering tunes. And if Mr. H. will examin [sic] their works comparing them with the old copies, he may perhaps perceive that they have made some alterations where no correction was necessary, and that in their books are some passages which still need to be corrected in order to bring them within the rules of harmony. . . . Mr. H. farther [sic] proposes that I should bring forward much foreign music. . . . Perhaps Mr. Hart does not know that many of the tunes which appear in American publications under the names of Handel, Hayd'n [sic], Mozart, &c. are scraps cut out of the oratorios of those authors, patched up and altered to make metre of them; like cuting [sic] scraps out of West's or Trumbull's historical paintings, as if, because the whole peice is beautiful, it must also be beautiful in its parts seperately [sic].[31]

31. From Letter F to the Rev. Samuel Merwin, dated May 7, 1829.

Read completed the tune-book in 1832 despite lack of encouragement and decided to present the manuscript to the American Home Missionary Society with the understanding that the Society was to arrange for its publication and to use the entire proceeds for missionary purposes. The old man must have been extremely shocked to discover that his well-meant offer had been rejected.

I am sorry to learn that my offering to your Society cannot at present be so used as to add something to its funds for missionary purposes. I had hoped that, if it was published and brought into use in the American Churches, it would have produced an income sufficient to have supported one or more missionaries for many years. . . . I was desirous of contributing to the cause of missions, and not having an abundance of silver and gold, I offered such as I had. But since it appears that, (under existing circumstances,) no available funds are likely to be derived from it, I feel it my duty to submit to the providence of God without a murmur.

The two principal obsticles [sic] in the way of accomplishing the object I have so ardently desired are, first the want of funds to effect its publication and second the want of efficient patronage to introduce it into extensive use. . . . As to the second obsticle I have only to say, that if the merits of the work itself . . . are not sufficient to engage a portion of the teachers of music and of your society's missionaries to lend their influence toward introducing it, I see not but its publication must, for the present, be given up.[32]

Thus Read abandoned the product of nearly five years of intensive labor.

IT IS obviously impossible to do more than hint at the content of the Read letter-books. Snippets can only give the reader a vague sense of the man's style and personality; one cannot summarize the content of a thousand letters in a few thousand words. Here is a most significant fresh source of authentic information about certain important facets of American musical life during the late 18th and early 19th centuries, particularly valuable in view of the paucity of pertinent documentation in this field.

32. From Letter X to the Rev. Absolom Peters, dated Aug. 16, 1832.

The reader may have observed that Read has not been referred to as a "composer of hymn-tunes" or as a compiler of "sacred" music. This has been done quite deliberately in order to avoid the perpetuation of an almost universal misconception regarding early American music. Such collections as *The American Singing Book* and *The Columbian Harmonist* were *not* designed for church use; they were intended for the use of singing-schools and musical societies. Sacred texts were largely (but not by any means exclusively) utilized because the poetry of Watts and others writing in similar vein was the popular poetry of the period, that which was loved and understood by the people. It is true that the singing-school grew out of the church, but during the heyday of the American idiom, it was not a church institution. The use within the church of some of the music selected from the tune-books was quite accidental; the tune-books themselves were compiled for educational purposes. In a very real sense, here was the popular music, the music of the people. The artisan hummed snatches of Read's SHERBURNE, or Edson's LENOX, or Billings's JORDAN as he drank his dram or sawed his wood, not Hopkinson's *My Days Have Been so Wondrous Free*. It is a convenient rough classification to divide all music into "sacred" and "secular" halves, but the music of early America just does not fit into these easy categories. To attach the label "psalmodist" with its unfortunate present-day connotations to Read and his fellow composer-compilers is to distort the nature of the music of an entire era and to misunderstand its historical role. These men were the *musicians* understood and appreciated by the people of their time.

9

---»» ««---

THE

MUSICAL EDSONS OF SHADY:

EARLY AMERICAN TUNESMITHS

ONE MEMORABLE May morning in 1952, I was in the Library of Congress trying to increase my scanty store of information about an obscure early American composer named Lewis Edson. The day was gentle and warm, of that typically Washington spring-fevery sort that makes one understand just why the wheels of government turn so slowly in the Nation's capital, and I was making spectacularly little progress. I was therefore more than usually delighted that fate provided me with a respectable reason to drop my work and do something more rewarding and pleasurable.

Sidney Robertson Cowell, whom I had not previously met, had dropped into the Music Division. We shared mutual friends and a mutual interest in early American music, and before long we were immersed in animated conversation. Ultimately I got around to mentioning my then current problem. I remember remarking, in passing, that Edson was an especially slippery customer, and that disentangling him from his complicated family tree seemed to be just about as impossible as locating the place he had died, a metropolis called Mink Hollow supposedly somewhere in New York State—but not according to the map spread out on my desk.

Since that first meeting, I have learned to take the incredible in regard to Mrs. Cowell with something approaching equanimity, but at that time I barely knew her. I still vividly recall my feeling of awe and utter astonishment at her matter-of-fact reaction to this information.

"Mink Hollow? I'm on my way there right now," she said briskly, just as if everybody in the world knew the place. "Why it's just over the hill from Shady!"

Parenthetically, I must explain that Mink Hollow and Shady—as I was to learn for myself later—are adjoining flyspecks in the foothills of the Catskills, still pretty much unspoiled despite their proximity to the resort town and art colony of Woodstock. In Shady, Mrs. Cowell and her famous husband, the composer Henry Cowell, spend their summers. There, in a modest but fantastically lovely cottage tucked into the woods out of sight of the highway, they work and play—writing, composing, talking, resting, and making friends with the felines who are bona fide members of the household as well as with every raccoon, opossum, woodchuck, porcupine, and four-legged skunk in the neighborhood.

Shortly after our talk, Mrs. Cowell piled into her battered and dusty green Chevrolet station wagon and departed for the North, but not before I had extracted from her a promise that she would keep her eyes and ears open for any hint of Edsoniana around Shady.

Within a few weeks, a long letter arrived. "Some preliminary rustling about in Ulster County discovered no living Edsons near at hand," she wrote, "but they are scattered to communities within 30 miles or so, and I will pursue them in July. Saw the ruins of the Edson house at Mink Hollow, and will try later to determine the extent of the old Edson place from the county records and take photos as of 1952 just for fun. The place is wild and overgrown, with a deep creek, and a very young porcupine playing in the ruins of the old chimneys . . ." (June 9, 1952). The letters came thick and fast. I cannot resist quoting from another:

My goodness, what a thing you got me into! I couldn't begin to tell all the things that have been happening, but among others we had a minia-ture Edson family reunion here over the week-end—object: to locate the burial place of the two Lewis Edsons. One great-great-granddaughter, and one great-granddaughter of the younger Lewis was present, along with two people from another branch of the family . . . then there were some nieces and a couple of friends. We had planned a picnic but it sprinkled and only three people had brought lunch anyway, so I fed 12 people on half an hour's notice, among other things. Another guest was an old lady who knew Lewis, Jr.'s grandson. She led us to an old "lost" dooryard burying ground. This was near the old Edson place which . . . now belongs to the city of Kingston so we had no permissions to ask there. Nothing left—no buildings, only chimneys of a much later house, and holes in the weeds that were probably old foundations. Unfortunately we drifted off Edson boundaries and three of us were thoughtfully stamping about in a corner by an old stone wall, trying if there were stones or only earth under our feet. No house was visible, but an irate land-owner who had had trouble with city hunters came charging down to order us off in a real passion and fury, and when I apologized and said we were looking for the possible burying place of a "famous composer" who lived up in Mink Hollow 150 years ago, he said: "A *likely* story!" I could see his point. We were a kind of improbable enterprise all around. (August 4, 1952)

By this time, Washington was going through its usual summer baking and I was getting pretty envious of Mrs. Cowell and her Edson hunt. So when I discovered from yet another letter that on August 10 the villagers were going to sing Edson tunes in the Shady Methodist Church, I suddenly conceived a strong dislike for the city. A few days later my wife and I drove off to Shady to participate in the first and last Edson "festival" on record, and to join Sidney Cowell in her expeditions in Edsonian archaeology.

BEFORE I continue with my own adventures, I suppose I should say something about the Lewis Edsons, father and son, in view of the fact that their names are absent from almost all standard reference works and they do not appear in the histories of American music currently available. Indeed, when they are mentioned, the two men are usually blended into one composite Lewis Edson with an enormous life-span. The conclusion that no one really knew that there were, in fact, two composers with the same name is inescapable.

The elder Edson was considered by his contemporaries comparable in importance to such prominent men as Billings, Read, Law, Holden, and Holyoke. Why was this so? His renown was not due to the large number of his compositions—he was one of the least prolific of the New England tunesmiths. He compiled no tune-books. He was not an influential teacher in a big city.

Lewis Edson, Sr. was a back-country amateur whose one-time great fame is comprehensible only in the light of the really extraordinary popularity achieved by three compositions that marked his debut as a published composer. So favored were the Edson fuging-tunes GREENFIELD, LENOX, and BRIDGEWATER (see Illus. 18) by tune-book compilers of the day that it is difficult to find a collection printed between 1782 and 1810 in which at least one of the three cannot be found. Only a single fuging-tune, the 34TH PSALM by the English psalmodist Joseph Stephenson, was more frequently reprinted, and Edson's work proved far more durable. As a matter of fact, the three Edson fuging-tunes proved more durable than the whole idiom, and their popularity did not begin to fade until the beginning of the 20th century. Indeed, LENOX is still to be found—in emasculated, de-fuged form—in the present official hymnal of the American Methodist church.

18. Lewis Edson, *The Social Harmonist*, 2nd edition (New York, 1801), p. 40. Courtesy of the Music Division of the New York Public Library.

No other early American composer began his career so auspiciously; no other ended it quite so ingloriously. Yet this obscure, all-but-forgotten rural was the composer of the *three* most popular American fuging-tunes ever penned. GREENFIELD, LENOX, and BRIDGEWATER were important in that they left their imprint on the subsequent development of the entire fuging-tune idiom, and the man responsible for them surely warrants rescue from total oblivion.

Lewis Edson, Sr. was born on a farm near Bridgewater, Massachusetts, in the southeastern part of the state, on January 22, 1748. As soon as he was old enough to make himself useful, he was undoubtedly set to work in the fields as were other Massachusetts farm boys of his time. There was little time for book learning, and Lewis probably grew to manhood without the benefit of formal schooling. He was apparently a strong, husky lad, somewhat big for his age, and in July, 1761, during his 13th year, he enlisted in the British army together with his father. Both father and son served as common soldiers in the same regiment for nearly two years and participated in several campaigns during the French and Indian Wars. When Lewis was mustered out in 1763, he returned to Bridgewater with his father and began to earn his living as a blacksmith.

What it was that transformed a 15-year-old ex-soldier and blacksmith into "Mr. Edson of Bridgewater," singing-master and tunesmith, between 1763 and 1769, will probably never be known. Perhaps his elder brother Obed, a chorister in later years, taught him the rudiments of the art of music. Perhaps some itinerant singing-master set up shop for a few weeks in Bridgewater and Lewis attended the singing-school. The fact remains that he learned enough to teach, and the annals of the church in neighboring Halifax record that in 1769 Lewis Edson was engaged to come there to instruct the church members in "the Science of Musick." Every year until 1776, he taught singing school in Halifax and there were no complaints about his teaching ability. A year after he began to teach music he married Hepzibah Washburn, and some 12 months later his only child, Lewis, Jr., was born.

The Edsons, a large family firmly established in Bridgewater for well over a century, suddenly began to move westward in 1773. The first to leave was Obed, who emigrated to the semi-wilderness country in the Berkshires, settling in a recently established village near the New York border called Lanesboro. He soon became one of the community's leading citizens. Obed was no doubt instrumental in persuading his brother Lewis and his father to join him, which they did in 1776.

There is a possibility that the migration of the Edsons to Lanesboro may have been forced by the politics of the day. In Bridgewater, the family had produced one prominent Tory, Colonel Timothy Edson, and anti-Loyalist sentiment, always strong in that part of the state, was becoming increasingly violent in the early 1770s. Obed, Lewis, and father Edson were active members of the Church of England, and in a family manifesting such close ties, it is a temptation to assume that the whole lot were sympathetic to the British cause. While this assumption would neatly explain the dispersal of the clan, there is no really incontrovertible evidence that it is true. Granted that Colonel Edson was a well-known Tory, Lewis's half-brother Thomas was an almost equally well-known patriot, and there is no indication that Thomas's views disrupted the cohesion of the family. Neither Obed nor Lewis fought in the Revolutionary War—a suspicious circumstance—but if they were Tories, they were very quiet about their political beliefs.

Lewis continued his musical activities in Lanesboro, sharing the office of chorister with Obed in the recently established Church of England there for three years and then supplanting him entirely. The duty of the chorister was two-fold: first, to select the music to be performed in church and, second, to "set the tune" for congregation and choir. Probably these responsibilities impelled him to begin to try his hand at writing tunes, something he does not seem to have done at Bridgewater.

It appears to have been his impressive voice, rather than his skill as a composer, that won Edson more than local fame. By 1780, he was widely known in the western Massachusetts counties as "the great singer." His reputation spread across state borders into New York and Connecticut, and some time before the end of 1782 his tunes came to the attention of Simeon Jocelin and Amos Doolittle of New Haven, who were preparing a new tune-book, the *Chorister's Companion*, for the press. One of its main attractions was that it was to include "a number of tunes, never before published, (composed by several Gentlemen in the country)," and when it was published in December, 1782, Edson's famous three were there.

Edson was never again to write a truly popular tune, and he seems to have made very little effort to do so. Fresh specimens of his skill (or lack of it) are found in the 1790 *Federal Harmony* of Asahel Benham and in his son's 1800 *Social Harmonist*, but the failure of the new music was as resounding as the success of the old. As compiler after compiler used GREENFIELD, LENOX, and BRIDGEWATER, Edson's reputation continued to grow, but as his name became an American household word, the man himself became a phantom figure, merely an identifying tag attached to a few tunes everybody knew and sang.

In 1791, Edson sold his land in Lanesboro and disappeared over the New York State border, perhaps settling unobtrusively in the Hudson Valley. During the 1790s, other members of the family turn up in Cooperstown—son Lewis in 1795, brother Obed in 1798—but of Edson himself there is no trace, and his whereabouts and activities between 1791 and 1806 remain a complete and tantalizing mystery. Late in 1806, Lewis Edson came to the farm and homestead in Mink Hollow where Mrs. Cowell had discovered the very young porcupine playing in the ruins. In those peaceful hills he died some time in 1820, forgotten by the world.

OF HIS SON Lewis even less is known. He was born in Bridgewater one day after his father's 23rd birthday and makes his first appearance on the stage of history at the age of 24 in Cooperstown,

New York, as post-rider, Freemason, and singing-master. This was in November, 1795. In 1797 he moved to Middlefield, New York—apparently he was one of the hamlet's founding fathers—and served the community as school commissioner until he departed, a year later, for Danbury, Connecticut. At the turn of the 19th century, he published a very interesting eclectic tune-book containing much music of his own composition. Although it is now one of the scarcest of tune-books—no copy of the first edition is known to have survived—the *Social Harmonist* was quite successful, going through three editions in four years.[1] Probably coincidentally with its publication in 1800, he shows up in booming commercial New York City to sample the heady wine of urban life.

Once in the big city, Lewis, Jr. turned his hand to building houses and teaching school in order to earn a living. The New York directories of 1801 through 1812 list him as teacher; from 1813 through 1815, in which year his name was dropped, he appears as a nail manufacturer.

THE

SOCIAL HARMONIST,

CONTAINING

First. The Necessary Rules of Music.

Second, A Collection of *TUNES* chiefly Original.

By LEWIS EDSON Jun.

SECOND EDITION

New York, Published according to act of Congress. A.D. 1801

19. Title page, *The Social Harmonist*, 2nd edition. Courtesy of the Music Division of the New York Public Library.

---

1. The 2nd edition title page (see Illus. 19) appears to be an amended version of the 1st edition title page, with the last digit of the date changed and the words "chiefly Original" engraved over a phrase that began: "with . . . . . ."

Throughout the earlier New York years, he was undoubtedly active as a singing-master. In 1806, he was the vestryman and clerk at Christ Protestant Episcopal Church on Ann Street. In the same year, he received as payment for services rendered as a house builder the Mink Hollow place to which his father moved.

Lewis, Jr. slips into the shadows in 1815, emerges briefly upon his retirement in 1830 to a farm in Bristol (now Shady), New York, a few acres away from the homestead occupied by his father, and fades from the scene permanently on May 23, 1845, when death overtook him. Both father and son were supposedly buried in Mink Hollow, perhaps in the dooryard burying ground on their property such as the one Mrs. Cowell was looking for in 1952. Neither she nor I succeeded in locating their final resting-place.

I CAN NOW pick up the story of the Edson hunt where I left off, en route to Shady to help the local folk sing Edson tunes in 1952. The pastor of the church had devised an elegant title for the affair, calling it a "program on the history of hymnology in America," and some 30-odd townsfolk showed up. Although the singing was crude, there was a peculiar fitness about the whole thing, and to me it was a moving experience. Thanks to Mrs. Cowell's trusty tape-recorder, there is a record of the whole thing for posterity, now on deposit in the Archive of Folk Song at the Library of Congress.

The rest of the stay at Shady was occupied in good talk with Sidney and Henry Cowell about a multitude of things and several forays into the countryside searching for Edson remains.

I had thought that the shallow vein of information Mrs. Cowell had struck had been exhausted, but it turned out that her diligence had an unexpectedly important coda. In one of her 1952 letters, she wrote:

There is one exciting tidbit which may turn out to be pure gold—and may not. Miss Jannette Edson, an elderly 6th-grade teacher in the Kingston public schools, was always told that her grandfather's father was named Lewis and wrote hymns. Moreover, she once possessed what she described as a handwritten music book, a small notebook half empty, with Lewis Edson's name in it and the date 1800. A niece carted this off to Florida on the ground that she was musical and her aunt was not! But because of the C-clef she found she could not make sense of the hymns. Miss Jannette had just written for it when I met her. (August 4, 1952)

Nothing further developed from this immediately, however, and the Edsons faded out of my life in the years that passed. I dismissed the existence of the Edson manuscript as another one of those family legends that prettily garland a family tree. But I turned out to be wrong.

In June, 1960, my wife and I took advantage of attending the summer meeting of the Music Library Association in Montreal to drop in on the Cowells on our way back to Washington. Suddenly we were faced with Edson *redivivus*. After a series of most improbable events which cannot be related for fear of straining credibility beyond the breaking point, it developed that the indefatigable Mrs. Cowell had once again located Miss Edson (who had meanwhile disappeared from view) when she learned we were coming. And, lo and behold, we were to visit Miss Edson at her Kingston house and have the privilege of seeing the Edson manuscript with our own eyes.

On Saturday, June 25, 1960, we did in fact meet Miss Edson and examine the manuscript. It was indubitably genuine and very interesting, and we urged her to make sure that it was suitably preserved for posterity. Within a few weeks after our visit, Miss Edson generously presented her grandfather's father's music book to the New York Public Library, where those interested in the music written in the early years of the Republic can study it in conjunction with one of the two known copies of the earliest surviving edition of Edson's *Social Harmonist*.

THE OBLONG notebook is 14 by 20 centimeters in size and bears the legend "Lewis Edsons Book, Danbury Ct., March 1st 1800."

on the marbled board cover. This is followed by two blank leaves; the stubs of five additional leaves show that these were torn out. The manuscript itself begins on a page numbered nine and continues on numbered pages through 110. Then come seven additional pages of manuscript, unnumbered. As well as the preliminary leaves, pp. 11–12, 17–18, 30–31, and 43–62 are lacking, having been cut out of the notebook at some undeterminable time before it arrived in the New York Public Library.

There appears to be little question that the notebook was kept by Lewis Edson, Jr., not by the composer of the famous three. The evidence to this effect seems quite conclusive: (a) the Danbury date-line on the cover; (b) the positive identification of the first three tunes, SOLITUDE, FRIENDSHIP, and HARLEM, as Lewis, Jr.'s in the *Social Harmonist*; (c) the dating of several of the tunes many years after the father's death; (d) the explicit notation of the last tune in the book, RESURECTION [sic], (see Illus. 20) as "by L. Edson sen.," the sole composer attribution in the entire manuscript.

The notebook was probably acquired by Lewis, Jr. on or about the date written on the cover and kept by him as a repository for his creative work in music for well over three decades. As evidence of the accuracy of this hypothesis, one might adduce the first four tunes, found published in the 1801 second edition of the *Social Harmonist*, and the tune TIDD, dated November 1, 1832. Of the 73 tunes in the notebook (there are also three duplications), only these first four ever achieved the permanence of print, and they appear only in the *Social Harmonist*. Two are the work of the father, the untitled fuging-tune without text on p. 13 which turns out to be DOMINION (attributed to Lewis Edson, Sr. in the *Social Harmonist*), and RESURECTION, already cited, apparently copied in the son's old age from some surviving manuscript of his father's. All the others are undoubtedly the work of Lewis Edson, Jr.

What can be deduced about Lewis Edson, Jr. as musician and man from these old tunes? Not much, but perhaps something. The

20. "Lewis Edsons Book," Leaf 75ᵛ. Courtesy of the Music Division of the New York Public Library.

names of the tunes follow the standard pattern for the most part, but a few are a little unusual. Edson occasionally used the names of poets as titles—HOMER, POPE, VIRGIL, and BYRON are examples. This might imply a certain literary bent. While it is hardly safe to assume that Edson was familiar with all the places he used as tune names, a pattern does seem to emerge from the 24 tunes with this sort of title. Very few place names are used in the early pages (HARLEM is a significant exception), but beginning with the tune LEMINGTON on p. 70, written around 1830 when Edson retired to Shady, they become common. It is difficult to avoid the conclusion that he must have been drawing on his memory of earlier years for titles, and the town, county, and state names should at least provide some scholar with a starting-point from which to pursue Edson's history further. Towns are named in New Hampshire (LEMINGTON), Connecticut (EAST CHESTER, DANBURY, CAN-

TON, BRIDGEWATER, PLYMOUTH), New York (SCHENECTADY, COOP-
ERSTOWN), New Jersey(PITTSTOWN, AMBOY, TRENTON), Massachusetts (LANESBOROUGH, RICHMOND), and Vermont (POWNAL);
counties in New York (ULSTER, WASHINGTON, ALBANY, SARA-
TOGA); states are OHIO, JERSEY, and YORK; there is also AMERICA.
Perhaps the large area covered can be in part explained by his
youthful work as post-rider.

Lewis, Jr. was not an especially gifted tunesmith, and few of
his unpublished tunes seem to merit revival. Those found early in
the notebook show some ties with the New England idiom which
his father used so brilliantly in LENOX, BRIDGEWATER, and GREEN-
FIELD, but the later ones are obviously influenced by the pale and
relatively characterless "scientific musick" which came into vogue
in this country in the second decade of the 19th century and which
drove the uniquely flavored tunes of the 1780s and 1790s out of
the cities and into the frontier areas. Not entirely without interest, however, is the fact that some 21 of Lewis, Jr.'s tunes were
composed in three parts rather than the customary four. One, the
tune POPE, was actually written in five parts—a great rarity in
that time. A few tunes are unusual in formal structure—CHRIS-
TIAN TRAVELLERS, which utilizes antiphonal men's and women's
voices followed by a mixed-voice chorus, is a fine example. Also
interesting is Edson's occasional use of secular texts—for instance,
an INDEPENDENCE ODE, a paean to the advent of the NINE-
TEENTH CENTURY, and THE WOODLAND HALLOO. But he cannot,
in all honesty, be classed as anything more than a very minor composer, even according to the standards of his own place and time.
Perhaps his most notable composition is the tune REFUGE, which
is not found in the manuscript notebook, but which appears in
the *Social Harmonist.*

Rather unexpectedly, the notebook reveals Lewis Edson, Jr. as a
not untalented primitive poet. The last few unnumbered pages of
the manuscript contain three poems, obviously original, and they
are so charming and illuminate his character so brightly that I cannot refrain from quoting at least two. The first is called

THE BRAG

Writing is what I do well understand
Printing is also at my own command,
Cut[t]ing down Trees, and sewing up Trouse[r]s;
Carving also to me's very handy,
Marking out statues or drinking of brandy;
Stamping of muslin I do very neat,
Engraving's an Art, I have it compleat;
Staining I do it both han[d]some and good,
Painting by me is well understood;
Inditing is what I well understand,
     He that don't b'l[i]eve it may dought & be d---d.

The second is quite moving, rather startling in rhythm, and completely comprehensible in mood to anyone who has walked
in the quiet green woods and meadows of Shady and Mink Hollow.
Edson entitled it

ODE TO THE FOREST

Let others tell [sing] of Cities and their Grandure
Of swelling tides and beauties of the Ocean,
Mine be the task to speak of humble stations,
    In lonely forests.

There nature's seen without a faulse dis[s]embler,
There all is truth and harmonizing system,
Hypocricy ne'er shoes its hateful features,
    In silent shadoes.

Where shall a Saint on Earth find safe retirement,
But in the wild and vast extended forest,
There all is simple and sincear, completely,
    Without temptation.

O, that I had a dwelling in the desert,
Where the false polish of the great ne'er enter'd,
There would I rest secure from Earth's deceptions,
    In contemplation.

O that the Lord would grant me this great blessing,
In shady groves, to walk with a kind partner,
There might we rest secure from Earth's temptation,
    And rise to'w[a]rds heaven

There should our prayer ascend like morning incense,
Sweetly perfum'd by real pure devotion,
And gratitude should rise, when ev'ning shadoes,
    Spread their dominion.

I WOULD BE the first to concede that the Edsons of Shady will never challenge the Bachs, Beethovens, or even the MacDowells and the Fosters as composers. Nor need Shakespeare and Robert Frost fear for their laurels. But I would nevertheless insist that they are deserving of careful scrutiny. There were in the early days hundreds (perhaps thousands) of humble artisans in the United States who hungered and thirsted for the arts. We are considered a materialistic people by those who note our addiction to gadgetry and our affinity for the dollar. I will not argue the truth of the indictment today—others have done that with great eloquence and power—but so far as late 18th- and early 19th-century America is concerned, I feel that this is a stereotyped distortion based on ignorance of the way in which our people really lived.

There is plenty of evidence that the musical Edsons were by no means a unique phenomenon. The music of the American singing-school period was omnipresent and deeply beloved. Musty town records show that carpenters, physicians, storekeepers, legislators, farmers, blacksmiths, printers, painters, schoolteachers, tavernkeepers, lawyers, newspaper editors, housewives, hatters, tanners, members of virtually every trade and profession that can be mentioned, not only sang and played music but taught it and wrote it.

The Edsons are prototypes of an American civilization as yet unexcavated, symbols of a strong drive towards non-material goods. This civilization has remained unknown to those who see only the rapidity of our technological progress and our affinity for creature comforts. The story of the Edsons should give pause to those who would apply to the history of music in America the same yardstick with which the progress of the art in Europe is measured. On this side of the Atlantic, the musical Edsons are significant because of their ubiquity. Any view of the American prospect which does not see their character is a false one, and this leads me to hope that this attempt to sketch the history of two such minor figures as Lewis Edson, father and son, may prove instructive as well as mildly entertaining.

10

—⟫ ⟪—

JAMES HEWITT:
PROFESSIONAL MUSICIAN

APRIL, 1789 WAS A BIG MONTH for New York. The town was bursting at its seams. Visitors had jammed every available tavern and private dwelling; from far and wide, everyone who could possibly manage the journey had flocked into the nation's capital to witness the presidential inauguration of General Washington.

Although it was smaller, dirtier, noisier, and poorer than Philadelphia, America's great metropolis, the village on the Hudson had an unmistakable charm of its own. Pennsylvania's Senator Maclay, who vacillated between damning its inconveniences and marveling at its fascination, admitted in his diary that "the allurements of New York are more than ten to two compared with Philadelphia." Even in those days, New York was a wonderful place to visit, but a nerve-wracking place in which to live.

Perhaps then as now, its distinctive character was due to its cosmopolitanism. Many diverse nationalities, jostling each other in its winding, busy streets, gave the town a racy and sophisticated aura. Numerically, the Dutch were still the largest group, but the influx of English, French, German, Scotch, Irish, and other nationals was well under way. The city directory for the year listed 11 intrepid souls who made their living, in one way or another, from music. Their mere names—Henry Capron, Christian Claus, Thomas Dodds, Melchior Ferch, George Gilfert, Joseph Harvey, William Hoffmaster, Andrew Picken, Abraham Turk, George

Ulshaffer, Charles Watts—demonstrated the town's mixed stock.

The melting pot boiled merrily, but it was still not much more than a small saucepan. New York's 20,000 inhabitants did not feel in the least cramped living on the southern tip of Manhattan island. An arc of a mile's radius, using the Battery as center, completely circumscribed the urban area. Outside of this arc, the countryside was still more or less virgin, dotted with farms and swampland. Even disregarding the hazardous condition of the streets, which distracted Gothamites described as "hills and Vallies . . . not passable with Carts and dangerous for foot Passengers after dusk," a half-hour was the absolute limit for a town walk in any one direction.

New York was small, but it was growing, lustily and noisily. The racket was terrific. At the first cock's crow, milkmen and milkmaids began their morning rounds to the accompaniment of bellows, meant to be musical, of "Milk, ho!" and "Milk, come!" Tradesmen of every description—notion-hawkers, ragmen, knife-grinders, orange-girls, lamp-menders, wood-vendors, chimney-sweeps—all with their distinctive shouts and cries, used the thoroughfares as a place of business. As the day really got under way, interminable traffic jams led to choruses of profanity. Barking dogs chased squealing pigs who dodged through the legs of bleating goats. The din was so great that it was found necessary to block off a section of Broad Street in order that the judges holding court might be able to hear what the lawyers and witnesses were saying. On Wall Street, the noise interfered with the smooth functioning of Congress. The hard-working legislators could not hear the speeches. Senator Maclay, after straining to make out what one of his colleagues was saying, despairingly noted in his diary that there was "such a noise I was not master of one sentence of it."

A FEW BLOCKS AWAY FROM from the nerve center of the newly-born republic, John Jacob Astor sold imported "Forte-pianos" on Queen Street to the musically minded. A couple of doors farther down the street, his neighbor and competitor, Thomas Dodds, manufactured his own instruments and undersold the future founder of the Astor fortune by as much as 25 per cent. Eventually, John Jacob left the music trade for the much more lucrative fur business and made out somewhat better.

Almost any day of the week, the most picturesque of New York's musicians, William Hoffmaster, could be seen parading through the streets. This eccentric character, known familiarly throughout the town as "Billy the Fiddler," was a dwarf, about four and a half feet tall, who was given to wearing oversized boots and outsized cocked hats. Billy was quite the raconteur and man-about-town, and claimed acquaintance and friendship with Mozart. He is known to have performed for his pupils a Mozart sonata which he said was really by William Hoffmaster. He set himself up as a music teacher, and in his public announcement of the fact, he was frank enough to say that he did so because he was incapable of earning a living in any other manner. Of his skill as a teacher there is no contemporary testimony, but excellent instruction was available at Henry Capron's or George Gilfert's establishments.

An important musical family had just arrived in New York, too late to be included in the 1789 city directory. Peter Albrecht Van Hagen, Sr., "organist, klokkenist, and componist," with his wife and his eight-year-old son Peter, Jr. came, and it did not take them long to conquer. The Van Hagen clan, excellent and extremely versatile musicians, had originally settled in Charleston, South Carolina in 1774, and were now seeking greener musical pastures. According to his first New York advertisement, Peter, Sr. was prepared to give instruction on any or all of the following: "violin, harpsichord, tenor, violoncello, German flute, hautboy, clarinet, bassoon, and singing"—all for the small sum of six dollars per month. As a one-man musical conservatory, Van Hagen was quite successful, and he soon demonstrated that he was more than a routine teacher. In October, he made his New York concert debut, and besides playing two concertos on the violin and one on the tenor (or, as we would call it, the viola), he delighted his audience with a solo "upon iron nails, called Violon Harmonika." His talented son, Peter, Jr., also performed, offering a pianoforte concerto and singing a ballad, and was also very cordially received.

The subscription concert was the backbone of New York's musical life. These affairs were socially exclusive events, and included dancing and refreshments in addition to the musical program. They had been going on since 1785, when William Brown had presented the first series, and no subsequent season had passed without a subscription series. As well as teaching and performing publicly, Van Hagen also entered the lists as an impresario. As he appears to have been a genial and astute businessman as well as a fine musician, he quickly established himself as New York's dominant musical figure, but his uncontested supremacy in the field was of brief duration.

In September, 1792, a tempestuous 22-year-old Englishman named James Hewitt (leading a formidable company of musicians including Jean Gehot, B. Bergmann, William Young, and a Mr. Phillips) landed in New York. Fresh from the brilliant atmosphere of London, these "professors of music from the Operahouse, Hanoversquare," who had played "under the direction of Haydn, Pleyel, etc.," immediately announced that they would give a concert at Corré's Hotel at which "they humbly hoped to experience the kind patronage of the ladies and gentlemen, and public in general." New York smiled on their efforts, and Hewitt and his associates proceeded to give Van Hagen very stiff competition indeed.

JAMES HEWITT, son of Captain John Hewitt of the British Navy, was born on June 4, 1770, in Dartmoor, best known to Americans for its prison, which was to house hundreds of American prisoners during the War of 1812. Hewitt's father, a brave and skillful officer, appears to have been distinguished chiefly for the length of time he lived—he died in the New World after he had reached the remarkable age of 101 years. Little is known of James's childhood except that, tiring of the rugged Devonshire moorland, he entered the naval service. According to family legend, he quickly resigned when he saw the cruel treatment inflicted upon the sailors on board his ship and abandoned any further attempt to follow in his father's footsteps. He thenceforward devoted his energy to studying music, a field in which he showed great talent. His industry must have been great and his masters excellent, for his progress in his chosen profession was very rapid. While he was little more than a boy, he became the leader of the orchestra at the court of George III, and counted amongst his intimates the Prince of Wales, who presented him with an Amati cello as a token of esteem.

In the light of his successful career in England, it must have been quite a coup for John Henry, of the Old American Company, to persuade the young man to emigrate to America as "leader of the band" for the dramatic troupe in New York.[1] Perhaps the death of his wife and infant in 1791 may have impelled him to seek his fortune and happiness across the seas.

It is not difficult to understand why the Van Hagens must have felt chagrined when Hewitt and his friends arrived in New York in 1792. Although he was young in years, he was a seasoned professional when he offered his first concert to the New York public. Hewitt's program, one of the most interesting of the period, was unusual in several respects. The standard works which served as the concert's framework—an Overture by Haydn, a *Quartetto* by Pleyel, and a Symphony and a Flute *Quartetto* by Stamitz—were indicative of the excellent taste of Hewitt and his associates, but of greater moment were the novelties. These were an original concerto for the cello by Mr. Phillips, Gehot's *Overture in 12 movements, expressive of a voyage from England to America,* and Hewitt's *Overture in 9 movements, expressive of a battle.* Unfortunately, the scores have been lost, and it is thus impossible to judge the musical value of these new works. It is pretty certain, however, that the Gehot piece was of autobiographical interest, while the Hewitt overture must have been modelled after Kotzwara's *Battle of Prague,* which enjoyed a tremendous popularity both here and

1. See Chapter 5 for further details.

abroad for many years.

This first concert was a benefit affair for the newly-landed quintet of musicians, and they promptly decided to challenge Van Hagen and invade the subscription concert field. An extremely ambitious series of 12 concerts was announced. Van Hagen, in turn, presented his own subscription series of three concerts in the fall of 1792, and had the satisfaction of watching the Hewitt combine run into one difficulty and postponement after another. It was not until 1793 that the Hewitt subscription series materialized. By then, the number of concerts had shrunk to six, and the number of sponsors to three. Gehot had departed for Philadelphia, and Young had followed him there, only to meet a melodramatic end a few years later, when he was sentenced to death for the murder of a constable who had come to arrest him for debt. In the next year, Phillips left also, adding insult to injury by joining the Van Hagens. Of the original five, only Bergmann remained with Hewitt.

The competition between the two rival managerial groups was extremely hot, and both suffered because of it. New Yorkers could not absorb more than a fairly small number of concerts, and between them, Hewitt and Van Hagen just about succeeded in glutting the market. In 1795, they declared a temporary truce and merged forces for a joint series of three concerts, but the union was shortlived. Hewitt withdrew and devoted himself to his duties as leader of the orchestra of the Old American Company. His talents as conductor were much appreciated; there is record of his leadership of several bands, including the one at the celebrated "Vaux Hall Gardens" summer concerts, where the admission fee entitled the listener to "a glass of ice cream punch" and the privilege of witnessing the amazing fireworks "made by the celebrated Mr. Ambrose."

Strangely enough, many of Hewitt's compositions are known, but these are only his smaller and less consequential works. They do indicate that he was a composer of real talent, but they are no accurate measure of his full capabilities, which could only be judged on the basis of his extended pieces—and these have all disappeared. One of his most important efforts appears to have been the music to *Tammany,* which was first performed (under the auspices of the Tammany Society) in 1794. The struggle between the Federalists and the anti-Federalists was particularly bitter at that time, and as the libretto was violently anti-Federalist, its presentation aroused considerable controversy. There was much excitement at the actual premiere. One Federalist writer accused the promoters of gaining an audience by circulating a story that a claque had been hired to hiss the work. As was to be expected, the anti-Federalists hailed *Tammany* with great enthusiasm, and the Federalists lambasted it as a "wretched thing, literally a melange of bombast." Since Hewitt's music has never turned up, and considering the temper of the times, to estimate its value is a hazardous thing. One thing is certain, however: it did make Hewitt a political storm center in New York for many months afterward.

Also in 1794, he anticipated Rossini with his opera *The Patriot, or Liberty Asserted,* founded on the well-known story of William Tell, the Swiss patriot, who shot an apple from his son's head at the command of Tyrant Grislor who first gave liberty to the cantons of Switzerland." The score of this too has disappeared.

A few years later, Hewitt purchased the New York branch of Benjamin Carr's music publishing establishment, and embarked upon a business that was to last through the middle of the 19th century, thanks to the business acumen of his eldest son, John Hill Hewitt. James Hewitt was not a good businessman and the firm brought him small profit; until John Hill took it over, it did not flourish.

DESPITE his spirited participation in publishing, composing, concertizing, conducting, and managing, Hewitt was apparently dissatisfied with New York as a center for his activities. At one time or other, he seems to have visited practically every orchestral pit on the Atlantic seaboard, proceeding as far south in his journeys as Augusta, Georgia. Something about Boston attracted him, and in 1810, despite the fact that New York was then three times its size, he decided to move his family there permanently.

As it had been in New York, Hewitt's entrance on the musical scene in Boston was marked by increased concert activity, and there are some striking resemblances between his opening New York and Boston campaigns. His chief competitors in Boston were the Graupners and there was no evidence of friendship between the two families. Although it was customary for local musicians to help newcomers and Gottlieb Graupner seems to have been a friendly and easy going sort, his name does not appear among those assisting at Hewitt's concerts. Between the two men there were no intimations of cordiality; each went his own way more or less successfully and managed to avoid the other as much as possible. Their concerts were generally held in different concert halls, and tickets to Hewitt's affairs were *not* for sale at Mr. Graupner's music store. When Dr. George K. Jackson, nabob of the Bostonian music world, presented an important concert consisting wholly of selections from Handel's works, the words "***Mr. Hewitt has declined" were boldly printed in the program. Gottlieb Graupner led the band.

Many concerts followed, and on rare occasions Hewitt took part in single events with other prominent musicians. Always, however, they were only single events, and Hewitt made his way alone. Eventually, even his wife left him; the couple were separated a year or so before Hewitt's death. Hewitt removed himself from Boston and lived in a boarding house in New York, while Eliza remained behind in the house of one of her sons. At the time of the breakup of his marriage, Hewitt was quite ill and had just undergone a serious operation. He despaired of his recovery, and the lonely man wrote moving letters to his son in Boston. "My sufferings are great and my death slow, but certain," he complained. "I hope my dear James you will be here to receive my last breath. I feel the want of home—tho every kind attention is paid me here—yet my heart longs once more to behold my family."

He was much concerned about his music, which he felt would be

11

---※➔※ ➔➔ ◄◄◄---

THE TRIUMPH OF
ANTHONY PHILIP HEINRICH

In 1846, NEW YORK AND BOSTON, cultural centers of a brash, vigorous, clumsy, rapidly growing young America, were hotly compet-
ing with each other in paying homage to a then living American
composer whose name has since virtually disappeared from memory. Even today, in our enlightened times, concerts consisting
solely of music by a contemporary American composer are extremely rare and widely heralded events. Yet, more than a century
ago, one Anthony Philip Heinrich completely conquered New
York and Boston with his music, if not with his personality. Within
the short space of six weeks, two concerts, both artistic triumphs
for the man, were given before immense and wildly enthusiastic
audiences.

Heinrich, called "the Beethoven of America" by the critics of his
time, was our most commanding figure as a composer during the
middle decades of the 19th century. His music has long since
passed into the limbo of oblivion. Nevertheless, he stood head and
shoulders above his contemporaries. If his music seems bombastic
and overambitious to us today, it must be remembered that he was
an artistic figure to be reckoned with in the turbulent years preceding the Civil War.

In a letter to a close friend, Heinrich paints a vivid and naively
pathetic picture of his struggles as a musician in the New York of
the 1840s. He writes:

I am trotting about from morning till night teaching little misses on the piano forte for small quarter money, often unpaid. Sometimes I have had good cause to sink under my exertions, but still my spirits remain buoyant on the heated and dusty surface of the summer earth. At night, I close my toilsome labors and lonely incubations, on a broken, crazy, worn-out, feeble, and very limited octaved piano forte. As this decrepit instrument has, alas, lost by moving on the first of May, one of its legs, and many other props and intestines of enchantment, it might be well worth the visit of some curious antiquarian to look at it and hear it.

Father Heinrich, as he was affectionately and universally called by the musical world in the last years of his long and eccentric lifetime, was having his troubles. In order to help the old man out, his friends decided to put on an all-Heinrich concert for his financial benefit. This concert, scheduled for May 5, 1846, at the Broadway Tabernacle, proved to be good copy for the newspapers. Many columns of lush prose were devoted to Heinrich's life and works; the press was delighted with a composer who actually starved in a garret and was, moreover, as "queer" as the genius of the romantic age is expected to be. On the day before the concert, Horace Greeley's New York *Tribune* gave space to an extended, last minute eulogy of Heinrich written by Mrs. Lydia Maria Child, his close personal friend and self-appointed New York publicity agent. This remarkable women is still remembered as a novelist and poet of some talent and as a firebrand abolitionist. In the purple prose characteristic of the day, Mrs. Child fervently implored the public not to let the composer down. Closing with a final burst of eloquence, she wrote: "I believe it will not be so, even in this selfish world, and this busy age. The numerous professional musicians who are preparing this concert . . . [for] the venerable object of their affectionate regard, will surely be cordially sustained by the public. . . . May this concert prove a bright sunset gleam in a life full of clouds and storms, and may it warm and cheer the good old man, with a soul full of music, and a heart full of love."

Although Heinrich was at the time 60 years old, the implication that he was feebly knocking at death's door must be attributed to poetic license on the part of Mrs. Child. Despite his numerous trials and tribulations, and "clouds and storms" which were to affect his later life, he was to live to the ripe age of 80 before he joined his ancestors.

IN DEFERENCE to the voracious musical appetite of the contemporary public, enough of Father Heinrich's music was programmed to blast a modern audience into insensibility. Among the more curious selections listed for performance was:

A MONUMENTAL SYMPHONY—"*To the Spirit of Beethoven.*" written for a grand orchestra. An Echo from America, to the inauguration of the Monument at Bonn . . .

Mr. Henry G. Watson, New York's leading music critic over a period of many years, compiled the very extensive program notes for the concert with a certain touch of abandon. His guide to the complexities of the "Monumental Symphony" is as follows:

SPIRIT OF BEETHOVEN

It depicts in glowing colors the whole ceremony of the inauguration of the Statue to the immortal Beethoven, at Bonn. A detail of the principal points will afford some idea of the comprehensive and poetical conception of the poet-composer.

It commences with a ceremonious movement—a salutation to the citizens of Bonn. Then follows at the *signal of the Gong*—the assembling of the musical profession and the people.

Signal with the Gong—Approach of the clergy.

Signal with the Gong—Commotion of the multitude discovering the Royal Cortege.

Soli, Flaute, Oboe, Clarinetti, Fagotti, &c.—The melodious outpourings of the Celestial Genii hovering over the monument.

Tutti—The greeting of the Genii to the assembled hosts of admiring visitors.

Signal with the Gong—Arrival of the King of Prussia, Queen Victoria, and her royal Consort, and Dignitaries of the Courts.

Entrata of Trumpets, Horns, &c.—Hail to Beethoven.

Signal with the Gong—The uncovering of the monument.

Allegro Brillante—The enthusiastic admiration and praise of the convocation.

Signal with the Gong—The triumph of Beethoven's glory.
Signal with the Gong—*Coda religiosa*—Last homage to the shades
of Beethoven.
Farewell Salutation.

This grand work is written for an immense orchestra, and the subject
presents wide scope for the inventive faculties, in which particular Mr.
Heinrich is marvelously gifted.

From this description, it would seem that Father Heinrich must
be given credit for being the first American to indulge in the sport
of kicking the gong around. Unfortunately, the "Monumental Symphony" was not actually played. The orchestra was neither immense enough, nor skillful enough, to perform it. According to one
reviewer, it was "omitted, as, notwithstanding the very large
orchestra engaged, there were not instruments enough for its
execution."

Despite the omission of the "Spirit of Beethoven", it was apparent that Heinrich had taken the city by storm. Mrs. Child's pious
hope that the concert would prove "a bright sunset gleam" in the
composer's dark and gloomy existence was more than fulfilled.
Father Heinrich was a positive sensation. One utterly confounded
reviewer, dazzled by the extraordinary fervor the audience and
even the performers manifested, wrote that the concert was "in
many respects the most remarkable and never-to-be-forgotten
entertainment we have ever witnessed." According to this eye-
witness, the audience "seemed for a while to have gone partially mad"; it yelled, screamed, stamped on the floor, and almost
completely buried the "venerable beneficiary" under massive
"floral tributes." And a hilarious and completely unexpected side-
show added immeasurably to the great excitement of the assembled music lovers.

The signal for the outbreak of general pandemonium was given
during the intermission by "a child, which ascended to the platform and presented a beautiful bouquet to Mr. Heinrich." The
applause had hardly begun to subside when Mrs. Child (from
what point in the pit the reviewer does not tell us) tossed a laurel

wreath to the stage with such uncanny accuracy that she performed the almost unbelievable feat of landing it squarely on the composer's head. The reviewer remarked that "the lady must, in former days, have had some practice in the manly and athletic art of quoit-pitching." We are left to guess how much of the tumultuous acclaim that followed was directed towards Mrs. Child for her remarkable aim, and how much towards Heinrich for his music. Mrs. Child's guiding hand in the homage paid to the composer apparently annoyed another of the music critics. He noted that "a delicate card, which was attached to the wreath . . . bore the words, 'for father Heinrich, from L. M. C.' The tribute to the old man's genius was in no danger of being mistaken."

Although his music made a deep impression on those present, the unfortunate publicity attending Mrs. Child's antics made Heinrich somewhat of a laughingstock among those who read the reports of the concert in the newspapers on the following day. To its later embarrassment, the New York press emphasized beyond all reason the copious amounts of flowers received by the composer and the sentimental ceremonies attending the concert; more sophisticated Boston was soon to subject it to an unmerciful ribbing.

Heinrich's artistic triumph was incidental, of course, to the real reason for the concert—the raising of money. From this point of view, the concert was a dismal failure. The detailed financial statement credited Heinrich with a net profit of $118.97, but it apologized for its own inaccuracy with the following note, which was appended to it: "We regret to learn that there are 'sundries' to be charged in this balance, not included in the above. We look for a better result from the Bostonians."

HEINRICH's friends in Boston, where he had always been a great favorite, were not slow to take the hint. A Heinrich benefit was announced for June 13, 1846 in the Tremont Temple. His Boston admirers worked hard to make the concert a success and to shame New York. As one of his partisans wrote: "We hope that it may yield for the beneficiary—not crowns and garlands of flowers or odes of sentimental poetry—but rather that better produce for the practical man, which can provide comforts for age and gratify the generous heart in its dictates. The *Boston* concert must sound of silver, and surpass that of New York."

In those days, Bostoners were fully as hardy as New Yorkers. In length, breadth, and magnitude, the program of the Boston concert even managed to surpass the one at New York. Among other large-scale pieces, the following were announced:

TECUMSEH, or *The Battle of the Thames*—A martial Ouverture—for full Orchestra.
>   Introduction—the Indian War Council.
>   Allegro Eroico—The Indian War Dance—Advance of the Ameri-
>   cans—Skirmishing—Battle, and Fall of Tecumseh.
OUVERTURE—*"To the Pilgrims,"*—Full orchestra, with Trumpet Ob-
ligato by Mr. Bartlett,—comprising the following Tableaux:
>   1st—Adagio Primo,—The Genius of Freedom slumbering in the
>   forest shades of America.
>   2d—Adagio Secondo,—She is awakened into life by those mov-
>   ing melodies, with which nature regales her votaries in her pri-
>   meval solitude.
>   3d—Marcia,—The efforts of power to clip the young eagle of
>   liberty.
>   4th—Allegretto Pollaca, [sic]—The joyous reign of universal
>   freedom and universal intelligence.

This time, the entire program was given as advertised, although Heinrich must have wished that the most ambitious works had been passed over. He complained bitterly of the concert in a letter to a friend in Boston: "The musicians of Boston have in their zeal and refined accomplishment nearly chopped off my head . . . Upon the imperfect, nay slovenly, confused execution of my orchestral works in Boston, I cannot accept any criticism or forecast of judgment on my musical ways—in common justice beyond that miserable fact of instrumental bankruptcy with which I was cruelly served by many delinquent performers . . ."

Despite the composer's unhappiness about the concert, critical acclaim was again unanimous. He was most fortunate in having for his friend Cornelia Walter, who was the editor as well as the music reviewer of the powerful Boston *Evening Transcript*. Miss Walter, who was an ardent if not a very discerning critic, found the concert "completely successful." In regard to the botched performance, she wrote in her newspaper that "the various compositions of the venerable artist were rendered in a manner which showed that the performers had entered into the feelings of the dreamy and enthusiastic musician, and nothing was wanted of that energy and precision which could alone carry off the peculiarities of the music. They played well because they loved the man for whose benefit they played." At the close of the concert, the leader of the orchestra and chorus, unaware of Heinrich's dismay, announced from the stage that the entire company intended "to express their regard for the beneficiary by singing a song together, and, in accordance with this announcement . . . united in making the welkin ring with the touching and appropriate strains of 'Auld Lang Syne'." Miss Walter was delighted by this artful touch: it was "a hearty compliment and a most suitable finale." Not so Heinrich, who was in no mood to appreciate the niceties of etiquette after hearing how his music had been played by the Bostonians. He wrote peevishly to his Boston friend: "'Auld Lang Syne' can hardly atone for the incongruous manner, with which my 'Ouverture to the Pilgrims' was performed . . ."

In Boston, no laurels crowned Father Heinrich's head, and "sentimental ceremonies" were entirely lacking. The Bostoners leaned over backward in order to make sure not to duplicate New York's unnecessary fripperies. Miss Walter carefully noted that "care was taken at the outset that the expenses should not exceed the receipts." But despite the business-like attitude of the Boston enthusiasts and their insistence that the concert must "sound of *silver*," once again the concert failed in its real purpose, and the total return to Heinrich was probably no more than he received in New York. Miss Walter allowed her high spirits to get the better of her good judgment; once more her report was hopelessly at variance with the facts. She estimated that "the concert, we doubt not, will put some hundreds into the pocket of Father Heinrich . . . The pecuniary results, however large, will be but an inadquate reward . . ."

Reports of the fiasco reached New York quickly, and a notice appeared in the New York press denying that it had been a failure. The anonymous writer explained that Heinrich had "received more than twice the amount of pecuniary compensation there as he did in New York, besides many touching private testimonials of the love in which he is held by the good and the wise."

THE FOLLOWING notice appeared in *Dwight's Journal of Music* on March 23, 1861: "There is among us an aged artist numbering eighty years. Every reader of this paper knows him as a highly gifted musician. His many valuable manuscripts fill large trunks, and in face of these riches this old man lies sick and without money in the second story of the house, No. 33 Bayard St. Anthony Philip Heinrich is too illustrious a person to be suffered to make his debut before the world in the character of a beggar. He has worked much and the world owes him [much]." A few weeks later, he was dead.

In a letter to Mrs. Child, Heinrich quaintly describes his own creations: "I believe my music runs in the same vein as my letters to you; full of strange ideal somersets and capriccios. Still I hope there may be some method discoverable, some beauty, whether of regular or irregular features. Possibly the public may acknowledge this, when I am dead and gone . . ."

The public has not acknowledged this, and in all probability, never will. Heinrich was what one calls a "character"—his eccentricity made him a wonderful butt for the jokesters of his day. Nevertheless, he made solid contributions to our musical culture. He was a pioneer, and he should be judged as such. He should be honored for his numerous accomplishments rather than condemned for his equally numerous failures. Above all else, he was a serious and a sincere musician. At a time when the possibility of a native American music was hardly thought about, Heinrich attempted to create it singlehanded. He did the best he knew how to do, and if his best was not good enough, he at least made the task easier for the more talented men who followed him.

Heinrich was the first musician to introduce the symphonies of Beethoven to the New World. This he did 10 years before Beethoven's death. Strange as it may seem, the first performance of a Beethoven symphony (the First) took place under Heinrich's direction in the comparative wilderness of Lexington, Kentucky, in the incredibly early year of 1817. In 1842, when a committee of distinguished citizens met for the purpose of forming the Philharmonic Society of New York, Heinrich was chosen its chairman.

Despite incredible hardships, he composed vast tone poems, comparable in orchestral complexity and size to those of Richard Strauss, decades before Strauss had begun to write. He was handicapped due to the fact that he was an autodidact; in a different and more sympathetic age, he might have progressed much further along his chosen path.

Among the distinguished people with whom he corresponded were included such giants as Felix Mendelssohn-Bartholdy, Washington Irving, Thomas Moore, and Alexander von Humboldt. In his younger days in Kentucky, he was a close personal friend of John James Audubon and his family.

Although he made the eagle scream too loudly, he was our first, and by far the most enthusiastic, musical nationalist.

The music of worse composers than that of Father Heinrich is heard today, but perhaps it is just as well that his remains unheard. At least his name, however, should be remembered and honored.

12

WILLIAM HENRY FRY:
AMERICAN NATIONALIST

In 1820, THE REV. SYDNEY SMITH, sharp-tongued wit and reformer, regally surveyed Americans from his vantage point in Yorkshire. "During the thirty or forty years of their independence" he wrote caustically in the *Edinburgh Review,* which he had helped to found in 1798, "they have done absolutely nothing for the Sciences, for the Arts, for Literature, or even for the statesman-like studies of Politics or Political Economy. . . . In the four quarters of the globe, who reads an American book? or goes to an American play? or looks at an American picture or statue? What does the world yet owe to American physicians or surgeons? What new substances have their chemists discovered? or what old ones have they analyzed? What new constellations have they discovered by the telescopes of Americans?—what have they done in mathematics? . . . Finally, under which of the tyrannical governments of Europe is every sixth man a Slave, whom his fellow-creatures may buy and sell and torture?" More supercilious critics than Smith added a still more exasperating and difficult-to-answer indictment: no matter how low the status of American culture, things would never improve because there was something in the New World that made greatness impossible to achieve.

Leading figures in America's intellectual life squirmed in impotent irritation over such all-too-common attacks. The charges were then just about unanswerable, and they consoled themselves with the strong conviction that America must eventually shake off its cultural dependence on Europe, that it must eventually achieve uniquely American glories in the arts, the sciences, and letters. But despite the burning desire for intellectual self-sufficiency, it was still some time before this was to be achieved.

Some 15 years later, when Harriet Martineau and her ear trumpet returned to England after her American visit, she could still write with more or less justice that "the Americans have no national character as yet." A fellow traveler and commentator, Charles Latrobe, found (after a survey of the differences in origin, blood, style of life, and diversity of habits of the American people) that the only distinctively American characteristics were detestation of monarchy, admiration for republicanism, and extreme sensitiveness to foreign criticism.

It is, of course, no wonder that Latrobe found Americans somewhat touchy about criticism from strangers. For some two decades, they had been alternately patronized and excoriated by British travellers and men of letters, and they were only too conscious of their utter dependence on Europe. Even the coming of the steamship was looked upon fearfully by some intellectuals because it made intercourse between the new and the old worlds easier. When the *Great Western,* initiating the trans-Atlantic run, arrived in the United States in 1838, the journalist N. P. Willis lamented: "Farewell nationality! In literature we are no longer a distinct nation." The thoughtful Rev. Ezra S. Gannett of Boston was alarmed. Sermonizing to his flock, he said: "The arrival of a steamship every fortnight at our doors, freighted with the influences which the Old World is no less eager to send than we to receive, must increase the danger of our losing independence, as well as our neglecting to cultivate originality of character."

Observers searched diligently for signs of the coming of a distinctive American culture, but they could find very little. The distinguished painter and future inventor of the telegraph, Samuel F. B. Morse, deplored the tendency of American artists to imitate European techniques. The "stench of decay" that exuded from the art galleries of the continent disgusted him. Sculptor Horatio

Greenough wanted to stop all commerce with Europe in order to insulate America from foreign, denationalizing influences. Poor Greenough! The pull of tradition was so strong that in molding a gigantic statue of Washington, he clothed the first president in a Roman toga!

"Why," demanded an anonymous writer in 1839, "cannot our literati comprehend the matchless sublimity of our position among the nations of the world—our high destiny—and cease bending the knee of foreign idolatry, false tastes, false doctrines, false principles? When will they be inspired by the magnificent scenery of our own world, imbibe the fresh enthusiasm of a new heaven and a new earth, and soar upon the expanded wings of truth and liberty?" As late as 1853, one observer was led to remark that even the Capitol in Washington betrayed the imitative nature of the arts in America. Arabesques and Greek and Roman mythological figures, even when occasionally relieved by an eagle, were scarcely appropriate to an American capital. Where were American birds, trees, and flowers? Where were American heroes and American experiences?

In the clamor for an American art, impatient nationalists could not see what was under their noses. In 1853, Thoreau was completing *Walden*. The *Week on the Concord and Merrimack Rivers* had been finished for four years. Herman Melville's *Moby Dick* had appeared in 1851. So had Hawthorne's *The House of the Seven Gables*. *The Scarlet Letter* had come from the presses in 1850. For two years, Walt Whitman had been hard at work on *Leaves of Grass*. And Ralph Waldo Emerson was celebrating his 50th birthday.

Music, it is true, was not in quite so advanced a state of perfection as literature. But still, a genuine American music could be found in chanteys that the sailors sang, in the amusing ditties of the boatmen on the lakes, canals, and rivers, in the work songs and spirituals of the Whites and the Negroes, in the folk-songs and folk-ballads of the Appalachian highlands. By 1853, at least one great and peculiarly American composer was reaching the peak of his popularity, although no one considered him such at the time.

Americans by the thousand were humming and singing his *Oh! Susanna, Old Folks at Home,* and *My Old Kentucky Home.*

And on a wintry evening in February, 1853, a composer of American grand opera, the music critic for Horace Greeley's New York *Tribune,* William Henry Fry, an angry, bitter, and eloquent man, stepped out on the stage of Metropolitan Hall and spoke the first articulate words in the struggle for American musical independence.

IN 1846, William Henry Fry (a few months after the triumphant presentation of his opera *Leonora* in Philadelphia) went to Paris as foreign correspondent for the New York *Tribune.* For six years he lived in the French capital, filing his dispatches, savoring continental culture, and hobnobbing with musicians. Among his intimates was Hector Berlioz, who also wrote for a newspaper, but whose strange ideas about music were considered advanced and eccentric.

Fry wanted to hear his opera performed in Paris, and as a man of comfortable means, he was quite willing to foot the bill.

I took the best possible introductions, and offered to pay the expenses of a rehearsal (he later wrote) according to my invariable custom to expect nothing as a favor. I wished the music to be heard simply; given book in hand without dress or decoration, and so pronounced upon—a frightful hazard, but one which I was willing to abide by. . . . When I asked for this simple rehearsal—so easily accorded and so fairly required—the director of the opera in Paris said to me, "In Europe we look upon America as an industrial country—excellent for electric telegraphs, but not for art . . . they would think me crazy to produce an opera by an American."

Undoubtedly his experiences with avant-garde musicians on the continent had set him seriously thinking about the problems of a composer in the United States. His familiarity with the American scene and his own unique position had certainly made him particularly aware of the matter. At any rate, when he returned home in 1852, he was quite ready to take up the cause of the American composer and do battle. His new post as music editor of the *Tribune* gave him a forum from which he could speak more or less freely, but he was anxious to go directly to the people, and so in the fall of the year, he announced "a series of lectures upon the Science and Art of Music" of large proportions. Metropolitan Hall, one of the biggest and best in the city, was to be the scene, and the estimated expense ran close to $10,000. Ten lectures were proposed, and at a subscription price of five dollars for the series, it was a foregone conclusion that it could not possibly be profitable from a financial point of view.

"Mr. Fry's proposition," reported his own paper, "is nothing less than to give a general, and, to a fair extent, adequate comprehension of the whole subect of musical composition, including its scientific relations, its history, its ethics and its esthetics. To accomplish this design, which implies extensive illustration, the following essentials are named: a corps of principal Italian vocalists; a grand chorus of one hundred singers; an orchestra of eighty performers; a military band of fifty performers." But this was by no means Fry's complete plan.

The first lecture was given on November 30, 1852, and was concerned with "the elementary ideas and technical expressions and rules of music." Even in dealing with this innocent subject, Fry's viewpoint (making allowances for the florid prose of the periods) sounds surprisingly modern. Many of today's estheticians hold a similar point of view. "Of all arts music is the most soul-like," said Fry. "It records nothing, proves nothing, cannot satirize, flatter, count, or calculate. It is the only art which in itself, and dissociated from all others, is immaculate. Not necessarily allied to fabricated words or perishable fiction, it is even a living tongue; requiring neither dictionary nor interpreter to fetch back its departed illusions."

The lectures that followed dealt with many diverse aspects of music. Fry discussed (for example) "the difference between formal and inspired music," the connection between literature and oratory and music, the nature and progress of musical ideas, the human voice, and the orchestra. But the point to which he had been leading appeared only in the final lecture.

THE SERIES had been, of course, a great expense for Fry. It is estimated that he had lost as much as $4,000 on it. But despite this, he dug into his pocket once more to the extent of $1,200, and added an 11th lecture in which he pulled no punches and dropped completely the flowery phrase. Seldom has a man of the arts so bitterly castigated those for whom he ostensibly creates his masterpieces.

The influential *Musical World and New York Musical Times* dealt with this astonishing lecture at great length and with great disdain. "Mr. Fry is a manly, vigorous and forcible writer," commented its critic. "His manner and address corresponds with this, and his personal impress is that of a superior, though—we could not but think—irregular, and undisciplined intellect . . . His mind, like an eagle, seems to soar, untrammelled—but wayward and uncertain."

Fry was far from uncertain in his views. "There is no taste for, or appreciation of true Art in this country," he said. "The public, as a public know nothing about Art—they have not a single enlightened or healthy idea on the subject." The audience, as an audience, who had paid good money to attend the lecture, must have been quite amazed to hear itself so described. "As a nation," he continued, "we have totally neglected Art. We pay enormous sums to hear a single voice, or a single instrument, the beauties and excellencies of which (if it have any) we cannot discover. We will pay nothing to hear a sublime work of Art performed, because we do not know enough to appreciate it, and consequently such a performance bores us terribly."

He then turned his attention to the American composer and declared that

it is time we had a Declaration of Independence in Art, and laid the foundation of an American School of Painting, Sculpture, and Music. Until this Declaration of Independence in Art shall be made—until

American composers shall discard their foreign liveries and found an American School—and until the American public shall learn to support American artists, Art will not become indigenous to this country, but will only exist as a feeble exotic, and we shall continue to be provincial in Art. The American composer should not allow the name of Beethoven, or Handel or Mozart to prove an eternal bugbear to him, nor should he pay them reverence; he should only reverence his Art, and strike out manfully and independently into untrodden realms, just as his nature and inspirations may invite him, else he can never achieve lasting renown.

As Fry warmed to his subject, he spoke more bluntly: the American people "can never say whether they admire a composition unless they see whose name is attached to it as author; an American composer cannot get his works brought out at home, unless he has a fortune which will enable him to bear the expense himself"—a transparent reference to his own experience which everyone present recognized. "No disposition is even now evinced by the American public to foster American Art, nor is there any indication that such a disposition will ever be evinced."

Those who came to hear Fry's lecture certainly got their 50 cents' worth. He wanted to wake people up, and judging by the excitement and discussion his words generated, he certainly achieved his purpose. He was attacked for his viewpoint from all sides, but invective was an old story to him, and he took it with equanimity, satisfied that he had made Americans more aware of the problems of a national art. And if his criticisms still have a contemporary sound, it might be remembered that some of them are still being made today with a certain measure of truth and justice.

It is an ironic and somewhat tragicomic fact that the music of this intensely nationalistic, yet peculiarly farsighted American should have been so notably derivative in character. Despite his battle for a uniquely American music, Fry was a quite typical product of the musical culture with which he was surrounded. He was an intelligent musician, but not a great one, and his works are to a great extent indistinguishable from those of the then flourishing Italian opera composers. When Fry's music was performed, his listeners heard only echoes of Bellini and Donizetti. Fry could hardly be blamed for this state of affairs, nor could his audiences; they were of their time, and probably thought that *Norma* was the ideal opera.

An interesting concert brought him temporarily into the spotlight in 1929. Under the auspices of the Pro Musica Society, Dr. Otto Kinkeldey, then Chief of the Music Division of the New York Public Library, arranged for selections from *Leonora* to be presented in conjunction with a number of modern works. The New York critics were present, and extended reviews appeared in the press. The sophisticated audience found the Fry excerpts hilariously funny. They were, of course, quite unaware that they were exhibiting one of the faults for which Fry had scolded unsophisticated Americans some 75 years before when he said: "They can never say whether they admire a composition unless they see whose name is attached to it as author." Oscar Thompson of the *Post,* echoing what Fry had once written, reminded his readers that "at last one tenor-soprano duet in melliflous thirds would not have been laughed at, it is fair to assume, if it had been held in a performance of *Norma, Puritani* or *Somnambula* at the opera." And Samuel Chotzinoff of the *World* noted that "*Leonora,* although outmoded, was found to contain tunes the absence of which was the main feature of the modern pieces which preceded the exposure of the operatic antiquity."

When the "operatic antiquity" was originally presented to the world in Philadelphia in 1845, Fry saw to it that it was lavishly and properly mounted; according to his invariable custom, he paid all expenses out of his own pocket. The Sequin opera troupe, one of the best in the country, together with an orchestra of 60 performers and a chorus of 80, were hired, and the settings were the finest that could be constructed. The performance was given in English, for Fry could see little sense in presenting an opera the meaning of which most of the audience could not follow. "Shall our American muse chant in a foreign tongue?" he asked, rhetorically. "Forbid it, national sense, pride, ambition."

The piece was a resounding success. Although the press was far from unanimous in its praise, *Leonora* ran for 16 performances before large and enthusiastic audiences. In general, reviewers found the music melodious and the instrumentation skillful, but complained that "like all early efforts, it is full of reminiscences." Although "it is full of delicious, sweet music," one critic found that it "constantly recalls the *Somnambula* and *Norma*." The *Musical Review and Gazette* found the opera boring. "Almost everything is poorly shaped and put together, and what is still worse, worked closely after the most common pattern. Mr. Fry can be passionate and inspired; he seems to be one of those men—of which our country seems to be richer than any other—who attempt everything grand and beautiful; but whether he has on the musical field, the power to finish his attempts successfully, can only be added when he favors us with another opera of more recent composition. *Leonora* makes us fear he has not."

It was 13 years before *Leonora* was again presented to an American audience. This time it was given in New York, and Fry, an early proponent of opera in English, suffered the indignity of having it rendered in an Italian translation because the troupe was incapable of mastering the intricacies of the English language. According to the New York *Spirit of the Times,* the opera met with the approbation "of the audience present, who displayed more enthusiasm throughout than had ever been elicited on any of the 'crowded' nights of *Les Huguenots* or *Robert le Diable.*" The reviewer (who was apparently familiar with earlier reviews of the opera in Philadelphia) found Fry's

invention evidently fertile; and if occasionally a few bars strike the ear, which you recognize as similar to something which you have heard before, he only errs as others of more ability have done before. Rossini, Bellini, and Donizetti have time and again, indulged in pleasant memories; and Verdi, the favorite of the moderns, continually indulges in self-repetition—for having once caught the inspiration of a good melody, he is exceedingly loth to part with it. It is but natural that the musical student should, in his first work, betray the evidence of his previous studies

—let him guard himself as closely as he will. In the instance of Mr. Fry, it has been so thoroughly compensated for by much that is good, beautiful, and perfectly original, that we forget and forgive the diminutive larcenies, or rather let us say, proofs of a good ear, and corresponding memory, which he has evinced.

QUIXOTIC FRY, "a splendid frigate at sea without a helm," opinionated, self-centered, afraid of no man, was probably the most quarreled with musician of his time. As a veteran journalist, he even crossed swords with the then editor of the New York *Herald*, the redoubtable James Gordon Bennett, and vanquished him in a celebrated lawsuit. Bennett, who knew a good story when he saw one and was none too scrupulous about how he got it, "fomented dissension among the Opera troupe which Mr. Fry was conducting," reported *Montgomery's Pictorial Times* in 1854. He "attacked that gentleman personally as a man of honor; denounced him as a fool, a cheat and speculator; insisted that the opera-house was maintained merely as a panderer to the bestial gratification of prostitutes, pickpockets and gamblers, and otherwise, in thought and word, did all that cowardly lampoon, vindictive sarcasm, mendacious abuse, or relentless fury could affect." Fry sued, and won.

He was not, however, so fortunate in his incessant polemics with other music critics. When Louis Antoine Jullien, who conducted with jeweled baton and white gloves, arrived with his orchestra in 1853, he found that conducting music by American composers was an easy and effective way to get an audience. He also undoubtedly realized that as music critic of the influential New York *Tribune*, Fry was a good person to cultivate. He therefore performed no less than four of Fry's symphonies—*Childe Harold, A Day in the Country, The Breaking Heart*, and the *Santa Claus Symphony*.

The presentation of the latter work inspired a ludicrous controversy in the press. According to one of Fry's colleagues on the *Tribune, Santa Claus* was a work "designed to be of religious and romantic character." The composer's intention was "to paint the songs of the stars—the fluttering ecstasies of hovering angels, the change from starlight to sunlight. The divine words 'Suffer little children to come unto me, for of such is the Kingdom of Heaven', make the artistic painting of children and their toys, as much of a mission of art as the writing of a hallelujah chorus. The finale, too, of this symphony, where an orchestra of drums is introduced to represent the rolling of the spheres, is among the composer's ideas of the necessity of towering sonority."

Fry was considerably put out when Richard Storrs Willis dismissed it with the comment that it was nothing more than "a kind of extravaganza which moves the audience to laughter, entertaining them seasonably with imitated snowstorms, trotting horses, sleighbells, cracking whips, etc." He wrote a long, indignant letter to Willis in which he expressed the idea that the length of the symphony and the seriousness of his intentions entitled him, at the very least, to more sober critical examination. "I think that the American who writes for the mere dignity of musical art, as I understand it, without recompense deserves better treatment at the hands of his countrymen," he complained. But regardless of his intentions, the *Santa Claus Symphony* was no masterwork, and Willis was quite correct when he coldly answered that "the length of a piece of music is novel ground, certainly, upon which to base its musical excellence, or its requirement for a very long criticism."

The attacking critics had the last word. Fry was no genius, and he could not justify his own music in the face of its detractors. His lasting monument, however, is not *Santa Claus,* or even *Leonora,* but rather his eloquence in behalf of American music.

13

---- ⫸⫷ ----

OUR FIRST MATINEE IDOL:
LOUIS MOREAU GOTTSCHALK

JUST ABOUT AN HOUR before the dancing was scheduled to start, the slaves began to arrive in the Place Congo. In the old days, the square had been a New Orleans eye sore, a barren, ugly plot of ground rutted and pitted by the shuffling and stamping of count-less black feet. Fifteen years earlier, Mayor Roffignac had changed its bleak aspect. Now it was lovely in the afternoon sun, verdant and sweet-smelling with the shrubbery and grass he had ordered planted. And Mayor Roffignac's young sycamores almost suc-ceeded in hiding the heavy iron fence that surrounded it, but not quite.

Inside the enclosure, the black men and women waited patiently. The women-folk wore gaudily spotted calicoes, and around their heads brightly colored Madras kerchiefs, intricately arranged to form the Creole *tignon*. The men-folk, their swarthy faces gleaming in the heat, proudly exhibited the cast-off finery of their masters. The ragamuffin children, in rags and tatters, played noisy games. Heavily armed and determined policemen kept a sharp watch over proceedings trough the bars. Gentle-born white men and women, impeccably attired in the height of fashion, languidly chatted and sipped ginger beer or lemonade while waiting for the dance to begin. Among them, a frail, shy, seven-year-old boy held tight to his mother's aristocratic hand and examined everything about him with wide-eyed wonder.

The captain of the police detachment shouted something to one of the slaves; the crowd hushed its chatter expectantly. In a far corner, a dark-skinned man seated himself gracefully before a cask and began a haphazard, shuffling tattoo upon its head, using two enormous beef-bones as drum-sticks. The dancers moved in toward the center of the square and took their places. Almost imperceptibly, the shuffle on the improvised drum settled into a hypnotic, insistent rhythm that pulsated steadily and monotonously. The dancers began to move.

Suddenly a hoarse cry went up: *"Dansez Bamboula! Badoum! Badoum!,"* and the rhythmic beat gathered impetus. The men, with bits of tin attached to ribbons tied about their ankles, pranced drunkenly back and forth, impetuously leaped into the air, or stamped fiercely on the ground. The women, barely lifting their feet above the clipped grass, swayed their supple bodies from side to side, chanting some African song redolent of the green jungle. Outside the circle of frenzied dancers, the children tumbled and cavorted in clumsy imitation of their mesmerized elders. The entire square became an almost solid mass of glistening black bodies stamping and swaying to the undulating beat of the bones upon the cask, the eerie intoning of the women, and the sharp metallic clink of the ankle decorations of the men.

The dance started slowly, but built in intensity as it progressed. Hours passed; finally, the sun began to sink beneath the horizon. The police charged in among the dancers, halted the drummer, and drove the slaves back to their hovels. The *Bamboula* was over.

A dozen years later, the little boy who watched with greedy eyes, now the celebrated pianist Louis Moreau Gottschalk, a teen-aged keyboard virtuoso whose extraordinary playing had aroused both Chopin and Berlioz to great enthusiasm, the pampered and petted darling of the Parisian salons, set the European musical world agog with his exotic new composition, *La Bamboula,* undoubtedly written out of a deeply-etched memory of the dancers in the Place Congo.

UNLIKE plebeian Stephen Foster, patrician Louis Moreau Gotts-chalk undoubtedly qualifies as a full-fledged child prodigy. His parents, an expatriate English intellectual and his aristocratic Creole wife, were convinced that the child possessed extraordi-nary musical talent almost before he was out of his infancy. They were determined to secure for him the best musical education that their wealth and social affluence could procure.

In 1831, a severe epidemic of cholera ravaged New Orleans. Medical men were helpless before it. Those who were financially able to afford the expense fled from the afflicted city. The Gotts-chalks had already lost one child to the malady, and two-year-old Louis Moreau, none too robust to begin with, was hustled out of town. In a sparsely populated spot on the Gulf of Mexico known as Pass Christian, the Gottschalks established their residence. There Mrs. Gottschalk occupied her spare time by singing her favorite airs in a light soprano voice, disturbed from time to time by melodramatic incursions from Indians who were attracted to the house by the strange sounds they heard issuing from it. Some few months after the arrival at Pass Christian, Mrs. Gottschalk came upon three-year-old Moreau, seated before the old square piano, repeating note for note an aria from Meyerbeer's *Robert le Diable* she had sung not more than 15 minutes before. When Mr. Gottschalk learned of this, he immediately decided that the family must return to New Orleans, cholera or no, in order that his son's talent might be properly nurtured and groomed.

Moreau's first teacher was a singer at the Théâtre d'Orléans, a re-putedly excellent musician named Letellier. Under his tutelage, the boy showed further signs of great aptitude for music. Letellier had never before experienced anything quite like Moreau's talent; he was constantly being astonished by it. He boasted to all who would listen to him that the boy could read at sight anything that was placed before him on the piano, although he had not been studying the instrument more than a year. Apparently this was not a fanciful tale. There is a well-authenticated story to the effect that seven-year-old Moreau substituted at the last moment for the organist at the Cathedral of St. Louis. The score of the mass being intoned was placed before him, and he sight-read the accompaniment to perfection—with one small exception. It seems that he was unable to reach the pedals with his feet. Letellier came to his aid, and played the pedals for him. When, at the age of 10, Moreau continued to progress in skill and musician-ship at the same pace, Letellier candidly admitted that he was incapable of advancing the lad any further. Greatly pleased with his son, the elder Gottschalk came to a fateful decision. The Gotts-chalks had influential relatives in Paris, and it well befitted the scion of so distinguished a family to go to the nerve-center of the musical world to continue his studies. Moreau would go to the French capital.

To the accompaniment of his mother's tears, the talented boy was placed on board the *Taglioni,* departing from New Orleans for Le Hâvre in May of 1842. On board ship, he celebrated his 13th birthday. Upon his arrival in Paris in July, he was placed with a genteel family who "never received more than six boarders at a time." He applied himself diligently to his studies under the great pedagogues Stamaty and Maleden, and through the good offices of his aunt, the Countess de Lagrange, gained immediate entry into the musical salons of Parisian society where reputations were made overnight. The gifted Creole youngster, blessed with a shy charm and nimble fingers, utterly captivated the fashionable circles in which he moved. His fame spread like wildfire, and when he made his public debut in April, 1845, he took Paris by storm. Chopin, tremendously moved, said to him: "Give me your hand, my child; I predict you will become the king of pianists."

And king of pianists he became. The years that followed were a triumphal grand tour of the continent. Gottschalk played before kings and workingmen's associations, was pampered and petted and lionized, dispensed largesse with a regal hand to the poor, and was everywhere acclaimed as a great genius. His compositions, which he had begun to write at the age of 15, brief *esquisses* with poetic titles such as *Le Mancenillier, La Savane, Banjo, Le Bana-*

nier, Les Colliers d'Or, and *La Bamboula,* are today little more than faintly perfumed memories; then, they roused his audiences to transports of enthusiasm. It was not only the delighted public that bowed the knee before him; hard-headed, sober critics fell under his spell. Julius Eichberg, later to be an important figure in Boston's musical life, called him a "grand artist truly, who knows no difficulty on his instrument, a marvellous composer and pianist, a meteor." Berlioz wrote that "his playing strikes from the first, dazzles, astonishes; and the infantine simplicity of his smiling caprices, the charming ease with which he renders simple things, seems to belong to a second individuality, distinct from that which characterizes his thundering energies." Adolphe Adam found that he had "all the grace and charm of Chopin, with more decided character." Barthélémon said that "the audacity and thunder of Liszt are tempered in him with the melodious sentiments of the German masters."

In 1852, his conquest of Europe completed, Gottschalk turned his attention to America. His native land was to be a much harder nut to crack.

ON JANUARY 10, 1853, Gottschalk arrived in New York. Almost immediately he was propositioned by P. T. Barnum, who sensed another Jenny Lind sensation. He offered Gottschalk $20,000 for a tour through the States, and the pianist might have accepted this large sum had not his father so strongly disapproved of such an undignified associate. He turned Barnum down, confident of his ability to draw the crowd and his pianistic prowess.

After resting a bit, Gottschalk gave his initial New York concert at Niblo's before a brilliant but rather small audience on February 11, 1853. The receipts did not pay expenses, but the enthusiasm and the reviews were strongly reminiscent of Europe. The New York *Tribune,* whose musical affairs were conducted by Americanophile William Henry Fry, climbed dangerously far out on a limb, implying that the music of Beethoven may have been all very well in its way, but Gottschalk's divine music, *American* music, was the real music of the future. This untoward enthusiasm brought vociferous protest from Boston, where John Sullivan Dwight ruled. Six days later another concert followed; the New York critics applauded, but Dwight was not convinced.

Gottschalk soon came to despise Dwight thoroughly. He had absolutely no respect for the man, whom he considered an opinionated, ignorant fool. For some 15 years the two carried on intermittent warfare. Neither could understand the viewpoint of the other. Dwight, who considered himself the defender of the great classical tradition fast disappearing in America under the onslaughts of such radicals as Gottschalk, really made valuable contributions to the cause of serious music and was by no means the ignoramus that Gottschalk made him out to be.[1] Despite his undoubted conservatism, he was usually a shrewd and discerning critic. His acumen did not prevent him, nevertheless, from falling into a pretty trap that Gottschalk prepared for him. During the course of one of his later Boston programs, the pianist scheduled a little known work by Beethoven, attaching to it his own name as composer; under the name of Beethoven, he programmed a composition of his own. Dwight did exactly what he was expected to do. In his review of the concert, he warmly praised the supposed Beethoven composition, comparing its plain virtues to the amateurish inanities of the brash American. Gottschalk then wrote to Dwight, apologized profusely for the printer's unhappy error, and politely thanked the critic for his generous praise and unfailing ability to distinguish the genuine from the spurious.

En route to his native New Orleans, where he made a triumphal entry to the extreme joy of his first master, Letellier, the young Creole paused long enough to give concerts in many cities along the way, becoming a familiar figure to hundreds of impressionable young ladies who thrilled to his virtuosity and swooned with delight over his romantic aspect.

Then, the following year, his castles crumbled when his father unexpectedly died:

1. See Chapter 5 for a summary of Dwight's Transcendentalist views.

From my birth I had always lived in affluence, thanks to the successful speculations entered upon by my father. Certain of being able to rely upon him, I quietly permitted myself to follow those pursuits in which I anticipated only pleasure and enjoyment. Poorly prepared for the realities of American life by my long sojourn in the factitious and enervating atmosphere of Parisian salons, where I easily discounted the success which my youth, my independent position, the education which I had received, and a certain originality in the compositions which I had already published, partly justified, I found myself taken unawares, when one day, constrained by necessity and the death of my father, hastened by a series of financial disasters, I found myself without other resources than my talents to enable me to perform the sacred duties bequeathed to me by him. I was obliged to pay his debts and to sustain in Paris a numerous family, my mother and six brothers and sisters.

Now playing and writing for money and not for art, Gottschalk stepped up the tempo of his concertizing. In New York alone he gave no less than 80 concerts during the next two years. This period saw the birth of *The Last Hope,* a composition that had a belated rebirth during the era of the silent motion pictures, when its perfumed, artificial elegance entered the repertory of every movie pianist. This work and *The Dying Poet* are the ones that immediately come to mind when Gottschalk's name is mentioned today. This is regrettable, as he himself was well aware of the nature of these compositions, and took very little pride in them. They were pure and simple pot-boilers, and he knew it. Asked why he wrote them, he replied candidly: "It is only mediocrity that pays, and, as I must live, I must be willing to please others, even if not myself."

Under the press of necessity, he settled down to a grueling chase after the almighty dollar. The great virtuoso lived on, but the inspired tone-poet of New Orleans gradually disappeared, and the composer of skillfully mechanical salon pieces for sentimental misses took his place.

Gottschalk did not give up his artistic aspirations without a struggle, however. In 1856, he suddenly abandoned the United States and moved to the more congenial atmosphere of Cuba.

There he spent five happy years doing exactly as he wished—wandering throughout the Caribbean islands, giving an occasional concert, writing music, and indulging in more earthly pleasures. Under the inspiration of the friendly Antilles, he composed his symphony, *La Nuit des Tropiques,* perhaps his most successful piece in a large form.

In an unusually candid vein, Gottschalk gives the reader a glimpse of his experiences in the Caribbean. "I began to live according to the customs of those primitive countries," he confided to his journal, "which, if they are not strictly virtuous, are, in retaliation, terribly attractive. I saw those beautiful 'Trigueñas,' with red lips, and brown bosoms, ignorant of evil, sinning with frankness, without fearing the bitterness of remorse. All this is frightfully immoral, I know it; but life in the savannas of the tropics, in the midst of a half-civilized and voluptuous race, cannot be that of a London cockney, a Parisian idler, or an American Presbyterian."

Fate, in the form of the impresario Max Strakosch, tempted him to leave his terrestrial paradise. Money was growing short, and although Gottschalk was quite happy in the tropical latitudes, he was beginning to miss the stimulation of the concert stage. Strakosch apparently wrote in a strategic moment, for when he offered Gottschalk a profitable contract for a grand tour of the United States, the pianist signed on the dotted line. In February, 1862, he arrived back in New York.

SUPERFICIALLY, Gottschalk seemed to have stepped almost immediately into a fascinating whirl of festivals and honors, but beneath the surface was a reality that was far from pleasant. At the end of his first concert tour, Gottschalk described his experiences:

I have given eighty-five concerts in four months and a half. I have travelled fifteen thousand miles on the railroad. At St. Louis I gave seven concerts in six days; at Chicago, five in four days. A few weeks more in this way and I should have become an idiot! Eighteen hours a day on the railroad! Arrive at seven o'clock in the evening, eat with all speed, appear at eight o'clock before the public. The last note finished, rush quickly for my luggage, and en route until next day to recommence always the same thing! I have become stupid with it. I have the appearance of an automaton under the influence of a voltaic pile. My fingers move on the keyboard with feverish heat, and for the moment it is not possible for me to hear the music, without experiencing something of the sensation of that hero of Alexander Dumas *fils,* condemned for one month to eat nothing but pigeon. The sight of a piano sets my hair on end like the victim in the presence of the wheel on which he is about to be tortured. Whilst my fingers are thus moving, my thought is else-where. Happier than my poor machine, it traverses the field, and sees again those dear Antilles, where I gave tranquilly a little concert every two or three months comfortably, without fatiguing myself, where I slept for weeks the sleep of the spirit, so delicious, so poetical, in the midst of the voluptuous and enervating atmosphere of those happy lands of the *dolce far niente,* whose lazy breezes murmuring softly bear on their wings the languid and distant harmonies of the country, and whose quiet and dreamy birds seem never to arouse from the contemplation of all the marvels of this terrestrial paradise except to love and to sleep. What an awakening for me after five years of this tropical gypsy life!

He was caught in a trap. The weary pianist travelled back and forth across the countryside, giving concerts almost daily. Entries in his diary vividly tell the tale.

Manchester, July 17, 1863. Manufacturing town, in which there is noth-ing remarkable. Only sixteen tickets sold. . . . Adrian, Michigan, Jan-uary 8, 1864. Infamous concert. Seventy-eight dollars!! The people say that they prefer "a good negro show." They are furious at the price of admission—one dollar. . . . February 24. Concert at New York. Crowded. It is the ninety-fifth or ninety-sixth concert that I have given in the City of New York within the last year and a half, without counting at least one hundred and fifty that I gave before my voyage to the Antilles. . . . Boston, March 11. Unpleasant weather. I play badly— too much fatigued, and have the influenza. . . . April 16. Concert at Binghamton. Very small but charming audience. . . . Schenectady, April 19. Detestable concert, hardly seventy-five persons, who ap-plauded at random with a free and easy frankness which was very amusing.

Diego de Vivo, the assistant impresario of Gottschalk's company, gives an authentic and sympathetic picture of the pianist during this time which was published in the New York *Sun* of March 4, 1897:

I hardly remember having seen Gottschalk idle for an hour. He was ever composing, reading or practicing. He was a constant reader on a railroad car, biting at the same time the forefinger of his right hand so much that at times it bled and he was unable to play for a day or two. Once he could not play for a week, and on another occasion for nearly three weeks. He was the most nervous man I ever saw. He was very fond of playing baccarat, monte, or poker, was a bold gambler and a bluffer, and also a good loser. It was, as he used to say, his greatest temptation in life to see playing cards. In New England cities the women worshipped him and were fascinated by his playing and charming personality. I remember how they used to mob the entrance of the stage door after the concert, struggling to shake hands with him, some even entering his carriage, and some following it to the hotel and remaining in the parlor until he reappeared. Then the next morning I would see a dozen or more women crying and bidding him goodbye. Such scenes before his departure I have witnessed not only in the New England cities, but in almost every city where he played, notably in New York, Philadelphia, Baltimore, Washington, Chicago, Cincinnati, and St. Louis. I have believed ever since that Gottschalk was the most fascinating and magnetic artist that I have ever known.

So Gottschalk traversed the land, indulging in his hobby of visiting insane asylums whenever possible, jotting down his thoughts about music and politics in his diary, which was later to become his fascinating *Notes of a Pianist,* carrying on flirtations with susceptible damsels, and frittering away his talent. After three years of it, he fled once again, and following his visit to the West Coast in 1865, departed for South America. On the way to his destination, Rio de Janeiro, he ran right into the middle of a Peruvian revolution which seemed to revolve, from the description he gives of it in his journal, almost entirely about the hotel in which he was stopping. Somewhere along the route, he contracted yellow fever, but continued concertizing despite the fact that he was dangerously ill. Finally, on November 26, 1869, during a performance in the Brazilian capital that he insisted upon giving, he collapsed at the piano. Twenty-three days later, he was dead.

History has dealt unkindly with Gottschalk—perhaps unduly so. Ironically enough, his reputation was almost killed with kindness. The stiffest blow that he ever received came a year after his death with the publication of a biography written by one of his most ardent admirers, Mary Alice Ives Seymour. From evidence in the book, it appears that Miss Seymour must have been Gottschalk's mistress. For this small immorality, Gottschalk paid dearly. Writing under the pseudonym of Octavia Hensel, Miss Seymour (in execrable prose) painted him as a cardboard figure. Unwittingly and unwillingly, he leapt from the pages of her biography as an insufferable prig, a dandified snob, and a towering fool. Gottschalk's own words, published in 1881 in a poor English translation by his brother-in-law under the title *Notes of a Pianist*, are still the one truly reliable source of information concerning his life. From his random jottings, an entirely different picture emerges, and he becomes the warm and vital artist that he undoubtedly was.

If ever a man was destroyed by an unsympathetic environment, it was Gottschalk. Essentially a creative musician of great talent, he was forced by circumstances to build his mature life around a struggle for money. He sacrificed himself on the altar of the gods of sentimentality then worshipped in every hamlet in the United States. Jumping from village to village like a trained monkey, performing his synthetic stunts at the piano like an automaton, his none-too-sturdy genius was slowly but surely beaten into the dust. The premature death of his creative impulse is surely one of the tragedies in the history of American music.

MISCELLANEA

14

THE ORIGINS OF THE AMERICAN FUGING-TUNE

ALTHOUGH ONE WONDERS WHY, certain 19th-century misconceptions about the nature of the American fuging-tune [1] are, to a large degree, still current today. Certainly one of the most widely held is the idea that the fuging-tune was merely a crude attempt by incompetents to write a fugue. One of the spokesmen for this point of view was the late Hamilton C. MacDougall, author of *Early New England Psalmody* (Brattleboro, Vt., 1940). In this quite unreliable book, the following is found on p. 95: "The 'fuguing tune' as written by the New England composers in William Billings's day was only a pitiful imitation of that part of the fugue known as the 'exposition.'" On p. 97, MacDougall varies the theme slightly by stating that "so far as the New England composers were concerned their 'fuguing' tunes were simply so many awkward bows and scrapes to the fugue itself." Even the most superficial examination of any of the hundreds of fuging-tunes composed in this country during the 18th and early 19th centuries is enough to reveal the patent absurdity of this contention. The fuging-tune bears no family relationship to the classical fugue of Bach, neither is it a rudimentary form of the classical fugue, nor could its composers possibly have intended it to be

1. I have adopted the expedient of utilizing the archaic spelling "fuge" and its derivative "fuging" when referring to the fuging-tune, reserving the modern spelling for the classical fugue. Were this practice generally followed, it would call attention to the clear distinction between the two forms and perhaps tend to reduce present confusion.

such. The fuging-tune is a distinctive variety of psalm- or hymn-tune, severely delimited in its structure by the metrical nature of the texts to which it was set and by the exigencies of practical performance. The very etymology of its name displays its pedigree: "fuging-tune" is a shortened version of the term "fuging psalm-tune" current in 18th-century England. Obviously, there is not the slightest point or validity in attacking the fuging-tune because it does not happen to be a fugue.

Another widely accepted fancy is the absurd idea that the fuging-tune is a uniquely American development with no apparent roots or analogues in European musical culture. In answer to a query from Professor MacDougall, James T. Lightwood, the eminent authority on English Methodist psalmody, wrote: " 'Fugal' tunes seem to be confined to America and to tunes in 'Reports' in early Scotch Psalmody. They do not belong to English psalmody. A notable feature of some of the tunes from 1761 was a 'Hallelujah' refrain, but in no instance is there any attempt at a 'fugal tune' (assuming that some form of imitation is meant) nor have I come across examples in other [than Methodist] books I have examined." [2] Lightwood's inability to discover any English fuging psalm-tunes can be explained only as a case of acute astigmatism. It is an indubitable fact that a considerable number of English tune-books published around the middle of the 18th century contain easily recognizable fuging psalm-tunes. Some of the collections even stress their presence on the title-page. On occasion, some of the psalmodists who bitterly attacked the form—such as John Arnold—were not averse to composing fuging psalm-tunes themselves. These attacks on the idiom alone, a popular form of polemic in England (and somewhat later in America), incontrovertibly establish the existence of the fuging psalm-tune in the Old World. Clearly, one attacks only what exists. By the time the first American-composed specimen appeared in print in William Billings's *New-England Psalm-Singer* (Boston, 1770), the form

2. Quoted in MacDougall, pp. 96–97.

already had a significant prehistory in both old and New England.

Still another misconception is the belief that the fuging-tune idiom was conceived and carried to full fruition by Billings. This myth is unfortunately being reinforced by the increasing interest in this unquestionably significant figure. To redress the historical balance, some of the other New England composers of the post-Colonial era—whose music is far more characteristic of the period—should be seriously studied. Billings's fuging-tunes are not really typical examples of the idiom in the heyday of its popularity. The compositional techniques he uses are not typically American; they are markedly similar to those used by his English contemporaries, perhaps more so than to those used by other New Englanders. His music owes its undoubted distinction more to his superior individual talent than to any specifically American style.

THE TYPE OF fuging-tune which attained a quite remarkable vogue on this side of the Atlantic, which *was* written in a uniquely American style, made its appearance first in Connecticut early in the 1780s. Very shortly afterwards, it spread to central Massachusetts, upper New York, Vermont, New Hampshire, and Maine. It was not notably popular, at least among composers, in the Boston area, where Billings held forth. The men who wrote these fuging-tunes were Daniel Read, Jacob French, Timothy Swan, Stephen Jenks, Supply Belcher, Abraham Maxim, Lewis Edson, Joseph Stone, Elisha West, Justin Morgan, Daniel Belknap, and a host of others equally little known today. It is quite likely that the later Billings, whose fuging-tunes do fairly well represent this native idiom, was more influenced by the work of some of these composer-compilers than he was their influencer.

It should be unnecessary to stress the fact that the fuging-tune must be accepted or rejected as music in its own right, but somehow or other the mistaken evaluations of the 19th century have been transformed into modern prejudices against the idiom. If one finds the music uninteresting, or sees no value in it as such, one is entitled to one's opinion. But the form cannot legitimately be regarded as merely an echo of some other of greater sophistication or higher musical interest. The Bach fugue is without doubt one of the peaks of musical achievement, but the American fuging-tune may well be considered at least a pleasant—and still pretty much unexplored—hillock. As Richard Franko Goldman says in the preface to his *Landmarks of Early American Music* (New York, 1943): "The 'fuguing tune' in Billings and his contemporaries is something much more exciting and musical than pallid imitations of 'correct' fugues and canons would be. The fuguing tune stands on its own feet, with no apologies needed."

The typical American fuging-tune (see Lenox in Illus. 21) usually begins with a homophonic section in the course of which a definite cadence is reached, frequently but not always on the tonic of the key. A fresh start is then made, in which each individual voice makes its entrance in succession, the order varying according to the inclination of the composer. In this second section—which was customarily referred to as the "fuge"—some form of imita-

21. Joseph Stephenson's THIRTY-FOURTH (*ca.* 1755) and Lewis Edson's LENOX (1782), as published in Daniel Read, *Supplement to the American Singing Book* (New Haven, Connecticut, 1787). Courtesy of the Library of Congress.

tion, in most cases quite free, was utilized for a measure or two. Normally, the fuge was then repeated, thus making the whole a small, rather tightly organized ABB form. Of course, variations in this basic pattern were of frequent occurrence, but all fuging-tunes roughly follow this formal structure. Techniques character-istic of the fuging-tune are often found in the lengthier composi-tions of the period, such as anthems or set-pieces, but as these lack the unique architecture of the fuging-tune, they cannot be consid-ered representative examples of the idiom.[3]

The English fuging psalm-tune, immediate predecessor of the American fuging-tune, was the end-product of a short-lived 18th-century union between metrical psalmody and contrapuntal tech-nique. Both sections of the fuging psalm-tune—the psalm-tune itself and the fuge—had long co-existed as independent entities before they briefly coalesced, and some conception of their devel-opment is essential to an understanding of the nature of the idiom as it was found later in both England and America.

UNTIL THE modern conception of the fugue gained ascendancy, in England the term "fuge" seems to have referred to an amor-phous contrapuntal form woven out of techniques ranging from the strictest canonic writing to the freest imitation. According to Christopher Simpson—and most other pre-19th-century theoreti-cal writers—fuges were "flying pieces." For nearly 200 years, this idea of what constituted a fuge remained basically unchanged. Thomas Morley no doubt would have accepted without question William Tans'ur's definition of a fuge as "a quantity of *Notes* of any Number; which is begun by any *single Part* and carried on; and afterward is sounded again, by some other Part; which re-

3. Even this simple point is not clearly understood. For example, an edi-tion of three Billings works was published in 1940 under the generic title *Three Fuguing Tunes.* None of the three can be considered fuging-tunes, two being short anthems, while the third is an orthodox canon. In passing, it might be mentioned that because a work happens to have been written by Billings, it does not necessarily follow that it must be a fuging-tune. Billings composed only 36 such pieces, a small fraction of his total output.

peats the same (or such like *Notes*) either in the *Unison*, or 8th; but more commonly in the latter; in a 4th, or 5th, or 8th, above, or below the leading Part." [4] This is no strange formulation of an eccentric original idea by Tans'ur (a much maligned figure whose presentation of the theoretical aspects of music is in fact not unskillful, once the camouflaging 18th-century verbiage is grasped); on the contrary, it is a rephrasing of a definition which had been accepted in England as standard at least since 1597, when Morley's *Plaine and Easie Introduction to Practicall Musicke* appeared. There, Morley wrote: "We call that a Fuge, when one part beginneth and the other singeth the same, for some number of Notes (which the first did sing)." The clear line of continuity between the musical thinking of the Elizabethan madrigalist and that of the Georgian psalmodist is plain from parallel definitions in other theoretical treatises of the intervening period, such as Christopher Simpson's *Compendium of Practical Musick* (1667) [5] and the 1694 edition of John Playford's *Introduction to the Skill of Musick*,[6] corrected and amended by Henry Purcell.

From these definitions, it can be seen that fuging is pretty well synonymous with what we today call the technique of imitative writing and, as a matter of fact, this is so obvious that R. Alec Harman, in his modern edition of the Morley *Plain and Easy Introduction* (London and New York, 1952), substitutes the term "imitation" for the term "fuge" wherever the latter appeared in the original, with no indication that the Morley text was in any way altered.

Fuging (or imitative writing) was, of course, the normal musical language of late 16th- and early 17th-century England. As

---

4. *A Compleat Melody, or Harmony of Sion,* 4th ed. (London, 1738), p. 63.

5. "[A fuge] is some Point (as we term it in Musick) consisting of 4, 5, 6, or any other number of Notes; begun by one single Part, and then seconded by a following Part, repeating the same, or such like Notes . . . the leading Parts still flying before those that follow; and from thence it hath its name *Fuga* or Fuge." Simpson, pp. 128–29.

6. "A *Fuge* is when one part leads one, two, three, four, or more Notes, and the other repeats the same." Playford, p. 108.

would be expected, this technique appears not only in the large works of Tye, Tallis, Byrd, and the other great masters of the late Tudor and early Stuart periods, but also, quite as naturally, in the psalm-tune settings then being sung. Even the psalters designed for congregational use came under the influence of the prevailing contrapuntal style. For example, in Thomas Est's *Whole Book of Psalmes* (1592) may be found psalm-tune settings which are actually small motets, excellent examples in miniature of late 16th-century fuging techniques. Psalm-tune settings demanding an even higher degree of musical skill can be found among the "tunes in reports" [7] of the 1633 and 1635 Scottish psalters. The same tendency toward fuging is found in other psalters of the period.

The situation changed markedly during the era of the Commonwealth, however. As Percy Scholes demonstrated in *The Puritans and Music in England and New England* (London, 1934), the Puritans were not opposed to music *per se*. They were not opposed to secular music outside the church or to what they considered appropriate music within it. Nevertheless, their tolerance did not include the elaborate, motet-like psalm-tune setting, and this genre gradually disappeared. The Commonwealth lasted just long enough to change the direction of England's musical development; under it, a new generation with different and perhaps less sophisticated musical tastes grew up. The Restoration saw the rise to popularity of a new psalmody, in which the contrapuntal style was replaced by a homophonic style of somewhat less sensual appeal, with stress on dignity and simplicity. Shortly after the beginning of the 18th century, the comparatively severe lines of the Restoration psalmody began to disintegrate as the ornate Italianate style began to make its influence felt in the church as well as in the opera house, and by 1750 the tunes had virtually disappeared in a pastiche of trills, gruppettos, and ornaments of every conceivable nature. Parenthetically, it is worth noting that these

7. "There is another diminutive form of Fugeing called *Imitation* or *Reports;* which is, when you begin *Counterpoint* and answer the Treble in some few Notes as you find occasion when you set a bass to it." Playford, *loc. cit.*

"excesses" of the early 18th century were a major factor in setting the trend followed by American as well as English psalmody. The New England singing-schools of the time were partly a protest against the "gracing" characteristic of the period as they were also a creative solution to the problem of musical literacy in the New World. And from these singing-schools grew the native idiom of the post-Colonial era, which had for its particular hallmark the American fuging-tune.

As THE ornate psalm-tune gained in favor, a new type of church musician, apparently unknown to the 17th century, appeared on the scene in England in increasing numbers. This was the itinerant singing-master, often ill-trained by orthodox standards, who wandered from village to village and eked out an existence by teaching the intricacies of psalm-singing and the rudiments of music to all who cared to learn. To supplement his generally meager income, he frequently sold self-compiled tune-books in which psalm-tunes of his own composition and new settings of old psalm-tunes were featured as examples of his skill and artistry. It is in tune-books of this general category that the earliest fuging psalm-tunes are found, but until much more study of these crude English collections and the men who compiled them has been accomplished, the exact identity of the first English psalmodist to publish a fuging psalm-tune will remain unknown. Already as early as 1724, however, the itinerants were numerous and influential enough to elicit a letter written to the country clergy by the Bishop of London, warning against "the inviting or encouraging those idle instructors who of late years have gone about the several counties to teach tunes uncommon and out-of-the-way (which very often are as ridiculous as they are new)." [8]

The idea of the fuging psalm-tune was quite simple: one merely took a psalm-tune and tacked a fuge (or fuging section) on to the end of it. At first, the fuge was a mechanical addition, an optional

8. Quoted in John S. Curwen, *Studies in Worship Music*, 1st Ser., 2nd ed. (London, 1888), p. 9.

chorus to be included or omitted at the pleasure of the group performing it.[9] Here, of course, is the genesis of the cadence on the
tonic at the midpoint of the fuging-tune. Very shortly later, the
fuge became an integral part of the psalm-tune.

The fuging psalm-tune was welcomed with enthusiasm in rural
areas, but in the cities it met with a less cordial reception. Among
others, John Arnold fulminated at length about the abominable
plague of what he called, in his *Compleat Psalmodist*, "whimsical,
flighty Psalm-Tunes . . . these new-fashioned fuging Psalm-
Tunes," but nevertheless, despite opposition, the form had rooted
itself firmly in English soil and had already crossed the Atlantic.
By the time the 1760s had ended, it was without question as familiar in America as it had been in the old country.

ARNOLD'S attack on the fuging psalm-tune appeared in 1761; in
the same year, the first English fuging psalm-tunes to be published
in America were printed in James Lyon's *Urania*. The six examples
of the idiom to be found in this famous tune-book were, it is true,
the first to appear in print in an American collection, but they
were clearly not the first ones known in America. Lyon had been
working on *Urania* for at least several years before it finally came
from the presses, and except for a half dozen tunes of his own
composition, the tune-book was a potpourri of selections from
English collections in general circulation at the time in the Colonies. There is rather clear evidence that English collections were
available here in substantial numbers. By 1764, Josiah Flagg, in
the preface to his *Collection of the Best Psalm Tunes*, felt it "necessary, that some Apology should be made, for offering to the
Publick, a *new* Collection of Psalm Tunes, at a Time when there
are already so many among us." As the only significant American

9. "I have adapted Portions of the PSALMS of David, of either Versions;
which is neither too dull, nor yet too gay; but such as well becomes the subject of the Words; with many *Fuging* CHORUS's, which may be omitted,
where *Voices* can't be had to perform them according to *Art*." William
Tans'ur, *The Royal Melody Compleat, or New Harmony of Sion*, 3rd ed.
(London, 1766), preface.

tune-books published by that date—except for *Urania*—were John Tufts's *Introduction to the Singing of Psalm-Tunes* (Boston, 1721) and Thomas Walter's *Grounds and Rules of Musick Explained* (Boston, 1721), obviously Flagg must have been referring to English imports.

Thus, when Billings arrived on the scene in 1770, the English fuging psalm-tune had been part of the normal musical experience of the New World for at least a decade, and possibly longer. It can be seen that Billings was actually pouring his ideas into a familiar mold, familiar not only from the comparatively few examples in the few American collections published by then, but also from the relatively many examples in the English collections in use in the Colonies. A few of the more important of these English tune-books should be mentioned by name. Perhaps the best known today, because of its connection with Billings, is William Tans'ur's *Royal Melody Compleat, or New Harmony of Sion* (London, 1755), in effect a revised and enlarged edition of an earlier collection by the same compiler entitled *A Compleat Melody, or Harmony of Sion* (London, 1735). It is interesting to note that Billings appears to have gained his knowledge of Tans'ur not from the English original, but rather from an American reprint of the 3rd London edition which differs considerably from its prototype. What appears to have been Billings's own copy of this American reprint, published by the Boston printer William M'Alpine in 1767, is at present at the Library of Congress. This copy contains the only known Billings holograph. Also worth citing is Aaron Williams's *Universal Psalmodist* (London, 1763), a comparatively obscure tune-book in England. Reprinted in altered form by Daniel Bayley of Newburyport, it was to become one of the most widely used collections in New England. It was almost invariably issued by Bayley together with an American reprint of the Tans'ur work as a two-part collection; later in its printing history, Bayley dubbed the originally nameless amalgamation *The American Harmony* (Newburyport, 1769). Other influential tune-books known to have been in circulation

here were John Arnold's *Leicestershire Harmony* (London, 1759),
Abraham Adams's *Psalmist's New Companion* (London, *ca.*
1760), and William Knapp's *New Church Melody* (London,
1753).

To IDENTIFY the particular individuals whose music most strongly
influenced the development of the American fuging-tune—in con-
tradistinction the particular tune-books—is a much more per-
plexing problem. At that time, compilers were notoriously care-
less about furnishing accurate composer ascriptions. Most tunes
appeared in print without any composer attribution at all. In the
large majority of cases, such anonymous tunes cannot safely be
credited to the compilers of the tune-books in which they happen
to be found. Even the supposedly clear statements of authorship
found in Tans'ur's collections—"Composed in four parts, by
W. T."—does not mean that Tans'ur was the composer of the tune
in question; it merely signifies that the setting was arranged by
Tans'ur. The tune itself may well have been the work of some
other composer. It is obvious that the task of conclusive identification is one of considerable proportions, made still more difficult
because of the relative scarcity of 18th-century English tune-books
in American libraries. One name, at least, should be cited, that of
Joseph Stephenson, an obscure psalmodist who spent some portion
of his life at Poole in the south of England. Stephenson is known
to have compiled two tune-books, *The Musical Companion* (London, n.d.) and *Church Harmony* (London, 1770). The author has
been able to locate no copies of either on this side of the Atlantic.
Probably late in the 1750s Stephenson composed three fuging
psalm-tunes, 34TH PSALM, and MILFORD. These compositions enjoyed an extraordinary vogue in America, retaining their popularity pretty well undimmed until well into the 19th century. They are
unusually close to the American idiom in formal structure and in
general character, and as two of the three were published in
American tune-books during the 1760s, it is quite likely that they
served as actual prototypes for Billings's work and perhaps for

that of other early American composers as well (see Chapter 6, Illus. 13).

It CAN thus be seen that the American fuging-tune is a logical out-growth of certain trends plainly evident in 18th-century English psalmody, trends that can be traced back as far as the 16th century. There exists clear evidence that the parent body of English psalmody, from which the American fuging-tune developed, was shot through with fuging psalm-tunes. The fuging-tune struck roots in the New World just as its popularity was beginning to wane in England. It was well known here long before Billings began to write fuging-tunes of his own.[10] In America, the fuging-tune experienced a period of spectacular growth and popular favor after 1780, reaching a peak during the 1790s and gradually declining thereafter; in England, on the other hand, the form reached the apogee of its success around the midpoint of the 18th century. It was never as highly regarded there as it came to be in America; it was well received only in the rural areas and was generally rejected in the cities. The crucial decade in its history would appear to be that between 1750 and 1760. Thereafter, the fuging-tune began its independent existence and phenomenal development in the New World, and ended its growth in the old.

10. Although Billings was the first American to compose a fuging-tune of whom we have knowledge, he was neither the most prolific nor the most in-fluential protagonist of the idiom. At least four composers (Samuel Holyoke, Daniel Read, Stephen Jenks, Jacob French) wrote more fuging-tunes than did Billings, while at least five composers (Daniel Read, Oliver Holden, Joseph Stone, Lewis Edson, Elisha West) had more fuging-tunes reprinted by other compilers than did Billings. It is of some significance that of 286 American collections published before 1810, only 31 contain no fuging-tunes; in the majority, approximately one-quarter of the contents can be classified as ex-amples of the idiom.

15

MUSIC AND AMERICAN
TRANSCENDENTALISM (1835 - 50)

This class are not sufficiently characterized if we omit to add that they are lovers and worshippers of Beauty. In the eternal trinity of Truth, Goodness, and Beauty, each in its perfection including the three, they prefer to make Beauty the sign and the head.

The Transcendentalist
RALPH WALDO EMERSON

A GOOD INDICATION OF just how important music was as an element of the "Newness" is the fact that the subject was dealt with to a greater or lesser extent in just about every periodical with which the Transcendentalists had any editorial connection. Of the eight journals generally considered to be the more or less "official" organs of American Transcendentalism between 1835 and 1850,[1] only Theodore Parker's *Massachusetts Quarterly Review* (1847–50) failed to include at least one article entirely devoted to the art. The *Review* was the magazine Parker himself characterized as "*The Dial* with a beard." One might perhaps not expect any discussion of so frivolous a topic among the weighty pieces on—for example—the political conditions and prospects of Greece, the causes and prevention of idiocy, the philosophy of the ancient Hindoos, and the methodology of mesmerism, but Parker did manage to smuggle it in. The second issue contains his own article

---

1. See Clarence L. F. Gohdes, *The Periodicals of American Transcendentalism* (Durham, N.C., 1931), pp. 14–15.

on "Ballad Literature," which includes a brief but highly interesting discussion of singing in early New England.[2]

Examination of the seven other Transcendental periodicals reveals that during the years when the movement was at its peak, no less than 183 items of musical interest were published. A full list of titles is given in Appendix C.

This was, truth to tell, a considerable body of literature about music for the particular period in American life. It varies greatly in quality and interest, but it is well worth analysis for what it can tell us of the Transcendental aesthetic and as a running commentary on the musical life of the time.

WHO were the writers dealing with the art? What did they have to say about it? What periodicals were important from the musical viewpoint? Which articles were most valuable as signposts of American cultural development during those years? What was the uniquely Transcendental view of the role of music in life? These are some of the questions for which at least partial answers may be found in the pages of these journals of American Transcendentalism.

If we momentarily leave aside a consideration of John Sullivan Dwight (virtually the Transcendental pope of music), the most prolific musical contributor to the periodical literature under discussion proved to be—surprisingly enough—Charles A. Dana. The future Assistant Secretary of War and owner-editor of the *New York Sun* was the author of seven articles (44–50) [3] in *The Harbinger* on the 1847–48 Italian opera season in New York. Dana, an intelligent music lover with no more than a minimum knowledge of the art's technical aspects, apparently picked up what slight musical erudition he did have from Dwight during the years when the two men helped George Ripley in editing *The Harbinger* at Brook Farm.

2. I, 245–46.
3. The numbers in parentheses throughout refer to items in Appendix C, where full citations are given.

Dana was a forthright, positive, extroverted character who rubbed the dust of Transcendentalism from his eyes very quickly. By 1845, he was pretty thoroughly dissatisfied with the rarefied atmosphere of Concord idealism. He openly attacked Emerson and his disciples for being overbearingly arrogant about their intellectual gifts and for their intolerance toward ideas other than their own. As for the Transcendental movement itself, he noted in it a cold lack of concern for the plight of the ordinary human being.[4] It was primarily for this reason that he rejected it in favor of the more heady wine of Associationism.

Music criticism was very much of a sideline for Dana (241 articles from his pen on other topics appeared in *The Harbinger*), but one cannot deny that his pieces on Italian opera were urbane, well-written, and free from that tendency to pontificate which marred much of Dwight's better informed writings.

George W. Curtis was another important contributor of musical articles to *The Harbinger*. He was the charming baby of the Transcendental circle, five years younger than Dana and 11 years younger than Dwight. He had sat at their feet as an 18-year-old boarder at Brook Farm, absorbing from the former instruction in Greek and German and from the latter, Latin and music. His most noteworthy addition to the literature of Transcendentalism was a long series of letters to Dwight begun when he was still in his teens. In letter after letter, his youthful ebullience and unabashed delight in music were most fetchingly reflected.[5] In later years, Curtis became a considerable power in American letters through his occupancy of *Harper's Magazine's* famous "Easy Chair" and his editorial connection with *Harper's Weekly*, but in 1845, when his articles on music began to appear in *The Harbinger* through Dwight's good offices, he was merely a bright young man of 21 with vaguely literary aspirations. His five musical articles for the

4. See particularly his review of *Studies in Religion* in *The Harbinger*, I, 362.
5. George W. Cooke, *Early Letters of George William Curtis to John S. Dwight* (New York, 1898), pp. 107–273.

Associationist journal (38–39, 41–43) tend to be rather breathless and juvenile; they are distinctly inferior to those of Dana. A much more interesting article from his pen was one which appeared in William H. Channing's *The Present* (40). Ostensibly a review of a concert by the famous violinist Ole Bull, it is in actuality a somewhat discursive formulation of his ideas about the nature of music.

The only professional musician to contribute to the columns of *The Harbinger* was Elam Ives, an important figure in the history of American public school music, about whom all too little is known. Ives was one of the first American converts to the educational theories of Pestalozzi and one of the first to attempt to apply them to the field of music.[6] He collaborated with Lowell Mason in the preparation of some of the first juvenile music textbooks to appear in this country. Just how he came into the Transcendental orbit is not clear, but it may have been through the three laudatory reviews of his works (134, 138, 144) written by Dwight in 1845–47. He was *The Harbinger's* first New York musical reporter after the journal moved to that city, and his four articles (170–173) demonstrate his adeptness in the field.

Also appearing in *The Harbinger* were single articles about music by Christopher P. Cranch (35), Albert Brisbane (26), Parke Godwin (169), and William Wetmore Story (181), as well as quite a number of "filler" paragraphs on musical subjects, most of which seem to have been translated by Dwight from the *Deutsche Schnellpost*, a highly-regarded German periodical. Of the articles, the most distinguished, both in style and content, was a long review of the sixth Boston Academy concert of 1846 by the sculptor Story (also lawyer, man of letters, and aesthete), who renounced the materialistic America of the 1850s to live in the more congenial intellectual climate of Italy.

But *The Harbinger's* big man—and the keenest critical intelligence on the entire American scene—was John Sullivan Dwight, who published 110 musical articles (51–61, 63–94, 96–162) in its

6. See Robert W. John, "Elam Ives and the Pestalozzian Theory of Music Education," *Jour. of Research in Music Ed.*, VIII (1960), 45–50.

pages during the journal's four years of existence. Dwight's stature as a music critic has received much attention. Through the medium of *Dwight's Journal of Music,* which he established in 1852, he became the major critical figure in American music for more than a quarter of a century. Before 1850, he was still in the apprentice stage of his career.

It is of some interest to note that he did not use the musical columns of *The Harbinger* in order to propagandize for Associationism. Dwight was primarily the practical reviewer concerned with reporting the musical happenings of the day. This he did through reviews of concerts, newly published music, and books about music. Only the first of his *Harbinger* articles (74) is devoted to Associationism and music. Thereafter, such matters were dealt with only in passing. It is true that he worked out his aesthetic in extensive discussions of the music of Beethoven, Mozart, Haydn, Schubert, Mendelssohn, and other giants of German Romanticism, but his most important pronouncements on the nature of music appeared elsewhere. Even the ideas of his friend Cranch received a more systematic exposition in the pages of *The Harbinger* than did Dwight's own, although it was through one of Dwight's articles (91) that this was effected.[7]

The Harbinger was far and away the most important medium through which Transcendental-colored ideas about music were disseminated. All but 26 of the 183 music articles listed in Appendix C were published there. Although *The Harbinger* was an official mouthpiece for a crusading sect of social reformers, its musical shoemakers stuck to their lasts, reported on what they heard, and left out the theorizing. It was because of this matter-of-fact attitude that the paper succeeded in becoming one of the country's leading musical journals. It is a bit overenthusiastic to say that "*The Harbinger* contained the first noteworthy criticism of the

---

7. The piece consists primarily of long extracts from C. P. Cranch, *Address Delivered Before the Harvard Musical Association, in the Chapel of the University of Cambridge, August 28, 1845* (Boston, 1845).

ethereal art in the history of American journalism" [8]—many earlier examples can be cited—but the really remarkably thorough
and detailed treatment of music found in it was unquestionably
one of the periodical's most noteworthy features.

Music was quite a different matter for some of the other Transcendental journals. *The Western Messenger* was primarily concerned with it as a church problem—as was fitting for the organ
of the Western Unitarian Association. Ten of the 12 articles on
music published there dealt with sacred music and its role in the
Unitarian service. Typical was James H. Perkins's "Public Worship" (177) which argued in favor of congregational singing and
against the use of a trained choir. James Freeman Clarke contributed several brief paragraphs on the state of church music in
Louisville, which are of interest because of their early date (31–
33). Samuel Osgood described church music in Nashua, N.H. as
he saw it during the course of a visit there in October, 1836 (176).
A long extract from a lecture on temperance by William E. Channing (29) praises music as a force for good. Perhaps the most
striking of the *Messenger's* musical articles was Cranch's spirited
defence of music teacher Timothy B. Mason (34) from an attack
characterized by "extreme ultraism and narrowness of spirit" in
which certain critics questioned the propriety of his use of a
Catholic text in a sacred concert held in a Presbyterian Church
in Cincinnati. Timothy, brother of the better known Lowell Mason,
was an important pioneer in Western music education, and the
fact that he had gained an ally in radical religious circles was an
unusual circumstance. The secular items are of no particular consequence. The most substantial contains a mildly interesting description of a musical festival held in New Granada, Colombia
(28) as reported by a traveler to that country.

The Dial contained eight articles with musical content, five of
which were penned by Margaret Fuller (164–168). Of these, only
the "Lives of the Great Composers" (166), a 55-page rhapsody

8. Gohdes, p. 113.

on Haydn, Mozart, Handel, Bach, and Beethoven, is of more than ephemeral worth. Reviews of the Boston music seasons of 1840, 1841, and 1842 were contributed by John F. Tuckerman (182), Dwight (62), and Fuller (165). Emerson's name appears here as a writer on music in his "Thoughts on Art" (163). In this essay, he advanced the famous dictum that "the laws of each art are convertible into the laws of every other."

The sole musical contribution to Brownson's *Boston Quarterly Review* was Tuckerman's unusually detailed examination (183) of the article on Beethoven which had appeared in Fétis's monumental *Biographie universelle des musiciens* (Paris, 1835). Dwight's most important statement of the Transcendental music aesthetic appeared in Elizabeth Peabody's short-lived *Aesthetic Papers* (95). The most noteworthy of the *Spirit of the Age* pieces was a three-part article on "Popular Music" by Charles Lane (175), an English Swedenborgian with some novel ideas about music, among them the belief that through music a people might achieve "national regeneration or earthly elevation." [9]

One can find brief flashes of Transcendental insight in the articles of virtually all the men who wrote about music for these periodicals. Cranch (37) felt that "the saying that in heaven there is music and celestial harping of angels, is no fable. It was said to me once by the Interpreter, that every human spirit was like a musical instrument—the Maker of these spirits, the all-skillful Performer upon them, is God. . . . There, music is the thoughts of their minds, the feeling of their hearts, the language of their lips." [10] Story (181) saw that "art is one; but there are many arts; to all of them there is one common centre to which they converge and which is their essence. The tone struck from one vibrates through all; and though each refuses to assume the form of the other, it is reflected in it partially, and can be in a measure reproduced through it. Music seems to contain every other art, but no other art wholly contains music. Therefore it reproduces itself

9. *The Spirit of the Age,* I, 353.
10. *The Western Messenger,* VI, 269–70.

in the mind of each in that form of art to which that mind is endeared." [11] Lane (175) wrote that "in the devout mind both the sentimental and rational natures are livingly present and ceaselessly active, but always in subordination to the supreme nature in the human being. Music is the chosen utterance from this central power." [12] These, however, were but sparks thrown off from the central fire. One must go to the writings of John Sullivan Dwight for anything like a complete system of Transcendental thought about music.

As early as 1835, Dwight expressed the root concept of the Transcendental attitude toward music. The idea was simple: if words were to be regarded as the language of thought, then music must be regarded as the language of feeling. The unfortunate person who was unable to sense the uniquely communicative nature of music was debarred from comprehension of some of life's deepest mysteries. Not everything could be said in words. "Love, striving to amalgamate with all,—devotion, reaching forward to eternity—all that mysterious part of our nature, which binds us to one another, to the beauty of the world, to God and to an hereafter"—these things, thought Dwight, "require a different language from that of common sense or intellect, which looks coldly upon the outward world, only to dissect it, and which occasions separations, instead of harmony, in human hearts." [13] That "different language" Dwight felt must be music.

Moreover, music was destined to play a social role of the greatest moment, he believed. The society which had for its standard of excellence money or power was a defective one, and it was the holy mission of music to remedy the defect by "familiarizing men with the beautiful and the infinite." The art was given to mankind

11. *The Harbinger*, II, 219.
12. *The Spirit of the Age*, I, 311.
13. "On Music," p. 5, an unpublished essay in the Boston Public Library, as cited in Walter L. Fertig, "John Sullivan Dwight: Transcendentalist and Literary Amateur of Music," unpubl. diss. (Univ. of Md., 1952), p. 35; subsequent quotations *passim*.

to "excite common feeling, create common associations, and unite individuals in common sympathies founded in things eternal."

An important element of his thinking was the idea that the aesthetic, spiritual, and moral qualities inherent in music are made most easily available through the greatest music performed by the greatest artists. This was the reason why he so persistently campaigned for those he considered the world's most masterful composers—Handel, Beethoven, Mozart. It was also the reason why he was so impatient with technical inadequacy.

Of course, the music lover was not expected to speak this "language of feeling" himself; he must merely understand it. Through music, he was transcendentally propelled into another world. The enormous potential power of music was, however, entirely dependent upon the individual who was affected by it; what it communicated could be grasped only intuitively and was incapable of translation into words.

This led Dwight to the elaboration of another aspect of his theory, expounded fully in an address before the Harvard Musical Association in 1841, in which the common distinction between "sacred" and "secular" music was attacked as false and misleading. Dwight contended that it was the greatness of music that made it sacred, not its association with religious words, and that great music was "the language of *natural religion*." [14] Hence, a Beethoven symphony was for him sacred music. "Music stands for the highest outward symbol of what is most deep and holy, and most remotely to be realized in the soul of man," he told his listeners. The purpose of great music was "to hallow pleasure, and to naturalize religion."

Although music seems to have been a bridge to a better world for Dwight from the very beginning, the shape this better world was to take remained cloudy until he came into contact with Associationism, the American brand of Fourierism preached with

14. J. S. Dwight, "Address, Delivered Before the Harvard Musical Association, August 25, 1841," *Hach's Musical Magazine*, III (1841), 265; subsequent quotations *passim*.

magnificent eloquence by Albert Brisbane, who made an astonishing number of prominent converts to the cause. In brief, Fourierist doctrine held that the universe was so created that there was a harmonious connection between the organic and the inorganic, between man and God, between man and the world, and between the world and the universe. Human passions, although immutable, could be brought into equilibrium or harmony by making due allowance for individual differences in a planned community. Theoretically, Fourier held that all human passions would be included in a group of 800 people; as a safe margin of error he postulated twice that many as the best number of participants in the ideal community. The work in such a community, which was termed a phalanstery or a phalanx, would be divided according to natural inclination and ability, and the result would be the more or less automatic achievement of the good life.

It was seemingly Brisbane who made the observation that, in music, a proper arrangement of the notes brought about harmony and an improper arrangement discord, and who tried to apply this observation to the social scene. What was needed in human relations was merely a proper arrangement of parts, a new institutional framework. Given such a framework, human discord would cease. "Establish true social institutions," he wrote, "institutions in harmony with the laws of organization in creation (and consequently in harmony with the spiritual forces which are in harmony with the creation); and we shall see them producing as high a degree of harmony as they now produce in discord." [15] Thus music was seen as the ultimate guide to social harmony.

Dwight anticipated, in most remarkable fashion, the Brisbanian view of music, but the stress on unity, on interrelationship between man, God, and universe, was common to both Transcendentalism and Associationism. Both systems were characterized by the same Romantic idealism, the same unshakable trust in the awful power of the ineffable One, the same mystical yearning toward oblitera-

15. As cited in Redalia Brisbane, *Albert Brisbane: A Mental Biography* (Boston, 1893), p. 181.

tion of Self in All. The difference was that the Transcendentalist saw his relationship to the total environment as an individual problem, whereas the Associationist saw heaven achievable through an artificial community of 1,600 souls. The ultimate end was the same, but the means of getting to it were completely different.

DWIGHT's thinking on music was a synthesis of the two philosophies. He saw in the art not only the Transcendental intuition of God, not only the shared vision of Oneness, but also the grandiose Associationist scheme of universal harmony. The growth of music on American soil he regarded as a herald of the time when all would be one, a harbinger of the future. The substitution of the symphonies of Beethoven for the psalm-tunes of New England he saw as the victory of "natural religion," i.e., of Transcendentalism.

Nevertheless, Dwight never put into practice the idea, advanced in the first number of *The Harbinger*, that he would use its columns to develop the correspondence of music "as a Science with other Sciences, and especially with the Science of the coming Social Order, and the transition through which we are passing towards it." [16] As has been previously observed, his writings there were pretty well confined to hard-headed examinations of the art as it was practiced in Boston and New York, together with a certain amount of interpretation of music as the expression of the unknowable. And by the time he wrote his masterful essay for the *Aesthetic Papers* in 1849, very little Associationist dogma remained in his theorizing.

The "Music" (95) essay was the clearest and most succinct statement of the Transcendental view of the art that had appeared in print until then. Dwight rested his faith in the religion of beauty Emerson had expounded in the 1842 lecture on "The Transcendentalist" cited here as epigraph. For Dwight,

music is both body and soul, like the man who delights in it. Its body is beauty in the sphere of sound,—*audible beauty*. But in this very word

16. I, 13.

beauty is implied a soul, a moral end, a meaning of some sort, a something which makes it of interest to the inner life of man, which relates it to our invisible and real self. This beauty, like all other, results from the marriage of a spiritual fact with a material form, from the rendering external, and an object of sense, what lives in essence only in the soul. Here the material part, which is measured sound, is the embodiment and sensible representative, as well as the re-acting cause, of that which we call impulse, sentiment, feeling, the spring of all our action and expression. In a word, it is the language of the heart;—not an arbitrary and conventional representative, as a spoken or written word is; but a natural, invariable, pure type and correspondence. Speech, so far as it is distinct from music, sustains the same relation to the head. Speech is the language of ideas, the communicator of thought, the Mercury of the intellectual Olympus enthroned in each of us. But behind all thought, there is something deeper, and much nearer life. . . .[17]

This was "the heart . . . its loves, its sentiments, its passions, its prompting impulses, its irresistible attractions, its warm desires and aspirations,—these are the masters of the intellect, if not its law." Music was the natural language of the heart, and Dwight had returned full circle to the idea he had promulgated 14 years earlier in the first statement of his thoughts on music.

Yet, we now have a mature faith based on experience rather than a youthful intuition based on enthusiasm. The ideas set forth in the *Aesthetic Papers* time and again echo the concepts of the "On Music" paper of 1835, but they are clothed with authority, grace, and clarity. Dwight never wrote more eloquent lines than the following, which can stand as the distilled essence of the Transcendental aesthetic applied to music:

The native impulses of the soul, or what are variously called the passions, affections, propensities, desires, are, all of them, when considered in their essence and original unwarped tendency, so many divinely implanted loves. Union, harmony of some sort, is their very life. To meet, to unite, to blend, by methods intricate as swift, is their whole business and effort through eternity. As is their attraction, such must be their destiny; not to collision, not to excess followed by exhaustion; not to discord, chaos, and confusion; but to binding ties of fitness and conjunction

17. *Aesthetic Papers*, I, 27–28; subsequent quotations *passim*.

through all spheres, from the simplest to the most universal accords. Through these (how else?) are the hearts of the human race to be knit into one mutually conscious, undivided whole, one living temple not too narrow, nor too fragmentary for the reception of the Spirit of God. Is not this foretold in music, the natural language of these passions, which cannot express corruption nor any evil feeling, without ceasing to be music; which has no tone for any bad passion, and translates into harmony and beauty whatever it expresses? The blending of all these passions harmoniously into one becomes the central love, the deepest and most undivided life of man. This is the love of God, as it is also, from the first, the inbreathing of God, who is love; to whom the soul seeks its way, by however blind an instinct, through all these partial harmonies, learning by degrees to understand the universal nature of its desire and aim. . . . Music is its natural language, the chief rite of its worship, the rite which cannot lose its sacredness; for music cannot cease to be harmony, cannot cease to symbolize the sacred relationship of each to all, cannot contract a taint, any more than the sunbeam which shines into all corners. Music cannot narrow or cloak the message which it bears; it cannot lie; it cannot raise questions in the mind, or excite any other than a pure enthusiasm. It is God's alphabet, and not man's; unalterable and unpervertible; suited for the harmony of the human passions and affections; and sent us in this their long winter of disharmony and strife, to be a perpetual type and monitor, let us say an actual foretaste, of that harmony which must yet come.

Truly, the only thing left here of Associationism is its poetry.

EMERSON, honestly confessing that he was "untaught by nature or art in the mysteries of music," [18] used to delight in relating the following anecdote. A teacher was listening to a group of youngsters sing, among them Waldo. Pointing unmistakably at Emerson, the instructor (who happened to be blind) shouted: "Send that boy away, he has no ear."

There is ample evidence of Emerson's lack of musical receptivity. Perhaps the most poignant musical incident of his life took place during the visit to England in 1848. The great Chopin had sent him a complimentary ticket to a concert, and Emerson was both flattered and embarrassed by the gesture. "Could he only

18. *Journals*, II (1825), 48.

lend me ears!" he wrote to his wife in telling the story—not without a touch of envy.

Emerson did not hear much music, but what did come to his ears he reacted to in true Transcendental fashion—intuitively. Such ascertainable things as harmony, counterpoint, form (functions of tuition), he scorned to investigate. But in the art's mysterious systole and diastole, he sensed something beyond his grasp. Music, he confided to his journal in 1838, "takes us out of the actual and whispers to us dim secrets that startle our wonder as to who we are. . . . All the great interrogatories, like questioning angels, float in on its waves of sound." [19] Technical matters were for others in the Transcendental circle whose ears were less unmistakably tin; Emerson cheerfully admitted that he read his friend Dwight on the dark anatomy of music "as a mute reads of eloquence."

For the Sage of Concord, music was valuable as an asylum, as something to "imparadise the ear." The ear, however, was not his portal of entry into the magical worlds of Nature and Art. He lived through the eye, and to make up for his lack of musical ears, he had been blessed (as he said) with "musical eyes." He conceived himself a translator of cosmic harmonies into language. "I am a poet in the sense of a perceiver and dear lover of the harmonies that are in the soul and in matter, and specially of the correspondences between these and those," [20] he wrote to his bride-to-be in 1835. There can be little doubt that the harmonies he perceived and dearly loved were not aural.

Looking back on those early years in 1871, Walt Whitman summed up the entire Transcendental era with the brevity of genius: "The priest departs," he wrote, "the divine literatus comes." It is, of course, idle to speculate about what would have happened had Emerson been less anaesthetic to the language Dwight under-

19. As cited in Vivian C. Hopkins, *Spires of Form* (Cambridge, Mass., 1951), p. 190.

20. As cited in F. O. Matthiessen, *American Renaissance: Art and Expression in the Age of Emerson and Whitman* (New York, 1941), p. 47.

stood so well. Certainly, the "Newness" would have been much different. Perhaps it would have been in fact what Dwight dreamed it might become: "the priest departs, the divine musician comes."

16

---»»·«««---

AMERICAN DEMOCRACY
AND AMERICAN MUSIC (1830-1914)

FOR WELL OVER a century now, it has been argued that the "youth"
of the American nation both explains and excuses our supposed
lack of a noteworthy musical culture. This, I submit, is sheer non-
sense. First of all, national maturity is no precondition for the
creation of memorable art. Furthermore, there was no musical
vacuum here. Even during the very years of this country's birth,
noteworthy musical developments were in progress. It is surely
more accurate to say, along with the distinguished student of
American democracy, James Bryce, that the arts have flourished in
almost every environment, and quite without relation to the age of
the political state.

About music specifically, however, Lord Bryce felt somewhat
uneasy. This "most inscrutable of all arts," he wrote in 1921,
"seems to be quite out of relation to the other intellectual movements of the world." [1]

It is difficult for the music historian to be patient with such be-
wilderment. It may be true that some of us think the symbols of
musical expression have no discernible referents in the non-
musical cosmos. Nevertheless, we can hardly concede that music is
totally disconnected from the world. To do so would be to admit
that the art is not of this world and hence is totally inexplicable.
Can we not at least agree that the creation of music is a human

1. *Modern Democracies* (New York, 1921), II, 525.

activity? Must it not, then, somehow mirror—if only as in a glass darkly—something of those who create it?

Probably all musicologists accept as axiomatic the proposition that the functioning of music in a given society can be meaningfully interpreted in linguistic terms. Yet we tend to avoid this troublesome area and we concern ourselves almost exclusively with the inner, technical operations of music as an encapsulated phenomenon. Are we not perhaps a bit too eager to leave the broader problem to such social historians as Lord Bryce, who may be brilliant observers quite familiar with historiographical method, but who are all too frequently anaesthetic to musical values and woefully ignorant of the specialized techniques of musico-historical research? Should it not rather be musicologists who come to grips with this elusive matter of the connection between music and the society in which it exists?

In this essay, it is my purpose to focus your attention on one aspect of this connection, as exemplified in the history of American democracy and American music from approximately 1830 to 1914. I do not intend to wrestle with value judgments—whether the music of the then United States is good, bad, or indifferent in any absolute sense is entirely beside the point I hope to make. For my purposes, it is enough to say that American music did exist.

BEFORE any clear relationship between American democracy and American music can be shown, the terms must be precisely delineated. It is all too easy to regard these high-order abstractions as unitary concepts and thus be led astray. Of course, both are pluralistic. To borrow an analogy from chemistry, they are compounds made up of elements each of which is quite different separately from their combination, just as hydrogen and oxygen separately are quite different from water, one result of their combination. And as sometimes happens in a chemical reaction between two compounds, the affinity of an element in the first for an element in the second may be demonstrable.

The two main elements of which American democracy is compounded may be seen united in the familiar phrases of the *Decla-ration of Independence:* "We hold these truths to be self-evident: that all men are created equal; that they are endowed by their Creator with certain inalienable rights; that among these are life, liberty, and the pursuit of happiness." One element is the idea of equality; the other is the idea of liberty. These are not only differ-ent ideas—they are in some ways quite contradictory. Equalitarian-ism implies the individual's responsibility to and dependence upon the community; libertarianism implies the community's responsi-bility to and dependence upon the individual. The political mech-anism through which the United States has tried to reconcile these conflicting philosophical concepts has been the American Consti-tution, an intricate machine designed to thwart tyranny of major-ity and minority alike. Although the equalitarian and the libertar-ian tendencies were each predominant at one or another period in our history, neither alone defines American democracy. Rather, it is their imperfect fusion, their interconnection, and their interac-tion.

Nor does the term "American music" really refer to a single entity. Perhaps more distinctly in this country than elsewhere, it is apparent that we have at least two musics with which to contend —one the issue of an educated culture, an elite art; the other the issue of a popular culture, a mass art. One might characterize elite art (as did Matthew Arnold) as the best that has been thought and said by the few in a civilization. Similarly, one might charac-terize mass art (as did Max Lerner) as "the run of what is thought, felt, and liked by the many." [2]

Lest I be misunderstood, however, I should like to say plainly that as I use them, the terms "elite art" and "mass art" imply no hierarchy of value. The one is not better than the other; both musics include good and bad. I shall refer to elite music as "fine-art music" and mass music as "popular music"—both phrases are intended to be merely descriptive.

2. *America as a Civilization* (New York, 1957), p. 780.

In effect, fine-art music and popular music are the two main elements in the American musical compound, perceptible separately without difficulty, but in combination something else again. As with American democracy, it is the way in which the elements interfuse, interconnect, and interact in a particular environment that constitutes the individuality of the compound. Failure to grasp the mechanics of this process has led some to seize upon the "American vernacular" as the only true American music; it has led others to dismiss our popular music, claiming the laurel for fine-art music alone. Both interpretations are equally fallacious.

Summarizing, American democracy and American music are both compound concepts, each composed of certain divergent elements. Our democracy is compounded of equalitarian and libertarian impulses; our music of popular and fine-art components. The relative proportion of each element in each compound is continually changing. In the social sphere, equalitarianism or libertarianism may be predominant; in the artistic sphere, popular or fine-art music may be pre-eminent.

It is my contention that the past history of the United States has demonstrated a certain correlation between the dominance of the equalitarian urge and the vitality of popular music, and a similar correlation between the dominance of the libertarian urge and the vitality of fine-art music. I am not positing a new law in social dynamics or insisting that such a correlation must be universally found. My aim is merely to indicate the existence of this correlation in American civilization during the 1830–1914 period.

Demonstrating this correlation is made more difficult because both our democracy and our music were continuously altered and molded by distinctively European influences. Our society was not free to develop apart from these influences, and there was no way that the United States could renounce its European heritage, despite the loud clamor on the part of American nationalists for a cultural declaration of independence from the Old World. In 1820, Anthony Philip Heinrich could publish a musical work called *The Dawning of Music in Kentucky*, but only its title did not speak with a strong Bohemian accent. In 1853, William Henry Fry could advocate eloquently a distinctively American music, but his own operas echo Bellini. But notwithstanding this complicating European factor, the broad lines of the correlation still manage to emerge with surprising clarity.

Since 1830 marks the beginning of the second act of the American drama, it might be helpful to sketch in the action up to that point. Our nation's first half-century was a time when the ideas of the Enlightenment which helped bring it into existence—such ideas as natural rights, humanitarianism, human perfectibility, scientific infallibility—were fresh and strong. This was essentially the honeymoon period of American civilization, an era of exquisite balance between equalitarianism and libertarianism. Before the turn of the 19th century, a leaning in the direction of equalitarian excess was tempered by patrician leadership of the state and patrician direction of thought; after 1800, the levelling influence of the Western frontier at first tempered the libertarian thrust—and ultimately halted it. During the early Federal period, America's most vital music was that of the New England singing-school movement, an individualistic fine-art music with a substantial admixture of popular elements based on an ubiquitous Anglo-Celtic folk tradition. As the equalitarian triumph loomed, the influence of this music gradually receded.

The election of Andrew Jackson to the presidency in 1828 marked a spectacular victory for the ideas of equalitarianism. So thoroughly submerged were libertarian tendencies that even the perceptive Alexis de Tocqueville, who visited the United States at just that time to study the workings of our democracy, was deceived into regarding equalitarianism and the American system as identical. He may not have discerned the libertarian component of American democracy, but he was nevertheless an exceptionally accurate observer of the dynamics of the contemporary scene. As he foresaw, in later decades the plain people came to take a more active role than ever before in American intellectual life. This trend was stimulated by the continuing growth of the West, the rapid expansion of industry and the consequent urbanization of the population, and the great influx of immigrants from Western Europe who brought to their new home that equalitarian fervor so characteristic of mid-century democratic movements in Europe. Important in the spread of equalitarianism was the wide diffusion of literacy, in large measure due to compulsory education.

What about our music? The salient point about the history of the art between 1830 and 1865 was unquestionably the dramatic growth in prestige and acceptance of the popular component. Thanks to an influx of professional musicians from across the Atlantic, there was also much activity in fine-art music, but it was the camp-meeting songs, the white and Negro spirituals, the gospel songs, the mass-produced polkas and schottisches, the stereotyped sentimental ballads, the formula salon pieces, the black-face minstrel shows, which especially characterized the era. The personification of American popular music was Stephen Collins Foster, an unsophisticated figure equipped with a positive genius for synthesizing "what is thought, felt, and liked by the many" in terms of simple melodic lines. So potent were Foster's tunes that they successfully invaded Asia as well as Europe, and as early as 1853, Bayard Taylor tells that he heard a Hindu musician singing "Oh, Susanna!" in the streets of Delhi.

Of our fine-art composers, the Louisiana-born Louis Moreau Gottschalk (1829–1869) was probably the most significant. His most engaging works are those he wrote when he was a young virtuoso pianist in the Paris of the mid-1840s, a libertarian counterbalance in environment to the equalitarianism of the land of his birth. His not infrequent use of direct quotation from such popular music of the day as Creole, Latin-American, and Foster tunes is a startling anticipation of a technique more usually associated with the name of Charles Ives.

AFTER the Civil War, the greatest single controlling influence in American intellectual life came to be that exerted by a powerful small group, the big-business class. Ultimately, the ante-bellum tyranny of the majority was superseded by a new tyranny of the minority, a libertarianism much different in its crass materialism from the idealistic libertarianism of the first years of the American republic. The "almighty dollar" became the standard of value, infecting the country with contempt for things of the spirit.

At the same time, a gradual decline in the vitality of American popular music was evident, a development which coincided with a burst of creative activity from our fine-art composers. The 1880s saw the advent of the first consequential American school since the days of the 18th-century singing-masters. Four men in particular towered over their contemporaries: John Knowles Paine, George Whitefield Chadwick, Horatio W. Parker, and Edward MacDowell. The last was the only member of the quartet who appears to have been touched with true genius, but the others were thoroughly trained professionals whose best work hardly deserves its contemporary neglect. In view of the temper of the time, it is not surprising that all studied in Germany, where composers earned respect even if they did not earn much money. It is natural that they composed, for the most part, in the then current late-romantic European idiom. But they all returned home and achieved considerable status as teachers and composers of fine-art music in a wealth-oriented libertarian society.

The 20th century ushered in a reaction against the rampant individualism of the previous decades. Responsible individuals attempted to restate equalitarian values in the face of an irresponsible libertarianism. Little aroused more enthusiasm than the intellectual's protest against the political, social, and economic ailments and grievances generated by the excesses of the 1865–1900 period. The first decade of the new century saw the birth of "muckraking," the rise of the labor union and the grange, and the development of Utopian and socialist movements in the United States. A new attempt to balance the libertarian and equalitarian drives was launched.

As the equalitarian drive gathered impetus, popular music took on new life. The generative vigor of the marches of John Philip Sousa, the operettas of Victor Herbert, and the rags of Scott Joplin is manifest even in their lineal descendants of today—band music, musical comedy, and jazz. But we must turn to Charles Ives for an extraordinary reflection in music of the delicate balance between libertarianism and equalitarianism of those years. Ives was a composer of sonatas and symphonies, but he deliberately quoted extensively from such popular music as gospel songs, patriotic ditties, and marches. His curious synthesis of fine-art music and popular music, a purely musical resolution of the American social duality, seems to mirror the dynamics of the age with startling verisimilitude.

Allow me to conclude by repeating that the correlation I have described as existing between American democracy and American music pertains only to the 1830–1914 period. To try to trace it after this terminal date would be a hazardous and probably unprofitable undertaking. The society in which we live today is qualitatively as well as quantitatively different from that of the earlier era, and I would seriously question whether such concepts as "American democracy" and "American music" can be meaningfully abstracted from the complex of Western civilization as a whole in an age in which national boundaries are no longer vitally important cultural walls.

17

---»»«««---

THE WARRINGTON COLLECTION:
A RESEARCH ADVENTURE
AT CASE MEMORIAL LIBRARY

ABOUT 75 YEARS AGO, James Warrington, a Philadelphia account-ant of scholarly bent, began the accumulation of materials perti-nent to the history and practice of American psalmody. At the time he began his collecting activities, but little significance was attached to this field. Warrington was virtually alone in his inter-est in it. Fortunately, he was more than a mere book-collector; had he not been a scholar by inclination it is doubtful that he would have paid much attention to early American hymn- and tune-books. These were originally utilitarian rather than decorative objects; they were given heavy wear and were used until they were quite literally worn out. As a natural consequence, copies in good enough condition to tempt the bibliophile are scarce indeed and always have been; the battered and tattered remnants of most extant copies find their way into the working libraries of institu-tions and scholars. Legend had it that Warrington was successful in building an unrivalled collection of these materials.

As a student of certain phases of American music history, I first became aware of the probable existence of the Warrington collec-tion through my acquaintance with a comparatively little known bibliographical work by Warrington himself. In 1898, he pub-lished privately in a small edition a short-title list of books relating to American psalmody. It seemed quite apparent that a personal library of some magnitude must have been the cornerstone upon which it was based, although no direct statement to that effect appears in the bibliography itself. The check-list suffered from the flaws and defects characteristic of the pioneer work; its sins of omission and commission were many, and it served only as a crude chart to a hitherto unmapped sea of research materials. Nevertheless, it was a valuable work.

Although I was mildly curious as to whether Warrington's collection was still available intact, my urge to track it down was somewhat lessened because of the fortunate circumstance that the excellent research facilities provided by the Library of Congress in Washington were easily accessible to me. These proved to be adequate for my investigations until 1950, when I began serious work on a project entailing the examination and study of every known American tune-book published before 1810. As there are many unlocated titles in this field, the question of the possible existence and whereabouts of the Warrington collection became a matter of more than academic interest to me.

There was, of course, no definite assurance that the collection had not been dispersed after Warrington's death. One circumstance that led me to believe that this was not likely, however, was the mention in Frank J. Metcalf's 1917 *American Psalmody* (the bibliographical work, by the way, which supplanted Warrington's study) of a "Warrington collection" housed at the Western Theological Seminary in Pittsburgh. This proved to be a false lead, or, at any rate, only part of the complete story. Examination of the titles found in the Pittsburgh "Warrington collection" led to one of two conclusions: either his collection was not as extensive as I had expected, or else only a fraction of it was located in Pittsburgh. The latter assumption proved to be correct. The riddle was finally solved in the course of a discussion with Allen P. Britton of the University of Michigan, who was also deeply interested in the bibliography of 18th-century American tune-books. In the course of his work on his doctoral dissertation, Dr. Britton had found it necessary to visit a large number of libraries to establish locations. In relating his experiences, he remarked that he had found what seemed to be the largest bulk of the Warrington collection at the Case Memorial Library in Hartford; at the time he had not as yet personally examined its holdings in detail, but he expected to do so at the earliest opportunity. Dr. Britton's rough description of its extent aroused my own desire to inspect it at first hand.

JAMES WARRINGTON was among the first to realize that early America was no musical desert. He charted the bibliography of our religious music with sympathy and understanding (although with the limitations of every pathbreaker) with the intention of eventually studying its history and development. This he did not live to accomplish. Chronologically, he was followed by the great American scholar-librarian Oscar G. T. Sonneck, whose investigations of the 18th-century secular music, commenced at the turn of this century, are now among the classics of musicological literature. At the time they were written, however, interest in American music was at such low ebb that no American publisher willing to publish his *Early Concert-Life in America* could be located. Eventually it appeared in 1907 under the Leipzig imprint of Breitkopf and Härtel. Warrington's successor in bibliographical and historical research in sacred music was Frank J. Metcalf, whose labors began shortly before the First World War. None of the excellent work accomplished by these men succeeded in arousing interest outside a narrow circle of scholars; it was not until 1933 that the tide finally turned. In that year, the late George Pullen Jackson of Vanderbilt University began the publication of a brilliant series of studies in American spiritual folk-song, pointing out not only the unquestionable beauty of this music, but also establishing a hitherto undetected but none the less important link between the secular and the sacred music of our country. Other men followed, broadening and deepening investigations along both secular and sacred lines.

AN OPPORTUNITY to visit Case Memorial Library finally came my way toward the end of 1951. My wife (who is my co-worker and fellow researcher) and I had spent the major portion of the summer studying available materials at the Library of Congress; it became necessary for us to travel to New England in order to complete our survey of early American tune-books. Our time was rather severely limited and there was much to be done; certain items had to be seen at New Haven, Worcester, Boston, Providence, and New York. However, we did manage to schedule a brief stop at the Hartford Seminary in order to examine five titles, not easily available elsewhere, we had reason to believe were to be found there. We were hoping to be able to complete our task at Hartford in a few hours, a most optimistic miscalculation. We soon discovered that it would require not hours, but months in order to get an accurate idea of the wealth of the Warrington collection.

At one time or another, every researcher has undoubtedly experienced difficulty in finding the materials he has come to a library to see. It is always just these items, it seems, that are in the process of being cataloged, recataloged, bound, rebound, or are otherwise unavailable; they have a bad habit of not being where they are supposed to be at the proper time. In the course of our trip, we had run into this situation several times; in one instance, we had to leave a library without examining three of the books we had travelled some distance to see. In most cases, however, such recalcitrant items were eventually tracked down and placed in our hands by helpful and efficient staff members. We were therefore not particularly alarmed when a careful check of the catalog at Case Memorial failed to disclose more than one of the five titles in which we were interested. After a double-check by the reference librarian verified the fact that we had not misread the card catalog, we were guided to what turned out to be *the* Warrington collection and (so to speak) were turned loose among its treasures, an experience and an adventure we shall long remember.

THE collection was located in a cellar which was obviously not designed for the convenience of either librarian or research scholar; one of the really essential prerequisites for the use of books, that of light by which to read, was sadly lacking. This difficulty was overcome within the space of a few minutes. Extension cords were obtained and hung so that we could begin a search which turned out to be something in the nature of an archaeological expedition.[1]

The books were shelved, but in widely scattered sections of the cellar. With the exception of very few titles, the collection was uncataloged and in no discernible order. The only available guide to what it contained, a rough index-card file probably compiled by Warrington himself, was more tantalizing than useful. What was one to make of listings of no less than six separate editions of Thomas Walter's 18th-century *The Grounds and Rules of Musick Explained*? Were they actually there, or was this merely a reference to books Warrington was seeking? We could not find a single copy. Elsewhere, we might well be dubious about such a concentration of editions of a scarce and most important American tunebook; here, however, we were forced to concede at least the possibility that the cards meant what they said. Although no copies of the Walter turned up, much else of comparable interest did. The collection is by no means confined to 18th-century, or even to American imprints. We found beautiful, crisp copies of 17th-century English and Dutch psalters. We found many early English and American secular songsters, perhaps even rarer than tunebooks. We found an astonishing wealth of 19th-century American materials, including a great number of exceedingly interesting shape-note tune-books of Southern and Western origin. Perversely enough, many of these items, which we personally examined, were not to be found in Warrington's own index.

It was not possible for us to gauge with even a rough degree of

1. Since our trip to Hartford in 1951, the physical arrangement of the Warrington collection has been greatly improved, but as of this writing, it has not yet been fully put in order or cataloged.

accuracy the number of titles in the collection as a whole. Certainly there appeared to be thousands of books, ranging from unique copies to commonplaces. We were seeking five specific titles; had not these been printed in that characteristic oblong format which distinguishes them immediately from most others, our task would have been completely hopeless. As it was, there were hundreds in the collection of similar shape and size; working purely by instinct, we managed to locate four after removing approximately 100 volumes from the shelves. The fifth eluded us completely. No doubt it is there, hiding in some corner that escaped our notice.

IF THE books we examined are characteristic of the Warrington collection as a whole (and there seems to be no reason why they should not be, as our selection was basically a random one), Case Memorial Library must be ranked as a most important center of research materials for the study of early American music. Of course, until a catalog is available, any opinion regarding its exact place in the hierarchy of libraries specializing in this sort of Americana can be nothing better than a more or less informed guess.

Most of the books were bearing up well under the strain of carrying dust and grime accumulated over a period of perhaps three decades, but some had been attacked, at one time or another, by insects or rodents and were damaged almost beyond repair. Others suffered from inevitable time-damage; their bindings crumbled at the slightest touch. All suffered from neglect. It was disconcerting in the extreme to find a book of which perhaps no other copy was known only to discover that a portion of its pages had furnished a meal to some denizen of the animal world; the social waste embodied in such a situation is incalculable. Nevertheless, taking all factors into account, the collection as a whole was in remarkably fine condition, and copies of rarities so pristine that it would seem they had come from the presses just yesterday, not 200 years ago, were easy to find.

As a very rough objective verification of my subjective impression that the Warrington collection was quite important, I transcribed the titles of 75 items we examined in order to see to what extent they were available in other libraries we expected to visit later. At Union Theological Seminary (whose library also includes the collection of The Hymn Society of America), I could find but 19 of the 75. The Library of Congress, whose holdings in this field are probably exceeded solely by those of the American Antiquarian Society, owned 39. Of course, such comparisons are deceptive, and I have no desire to imply that the Warrington collection surpasses these two magnificent libraries in extent. These comparisons should be regarded as nothing more than a slight indication that it is a significant collection. Undoubtedly, similar lists of holdings from either of these libraries could be prepared which could not be duplicated to even a small degree at Case Memorial. The general point should be quite clear, however: the serious student of American music cannot afford to neglect what may seem to be minor sources. Thanks to past neglect of our musical heritage, they may, in fact, turn out to be anything but minor.

18

---—— >>> ‹‹‹ ———---

THE AMERICAN TRADITION

OF CHURCH SONG

BACK IN THE DAYS of Benjamin Franklin and Thomas Jefferson, the French savant Abbé Raynal, speculating on the peculiar nature of America and Americans, arrived at some remarkable conclusions. There must be something wrong with the American climate or the American soil, thought the Abbé. Otherwise, how could one explain the fact that human beings placed in an American environment showed an unmistakable tendency to deteriorate, both mentally and physically? Was not America totally devoid of men of genius? Why had it produced no art, no science? Obviously, America was a dark, barbarous land, where only savages could flourish, no fit place for a civilized European, and culture was too delicate a flower to survive the rigors of such a strange New World.

About a century later, the American historian John Fiske attempted to explain why, even by that late date, he had been unable to discover any native American culture worthy of the name. According to Fiske, civilization—European civilization, of course, for he recognized no other—depended on "carriers" for its dissemination. These carriers were the men of science and art: mathematicians, philosophers, artists, writers, musicians. What little civilization there *was* in America came *from* these carriers, from Americans who had worshipped at the shrine of European culture and returned to their native land, from cultured Europeans who had emigrated to America. Through these men and their works, the "transit of civilization" (to use Fiske's own eloquent phrase) took place. If we were lucky, some day in the future culture might take root here. Until then, America, a gawky child gracelessly imitating the subtleties of its parent, was condemned to lag behind. Until then, America's culture must remain a prosy paraphrase of that of Europe.

Both ideas—Raynal's and Fiske's—have a common fallacy. To them, the individual masterwork—the Bach fugue, the Raphael painting, the Notre Dame cathedral—was culture. To us, the individual masterwork is but the flower of the plant; the plant itself represents what we consider culture. And as the flower blossoms from the plant, so the masterwork blossoms from the culture of a society. Culture is the totality of artistic and scientific expression of any group, community, nation, or civilization—a society lacking a culture is a sheer inpossibility.

Thus, young America too had its culture. Raynal and Fiske did not recognize it and sought it in the wrong places. As a matter of fact, it is only within the past few decades that we have recognized it and become aware of it. Now we know that young America had its primitive painters, its carpenter-architects, its artisan-sculptors in abundance. The forms of art these men created were characteristic of young America—they reflected the warp and woof of community experience, and they were the genuine manifestations of our culture in art. Their analogue in music was 18th- and early 19th-century American church song, commonly referred to as early American psalmody.

THE TERM "psalmody" is here used in a very broad sense. It is a misnomer and yet no other word is quite so accurate. For this music was much more than a church song sung only of a Sunday morning in church—it was a music of the out-of-doors, of the kitchen hearth, of the blacksmith's forge, and even of the tavern. We do not usually think of church song in this way, as a religious music fulfilling many of the functions of secular song as well.

Nevertheless, this is the truth of the matter, and the peculiar secular-sacred nature of early American psalmody can be fully grasped only within the context of the society of which it was an integral part. This was a time when Tate and Brady and Watts (theology in meter to most of us) spoke to the people in secular as well as sacred accents. This was a time when psalm- and hymn-tunes grew out of the same creative instinct that produces folk-music, when secular folk-songs and folk-dances became psalm- and hymn-tunes. This was a time when the church was called the meeting-house, and when the meeting-house was the center of *all* community life, both sacred *and* secular.

Such was the dual function of this 18th-century music. It is quite characteristic of the time that, even though the best of it was sung by congregation and choir in worship throughout New England, it should be the product of a social institution quite distinct from the church although growing from its needs—The New England singing-school.

Singing-schools (whose secular character is clear from the fact that they were just as likely to hold sessions in the tavern as in the meeting-house) got started in New England around 1720, when musically illiterate congregations were apparently making some pretty awful sounds in church. A few young ministers (Thomas Symmes, John Tufts, and Thomas Walter, all Harvard men) who were forced to listen to what Walter called "an horrid Medly of confused and disorderly noises" every Sunday, determined to do something concrete about this unhappy situation. Gilbert Chase has pointed out that these so-called "noises" may well have been the origin of a style of singing which blossomed in the South a century or so later, but at the time, the intellectual leaders of the Colonies were aghast at the situation. How to get the congregations to sing together decently and with some semblance of art? The answer was Yankee-simple—teach them to read music and supply them with printed music from which to read. So were born both singing-school and tune-book.

There was nothing complicated about it. The pupils, generally teen-agers or young adults, met of an evening. Everyone brought his own candle. Everyone brought his determination to learn. And everyone bought a tune-book. After some weeks of intensive study, the scholars were presented in concert to show publicly what they had absorbed in the way of musical knowledge, and school was out. The singing-master, usually an itinerant, moved on to another village and placed a notice in the local newspaper similar to the following:

Mr. MUNSON respectfully acquaints the GENTLEMEN and LADIES of the town of SALEM that he opens a Singing-School THIS DAY, at the Assembly-Room, where Parents and other Subscribers are desired to send their Children at 5 o'clock P.M., and young Gentlemen & Ladies to attend at seven in the Evening. N.B. Subscriptions are taken in at Mr. SAMUEL FIELD's in School-Street, and at the Printing-Office.
Salem, September 14, 1773.

There, the process was repeated. That was all there was to it, and the passing of decades had very little effect in changing the form of the institution.

THE singing-school's enormous popularity during the 18th century was obviously due to more than a great love for music or for learning. Here was a rare chance for approved social intercourse between boys and girls. No doubt the youngsters welcomed the break in routine provided by the chance to learn to read music, but they also used the singing-school as a place where they could make new friends, exchange notes, flirt, walk home together after lessons, and, in general, enjoy themselves. As an example of what went on, one might cite a letter, written in an unguarded moment, from a Yale undergraduate to his friend Simeon Baldwin (later a distinguished New Haven attorney) in 1782:

. . . at present I have no Inclination for anything, for I am almost sick of the World & were it not for the Hopes of going to singing-meeting tonight & indulging myself a little in some of the carnal Delights of the Flesh, such as kissing, squeezing &c. &c. I should willingly leave it now, before 10 o'clock & exchange it for a better.

It is easy to see that many marriages must have grown out of singing-meetings, and the old tune-books show plenty of hand-written evidence of incipient love-affairs of long ago.

But the basic purpose of the singing-school was a serious one: to teach people to read music and to sing music. As the singing-schools multiplied in number and spread geographically, they generated an insistent demand for ever more music. And they wanted *new* music, not the same old things they had been singing last year. Imports from the mother country could not satisfy such expanding, hungry markets forever. What with the maturation of national consciousness, increasing self-sufficiency, and growing resentment against England, it was inevitable that sooner or later a native, home-grown product, composed and printed in America, should come into being. The inevitable finally came to pass in 1770, and with the publication of Billing's *New-England Psalm-Singer,* the floodgates were opened wide, and the first great outburst of American musical creativity began.

WHEN it was composed, this music was experienced rather than heard because it was not written for an audience's appreciation or to tickle an ear—it was written to be experienced in performance by performers. How it "sounded" to a non-participant was of very little importance. This is no novel concept; it is one of the essential pre-conditions of genuine church song. Clearly, a basic function of congregational song within the service should be to enable members of the congregation to participate actively in worship through music. This active participation in worship is, of course, one of the foundation-stones of Protestantism, a democratization of religion that was one of the great achievements of the Reformation. If congregational song is to fulfill this function, it is obvious that no performer-audience relationship is possible; all members of the congregation must participate actively in the process of making music. Thus, congregational music must make its impact felt not through the hearing experience, as with choir music, but through the performing experience. To my mind, this identification of the music with the performer rather than the listener, this inwardness, this lack of self-consciousness, is a fundamental though generally overlooked characteristic which early American church song shares with authentic church song of all times and all places.

The New England tunes are usually found in four-part settings. These were not "harmonizations" in the modern sense. We hear them today as a succession of vertical chords, but they were originally experienced as a fabric of interwoven melodic strands; the emphasis was on the horizontal, the melodic flow. The ideal toward which these composers reached was to make each individual melodic line as interesting, as expressive, and as grateful to sing as the other. Of course, they did not always succeed, but the vertical aspects of their settings were merely an incidental product of the conjunction of horizontally conceived lines.

It should be clear that the 19th-century harmonic analysis of music in the early American idiom we have inherited from such men as Thomas Hastings and Lowell Mason was grounded on root ideas characteristic of their time. They postulated certain immutable "laws of musical science" the observation of which supposedly resulted in artistic achievement. Paramount among these was a law of correct voice-leading based on a vertical conception of music. Ignorance of the law was no excuse; those who transgressed wrote "incorrect" and therefore "bad" music. And in truth, if one accepts the premise, the conclusion is inescapable. The idea of music as a "scientific art," implicit in nearly all music criticism of the period, explains much of its dogmatism and error. It would, of course, be gross oversimplification to condemn a whole era for lack of critical acumen; the thinking of those who shaped its ideologies makes perfectly good sense in its historical setting. Harmonic analysis does not, however, have any pertinence today; in the 20th century, the music itself must serve as the basis for a fresh value judgment.

Some indubitably poor tunes were current, but an astonishingly large number seem to have been of greater intrinsic merit and expressiveness than most of those then being imported from Europe. If the tunes in the American idiom possessed no other virtue, they were certainly alive musically, unsophisticated and untrammeled by the "laws of musical science" which reduced much of orthodox church song to a dead level of mediocrity. And they still remain very much alive today.

IT IS my belief that the music that grew from the singing-school tradition has pertinence and significance in today's world and promise for tomorrow's. It is no mere historical curiosity, no mere recovered treasure-trove of a musical antiquarian. It is rather a new source from which our congregational song may perhaps draw inspiration, strength, and vigor. I am fully aware of the slowness with which changes occur in church song, and of the many practical and ideological difficulties which stand in the way of such changes. Congregational song is by its very nature conservative in tendency, and perhaps rightly so. But I do feel that, if our congregational song is to grow and maintain its vitality, those entrusted with the heritage—the clergy, the choir directors, the graduates of conservatories, the organists, the hymnal committees —must counteract this conservative tendency with genuine personal progressivism, and with minds receptive to change. Otherwise, stagnation in church song is inevitable.

The potential role of early American music in today's church song can be most clearly explained by analogy. English church song just before the turn of the 20th century had reached perhaps the lowest point, qualitatively speaking, in its long history. To quote Percy Dearmer, "the bulk of the tunes [in common use] illustrated a period of British music which the musicians of today are anxious to forget." From that low point, few will deny that English church song has improved until today it is hard to find its equal. To what can this flowering vitality be attributed? To my mind, the cause of the change was the addition of a new yet old leavening agent, the ancient body of national folk-song that had been rediscovered by Cecil Sharp, Ralph Vaughan Williams, and other leaders of the 20th-century renaissance in English music a decade or so before it made an appearance in English hymnals. It was this more than anything else that brought about the regeneration of English psalmody. Primarily because of the sensitive musicianship of those who adapted this music to the particular needs of the church (and I by no means underestimate the practical difficulty of this task), music from the folk tradition was successfully integrated into the main stream of English sacred song. The progress of this process of integration can be traced from its beginnings, in the *English Hymnal* of 1906, to maturity in *Songs of Praise*, certainly one of the great hymnals of our time. And by integration, I do not mean the quantitative number of British folk-tunes included by the editors, but rather the qualitative change that took place. In *Songs of Praise*, a folk quality pervades the entire book and lends it its distinctive character. This folk quality is found in many of the new and excellent hymn-tunes there introduced for the first time. The extent to which this revolution in church music has conquered may be gauged by the most recent edition of *Hymns Ancient and Modern* (once the very bastion of English Victorianism), in which this same folk quality is plainly evident.

The analogy should be fairly clear. In England, the catalyst appears to have been the national folk-song. In America, may not the catalyst well be our native church song, which encompasses that portion of the Anglo-Celtic heritage of folk-music that took root here, and adds to it something more? The similarities between the two traditions are too striking to require particular comment; it is surely enough to point out that early American music should have a unique and special importance for us, because it was born of the cultural traditions of our own land, and because it somehow reflects, in microcosm, our world, the New World, and its development.

APPENDICES

Appendix A

---※---

THE COMPLETE TEXT OF JOHN TUFTS'S
"Short Introduction to the Singing of Psalm-Tunes" (1726)

THE Tunes which follow are set down in such a plain and easy Method, that a few Rules may suffice for Direction in Singing of them.

The Letters F, S, L, M, mark'd on the several Lines and Spaces in the following Tunes, stand for these Syllables, viz. *Fa, Sol, La, Mi,* and are to shew you,

I. The Distance of the Notes one from another, or to give you the true Pitch of every Note. Therefore observe from *Mi* to *Fa,* and from *La* to *Fa* ascending; or, from *Fa* to *La,* and from *Fa* to *Mi* descending, are but Semi-tones, or half Notes. From *Fa* to *Sol,* from *Sol* to *La,* and from *La* to *Mi,* ascending; or, from *Mi* to *La,* from *La* to *Sol,* and from *Sol* to *Fa* descending, are Tones, or whole Notes.

Mi is the Principal Note, and the Notes rising gradually above *Mi,* are *Fa, Sol, La, Fa, Sol La,* and then *Mi* again: And the Notes falling gradually below *Mi,* are *La, Sol, Fa, La Sol, Fa,* and then comes Mi again, in every Eighth. For, as every Eighth Note gives the same Sound, so it has the same Letter and Name.

The Place of *Mi* is alter'd by *Flats* and *Sharps* put at the beginning of the five Lines on which the Tune is prick'd.

The natural Place for *Mi* is in the line which is called *B,* and there you will find it in the following Tunes, provided there be no Flats or Sharps at the beginning of the 5 lines, as in *Windsor,* &c. If you find a Flat mark'd thus (♭) in *B,* as in *London new,* then you shall find *Mi* stand in *E.* If there be a Flat in *B* & *E* too, as in *Manchester,* then is *Mi* in *A.* So also for *Sharps* mark'd thus (✕) [.] When you find a *Sharp* in *F,* as in *Canterbury,* then *Mi* is in *F.* If there be *Sharps* in *F* and *C* too, as in 148 Psalm Tune, then *Mi* stands in *C.* And if you find *Sharps* in *F, C* & *G,* as in 100 Psalm Tune, then *Mi* stands in *G.* And always remember, if *Mi* is in *B* in the *Treble,* it is also in *B* in the *Bass,* and *Medius,* for it is in the Letter of the same Name, in all Parts of the same Tune, altho' its Place may be varied to the Eye.

A *Flat* set over, or before any Note in the body of the Tune, signifies that That Note must be sung a Semi-tone or half Note lower than if there were no *Flat*. And on the contrary a *Sharp* signifies that the Note over which it is plac'd, must be sung half a Note higher than it should be if there were no such *Sharp*.

When a *Flat* is plac'd before that particular Note, which (had there been no *Flat*) ought to have been called *Mi*, you must call it *Fa*, altho' you have just descended from *Fa*. You will find an Example in the 148 Psalm-Tune.

A *Sharp* has influence upon several Notes adjoining in the *same line* or *space*, until you have a Note on some other line or space, or it be contradicted by a *Flat*. You have an Example of this in *Oxford* Tune.

II. These Letters will serve also to measure the *Length* of the Notes, or to show how long each Note is to be sounded. For Instance in Common Time, A Letter with two Points on the right side of it thus (F:) is to be sounded as long as you would be distinctly telling *One, Two, Three, Four*. A Letter with but One Point thus, (F.) is to be sounded while you are telling *One, Two*. A Letter without any Point thus (F) only half so long.

Where you find Two Letters tied together with a bow, thus (FF) they are to be sounded no longer than you would be singing a Letter without any Point; and to be Sung to one Syllable in the Psalms.

The Tunes in *Common Time,* are mark'd thus (C) at the beginning. Tripla (or *Triple*) *Time* Tunes are mark'd thus (3) at the beginning, and are sung about One Third swifter than Common Time.

There are two *Cliffs* made use of in the following Tunes.

The first of these is the *Bass Cliff* mark'd thus (ɔ:) and is proper to the lowest part of *Music,* and generally placed on the uppermost Line save one. Wherever that *Cliff* is found, the Line on which it stands is called F, and the *Lines* and *Spaces* ascend[ing] are G, A, B, &c. and descending are E, D, C, B, A, G, &c.

The second is the *Treble Cliff* mark'd thus, (gs) and is usually plac'd on the lowest Line but one. Wherever this is placed, call that Line G, & the *Lines* & *Spaces* ascending, A, B, C, D, E, F, and then comes G again; and descending F, E, D, &c.

A *Direct* (whose mark you will find among other Musical Characters in the first Page of the Tunes) you will find always at the end of the first 5 Lines of long Tunes, as in the 18 Psalm-Tune, &c. and is to inform you in what Line or Space your next Note stands, that you may more readily give it its proper sound.

Repeats, as you will find them mark'd in the 113 Psalm-Tune, are to shew that so much of the Tune as is included between those *Repeats* is to be *sung twice* before you proceed further.

The Comparison between the *Letters* made use of in the following Tunes, & the Musical Characters commonly used in Psalmody, may be of advantage to some.

A few Lessons are next plac'd to assist in *Raising* & *Falling* of Notes, either Gradual or by Leaps; the *Ground-work* of all good Singing, & is not to be attained ordinarily, without the help of some skilful Person, or of an Instrument. But being attained, and observing the few foregoing Rules, you will be able to leap with your Voice from one Note to another, as they occur in their various Distances, and with a little Practice, to sing all the Tunes in this Book [1] in any of their parts, with Ease and Pleasure.

1. In the 7th and subsequent editions, the phrase "or other prick'd after this method" was here inserted. This appears to be almost incontrovertible evidence that other collections making use of Tufts's letter notation (unknown to us today) were in circulation before 1728. It also supports the speculation that the collection described in the June 27/July 4, 1726 issue of the Boston *Gazette* was *not* an announcement of a forthcoming 5th edition of Tufts's *Introduction.*

Appendix B

—————— ≫≫ ≪≪ ——————

The Easy Instructor: (1801-1831):
A CHECK-LIST OF EDITIONS AND ISSUES

THIS CHECK-LIST is an attempted solution to one of the most complex bibliographical problems in the entire range of American printing history. It cannot be presumed that all the snarls have been completely untangled and all the booby-traps hidden in the jungle of *Easy Instructor* editions and issues have been circumnavigated, but it is fairly certain that the chronology of editions located has been accurately established, and exact dates of publication (within one year) have been ascertained. The solution of the problem is of more than bibliographical interest. With each printing dated and placed in proper chronological order, *The Easy Instructor* becomes an extremely accurate barometer of musical tastes in one area of the country over a period of nearly three decades. The tale told by the addition of one tune and the deletion of another is invaluable, highly detailed documentation of a significant, through much neglected aspect of our cultural development.

Two bibliographical studies of *The Easy Instructor* have previously appeared in print: one by Frank J. Metcalf [1] and the other by Lester Condit.[2] The Metcalf study, although fragmentary and based on incomplete data, is quite valuable; those interested in comparing his results with those arrived at here should consult

1. "*The Easy Instructor:* a Bibliographical Study," *Musical Quarterly,* XXIII (1937), 89–97.
2. "Editions of Little & Smith's *Easy Instructor,*" *Papers of the Bibl. Soc. of Amer.,* XL (1946), 233–36.

Table XIII, where the numbers assigned to the editions examined by Metcalf are listed in conjunction with the letters assigned in this study.

In the following list, each edition is assigned a letter in accordance with the chronology of its publication. Separate printings which embody no special changes of title, imprint, or content have been defined as issues of a given edition and are indicated by combining a lower case italic letter with that assigned the edition (e.g., A*a*, A*b*). Unless otherwise indicated, omitted titles and imprints or various sections thereof may be presumed to be the same as those of the edition or issue next above. Except for NeWsMMF (Moravian Music Foundation, Winston-Salem, N.C.), location symbols are those used by the National Union Catalog at the Library of Congress. Capitalization of initial letters has been followed exactly, but no attempt has been made to indicate original typography; however, reference is made to the method of printing (i.e., whether from engraved plates or from type). Title pages of key editions have been reproduced in facsimile. Although dozens of points of distinction among editions and issues were ascertained and tabulated in preparing the chronology given below, only those unique points are given which may serve to identify a particular edition or issue easily. Special attention is called to the eight tables, which are designed to give comparative data succinctly. Table VI distinguishes all undated typographically printed editions, and Table XIII is a conspectus of all editions and issues. Since William Smith's *The Easy Instructor, Part II* is a completely separate work, its two editions are not included in this list.

EDITION A*a*: [see Illus. 22] The Easy Instructor, or A New method of teaching Sacred Harmony. Containing the Rudiments of Music on an improved plan, wherein the naming and timing the notes are familiarized to the weakest capacity.—With a choice collection of Psalm Tunes and Anthems from the most celebrated Authors, with a number composed in Europe and America, entirely new; suited to all the metres sung in the different Churches in the United States.

Published for the use of singing Societies in general, but more particularly for those who have not the advantage of an Instructor. By William Little & William Smith Copy right secured according to Act of Congress. [Philadelphia, 1801]

[2], 105 (i.e., 106) pp. No. 12 is repeated in the paging. T.–p. and pp. 12*b*–105 engraved; pp. [1]–12*a* typeset. 14 x 23.5 cm. CtHC.

This issue may readily be distinguished from Ed. A*b* by the presence of a printed key signature of A major on p. 87, at the beginning of Daniel Read's tune STAFFORD. A notice of the publication appears in the *Philadelphia Repository and Weekly Register,* August 22, 1801.

EDITION A*b*: [same] [New York: G & R. Waite, 1802]

CtHT–W, DLC, MWA, RPB.

This issue, otherwise identical to A*a,* lacks the key signature on p. 87 referred to above. Apparently, the signature was originally engraved as an oversight and later expunged from the plate. It shows through faintly in the DLC copy. Other key signatures may be found in both issues only in Morgan's *Judgment Anthem,* pp. 99–105, and Babcock's ADMONITION, pp. 63–64. Advertised as just published in the New York *Chronicle Express,* November 25, 1802.

EDITION B: [see Illus. 23] . . . By William Little and William Smith. Albany: Printed by Charles R. and George Webster, and Daniel Steele, Proprietors of the Copy-right; and sold at Webster's Bookstore, corner of State and Pearl-Streets, and at Steele's Bookstore, near the Court-House, in Court-Street. 1805.

108 pp. T.–p. and pp. [2]–12 typeset; pp. 13–108 engraved. 13.5 x 23 cm. NN.

The engraver's signature, "Snyder Sculp," appears at the foot of p. 108.

EDITION C.: . . . Smith. Albany: Printed by Websters & Skinner, and Daniel Steele, Proprietors of the Copy-Right; and sold at their respective Bookstores at the corner of State and Pearl-Streets, and near the Court-House, in Court-Street. 1806.

108 pp. T.–p and pp. [2]–12 typset; pp. 13–108 engraved. MWA, NcWsMMF(2).

EDITION D*a*: . . . Albany: . . . Pearl-Streets, and a few Doors South of the Court-House, in Court-Street. 1807.

108 (i.e., 104) pp. Nos. 9–12 are omitted in the paging because smaller type was used to print the introductory matter. T.–p. and pp. 13–108 engraved; pp. [2]–8 typeset. NjR, NcWsMMF.

This is the last edition in which the full phrase, "which is submitted to," appears immediately preceding the names of Edward Stammers and Richard T. Leech at the foot of p. [3].

EDITION D*b*: [same]

DLC, ICN, MWA, NjR, NN, WaU.

This issue, otherwise identical with D*a*, has a new type set-up for the introductory matter which may quickly be identified by the absence of the word "to" from the phrase on p. [3] referred to above and by the presence of a misprint "INSTUCTOR" in the caption on p. 7.

EDITION E: . . . Albany: . . . 1808.

108 (i.e., 104) pp., as D*a–b*. CtHT-W, IU, MWA, NcWsMMF; NNUT.

EDITION F: [see Illus. 24] . . . Containing I. The Rudiments of Music . . . II. A choice Collection of Psalm Tunes . . . Printed, Typographically, at Albany, By Websters & Skinner and Daniel Steele, (Proprietors of the Copy-Right,) And sold at their respective Bookstores, at the corner of State and Pearl-Streets, and a few doors south of the Old City-Hall, in Court-Street; by T. & J. Swords, Evert Duyckinck and William Falconer, New-York; Mathew Carey, Johnson & Warner, William W. Woodward and Hopkins & Earl, Philadelphia; and Increase Cook, New Haven. [1809]

104 pp.; typeset. 13.5 x 23 cm. See Tables VI and VII. DLC, MiU-C, NcWsMMF, NN.

At foot of p. 104: "Van Benthuysen & Wood, Typographers." In this and all succeeding editions, the music is printed from type. Obadiah R. Van Benthuysen and William Wood advertised the establishment of their firm in the Albany *Register* of November 2, 1807; in the May 15,

Table VI

A CONDENSED IDENTIFICATION CHART FOR UNDATED ALBANY EDITIONS

• 104-PAGE EDITIONS •

		Title page points	
Edition		*Typographer*	*Last dealer's name*
F	[1809]	none	Increase Cook
G	[1810]	Van Benthuysen & Newton	Increase Cook
H	[1810]	Van Benthuysen & Newton	M. Cary [sic]
I	[1811]	O. R. Van Benthuysen	D. Allenson & Co.

• 112-PAGE EDITIONS •

		Title page points		*Other points*	
Edition		*Typographer*	*Last dealer's name*	*Page 61**	*Page 81*
J	[1812]	O. R. Van Benthuysen	E. Lewis	Salisbury	Judgment Anthem
K	[1813]	Packard & Van Benthuysen	E. Lewis	Salisbury	Judgment Anthem
L	[1813]	Packard & Van Benthuysen	William Norman	under "n"*	Judgment Anthem
Ma	[1814]	Packard & Van Benthuysen	E. Lewis	under "m"	Judgment Anthem
Mb	[1814]	Packard & Van Benthuysen	E. Lewis	under "e"	Judgment Anthem
Mc	[1815]	Packard & Van Benthuysen	E. Lewis	before "D"	Judgment Anthem
N	[1815]	Packard & Van Benthuysen	E. Lewis	between "n" and "m"	Judgment Anthem
Oa	[1816]	Packard & Van Benthuysen	E. Lewis	between "n" and "m"	New York
Ob	[1816]	Packard & Van Benthuysen	E. Lewis	under "D"	New York

Edition

• 120-PAGE EDITION •

P	[1817]	There is only one edition of 120 pages

• 127, [1]-PAGE EDITIONS: "REVISED AND ENLARGED" •

	Title page points			Other points
Edition	Steele's firm name	Steele's address	Page [3]†	Miscellaneous
Q [1817]	Daniel Steele	472 S. Market St.	roman	Anthm [sic], p. 89
R [1818]	Daniel Steele	472 S. Market St.	roman	Endfield [sic], p. 23
T [1819]	Daniel Steele	472 S. Market St.	roman	Armeley [sic], p. 41
V [1820]	Daniel Steele	472 S. Market St.	italic	Armley, p. 41
X [1822]	Daniel Steele	435 S. Market St.	italic	Armley, p. 41
Ya [1824]	D. Steele & Son	437 S. Market St.	italic	Armley, p. 41
Yb [1826]	D. Steele & Son	437 S. Market St.	roman	Armley, p. 41
AA [1830]	Oliver Steele	437 S. Market St.	roman	Armley, p. 41

* On page 61 of Eds. L-0b the continuation of the tune DENMARK appears; the point listed under "Page 61" indicates where the first letter of the word "soft" is printed in relationship to the various letters in DENMARK.

† The phrase "Philadelphia, August 15, 1708" appears in the middle of page [3] of the 127, [1]-page editions; the point listed under "Page [3]" refers to the typeface in which the phrase is printed.

1810, issue of the Albany *Gazette,* the following notice (dated May 8, 1810) appears:

> The Co-Partnership of Van Benthuysen & Wood being dissolved, and Mr. Wood having disposed of his right to Mr. George Newton, the business in the future will be conducted under the firm of Van Benthuysen & Newton at the Sign of the Bible, in Court-Street.

Of the booksellers mentioned, Hopkins & Earl of Philadelphia went into business on February 15, 1808, and continued only through February 1, 1810. Ed. F must therefore have been published between these two dates, and since Ed. E appeared in 1808, probably was released in 1809. It may, however, have been the "new edition" advertised in the Albany *Balance & New-York State Journal* as "just published" on February 6, 1810.

Table VII

CONTENT CHANGES IN 104-PAGE EDITIONS

Page	F	G *and* H	I
34	Southwell	Mount Sion	. . . .
35	Sherburne	Williamstown	. . . .
38	Caldwell, Williamstown	Sherburne	. . . .
70	Babel, Plymouth	. . . .	Concord . . . .
93	23rd Psalm, 29th Psalm	. . . .	Arnheim, *Arlington
100	Crucifixion	. . . .	*Newark
101	(cont.), *Newmark	*	*Columbia * . . . .

* Of European origin.

EDITION G: . . . Albany, . . . by T. & J. Swords, Everet [sic] Duyckinck and William Falconer, New-York; Wm. J. M'Cartee, Schenectady; A. Seward, Utica; Tracy & Bliss, Lansingburgh; Parker & Bliss, Troy; and Increase Cook, New-Haven. Van Benthuysen & Newton, Typographers. [1810]

104 pp.; typeset. See Tables VI and VII. CtHC, DLC, ICN, MWA, N, NcWsMMF, NjR, NNUT (2), RPB.

Could not have been issued before May 8, 1810, when Van Benthuysen & Newton went into business.

EDITION H: . . . Albany, . . . Troy; Increase Cook, New-Haven; and M. Cary [sic], Philadelphia. Van Benthuysen & Newton, Typographers. [1810]

104 pp.; typeset. See Tables VI and VII. ICN(2), MiU-C.

While it is theoretically possible that Ed. H could have been issued in 1811, since George Newton did not die until November 20 of that year, it is more likely that it appeared in the previous year in view of the fact that E. Lewis (mentioned for the first time in the list of agents for Ed. I) apparently was in business for himself in Newburgh only after January, 1811. Furthermore, M. Car[e]y of Philadelphia, here listed for the first time, sent a receipt to the firm of Websters & Skinner for books received on November 29, 1810, according to the Carey papers.

EDITION I: . . . Albany, . . . New-Haven,; [sic] M. Cary [sic], Philadelphia; J. Bogert, Geneva; J. D. Bemis, Canandaigua; P. Potter, Poughkeepsie; E. Lewis, Newburgh, [sic, comma] and D. Allenson & Co. [sic, no comma] Burlington, N.J. O. R. Van Benthuysen, Typographer. [1811]

104 pp.; typeset. See Tables VI and VII. ICN, N, NcWsMMF.

Table VIII

CONTENT CHANGES IN 112-PAGE EDITIONS

Page	J	K	L	M*abc*	N	O*ab*
16	Whitestown	....	....	....	°Dalston, °Martyrs	°........ °........
24	Calvary, °Mear	.... °........	°Mear, °Evening Hymn	°........ °........	°........ °........	°........ °........
34	Mt. Sion	....	°Tunbridge	°........	°........	°........
35	(cont.), Williams- town	....	Williams- town, °Pleyel's	.... °........	.... °........	..·..... °........
39	Sharon	....	°St. Asaph's	°........	°........	°........
42	Grafton	°Bethesda	°........	°........	°........	°........
43	(cont.), Coronation	Coronation Sutton	....	....	....	....
53	Stratfield	....	....	....	°Portugal, °Hymn	°........ °........

Page	J	K	L	Mabc	N	Oab
57	Ballstown	....	....	....	°Pelham	°........
61	Salisbury	....	°Denmark	°........	°........	°........
62	Lena	....	°(cont.)	°........	°........	°........
64	Rome	....	....	....	°Sunday, °Bedford	°........ °........
65	Judgment	....	....	°Pleyel's 2d	°........	°........
68	Berne	....	Lena			
69	Providence	....	Salisbury	....	New Jordan	....
71	Brentwood, °Bangor	.... °........	.... °........	°Bangor, °Salem	°........ °........	°........ °........
77	Heavenly Vision (cont.)	....	.... °Portugal	.... °........	.... °Irish	.... °........
81– 84	Judgment Anthem	....	....	....	....	°New York
85	(cont.)	....	....	....	....	°(cont.), °Munich
86	(cont.)	....	....	....	....	°Musick
87	(cont.)	....	....	....	....	°German
88	(cont.)	....	....	....	....	°Green's 100, °Dunchurch
92	°Piermont	°........	°........	°Portsmouth	°........	°........
95	Westminster	....	°Rutland	°........	°........	°........
96	Exhortation	....	....	°Portuguese Hymn	°........	°........
97	Milton	....	....	°Plympton	°........	°........
98	Christian Song	....	°Ashley China,	°........	°........	°........
99	(cont.), China	....	°Bethel	....	....	....
101	Columbia, °Newmark	.... °........	.... °........	°New-mark, °St. Thomas	°........	°........
105	°Pleyel's, °Silver St.	°........ °........	°Silver St.	°........	°........	°........
110	Winter, Funeral Thought	....	....	°St. Michael's	°........	°........

° Of European origin.

Condit (see fn. 2 above) reports an edition identical with Ed. I except that the name of M. Carey [Cary] is missing from the list of booksellers. The author has been unable to locate such an edition. As the title page is incorrectly transcribed in other respects, the omission of the bookseller's name may perhaps have been an oversight or a typographical error.

EDITION J: . . . Albany, By Websters & Skinners and Daniel Steele, . . . Duyckinck [sic, no comma] New-York; Wm. J. M'Cartee, . . . E. Lewis, Newburgh. O. R. Van Benthuysen, Typographer. [1812]

112 pp.; typeset. See Tables VI and VIII. RPB.
Perhaps issued as early as 1811, since the Websters & Skinners firm was in existence when George Newton died on November 11 of that year. However, if Ed. I appeared in 1811, it must have come out after that date, and it is not very likely that two editions so radically different could have been published within less than two months of each other. An 1812 date seems more reasonable.

EDITION K: . . . Albany, . . . Evert Duyckinck, New-York; . . . Packard & Van Benthuysen, Typographers. [1813]

112 pp.; typeset. See Tables VI and VIII. DLC, ICN, OCHP.
The firm of Packard & Van Benthuysen was not established until 1813.

EDITION L: . . . Albany, . . . New-York; A. Seward, Utica; Tracy & Bliss, Lansingburgh; Parker & Bliss and Solomon Wilber, Jun. [sic, no comma] Troy; Increase Cook, New-Haven; Matthew Cary [sic], Philadelphia; J. Bogert, Geneva; J. D. Bemis, Canandaigua; P. Potter, Poughkeepsie; William E. Norman, Hudson. Packard & Van Benthuysen, Typographers. [1813]

112 pp.; typeset. See Tables VI and VIII. MWA, MiU-C, NN, NcWsMMF.
Solomon Wilber, Jun., mentioned among the agents here for the first time, was in Troy only until 1813.

EDITION Ma: . . . Albany, . . . New-York; Riggs & Stevens, Schenectady; A. Seward, Utica; Tracy & Bliss, Lansingburgh;

Parker & Bliss, Troy; M. Carey, Philadelphia; . . . Poughkeepsie; E. Lewis, Newburgh. Packard & Van Benthuysen, Typographers. [1814]

112 pp.; typeset. See Tables VI, VIII, and IX. CBB (2), DLC, ICN (2), MWA, (2), NcWsMMF, NN, NNUT, RPB.

Riggs & Stevens, mentioned among the agents here for the first time, began business in Schenectady on July 16, 1814, and advertised "Smith & Little's singing book for sale" in the Schenectady *Cabinet* of August 10, 1814.

EDITION M*b*: [same, except comma omitted after "T. & J. Swords"] [1814]

See Tables VI, VIII, and IX. CtHT-W, MBC, N.

EDITION M*c*: [same] [1815]

See Tables VI, VIII, and IX. CtHC, MWA.

EDITION N: [same] [1815]

112 pp.; typeset. See Tables VI, VIII, and IX. N, NcWsMMF, NN, NNS, RPB.

EDITION O*a*: [same] [1816]

112 pp.; typeset. See Tables VI, VIII, and X. MB, N, NcWsMMF, NNUT.

EDITION O*b*: [same] [1816]

See Tables VI, VIII, and X. MWA (2), NcWsMMF.

Table IX

COMPARISON OF ISSUES, EDITION M

Page	Points	Ma	Mb	Mc
17	Last two words, upper line of text, "Sutton"	Surprize, And	Surprize, And	Surprise [*sic*], and
61	First letter of word "soft" in relation to letters in "Denmark"	under "m"	under "e"	before "D"

EDITION P: [see Illus. 25] . . . The Music Types used in printing this Book are secured to the Proprietors by Patent Right. Albany: Printed for Websters & Skinners and Daniel Steele, (Proprietors,) And sold at their respective Book-Stores, at the corner of State and Pearl-streets, and at No. 472 South Market-street [sic]; by T. & J. Swords, E. Duyckinck, Collins & Co. and D. Smith, New-York; M. Carey, B. Warner, W. W. Woodward and A. Small, Philadelphia; J. Cushing, Baltimore; H. Howe, New-Haven; Wells & Lily, Boston; G. Goodwin & Sons, Hartford; P. Potter, Poughkeepsie; B. F. Lewis, Newburgh; E. Norman, Hudson; Parker & Bliss, Troy; Tracy & Bliss, Lansingburgh; Dodd & Stevens, Salem; H. Stevens, Schenectady; W. Williams, Utica; J. Bogert, Geneva; J. D. Bemis, Canandaigua; Skinner & Crosby, Auburn; S. H. & H. A. Salisbury, Buffalo. Packard & Van Benthuysen, Printers. [1817]

120 pp.; typeset. CtHT-W, DLC (2), MWA, MiU, NcWsMMF. PPeSchw, RPB, SCU.

This is evidently the earliest edition printed after the lapse, on December 10, 1816, of the original New York copyright, which ran for 14 years; a patent notice is substituted for the copyright notice appearing on the title pages of previous editions. A patent on the casting and use of the shape-note types was issued to George Webster, of the firm of Websters & Skinners, on February 28, 1816. The original notice of the patent was apparently destroyed in one of the fires which ravaged the U.S. Patent Office early in its history, and so no details as to the exact nature of the patent are available. See also Eds. S, U, and W, which are derivatives of this edition, apparently printed by license of the holders of the patent.

EDITION Q: [see Illus. 26] Revised and Enlarged Edition. The Easy Instructor; . . . The Music Types of this Book, as to casting and using, are secured by Patent Right to George Webster, of the city of Albany. Rights to make or use them may be obtained of him. Albany: Printed for Websters & Skinners and Daniel Steele, And sold at their respective Book-Stores, at the corner of State and Pearl-streets, and at No. 472 South Market-street. Packard & Van Benthuysen, Printers. [1817]

127, [1] pp.; typeset. See Table XI. CLU, DLC, MdBJ, NcWsMMF. This edition was advertised as "just published" in the Albany *Gazette & Daily Advertiser* on November 6, 1817.

EDITION R: [same] [1818]

127, [1] pp.; typeset. See Table XI. CSU, MHi, N, NcWsMMF, NHi, NN.

EDITION S: [text of title page same as Ed. P through "Patent Right," then:] Utica: Printed by William Williams, No. 60, Genesee Street. 1818.

126, [1] pp.; typeset. CtY, DLC, ICN (2), MH, MWA, NcWsMMF, OClWHi.

EDITION T: [same as Ed. Q] [1819]

127, [1] pp.; typeset. See Table XI. ICN, NcWsMMF.

Table X

COMPARISON OF ISSUES, EDITION O

Page	Points	Oa	Ob
61	In line beginning, "The Committee . . ."	URANIAN SOCIETY	URANIAN SNCIETY [*sic*]
5	First word, second line	ample	the
	Last word on page	of	ensue
[4]	First letter of word "soft" in relation to	between "n" and "m"	under "D"
[3]	letters in "Denmark"		

EDITION U: [text of title page same as Ed. P through "the advantage of an instructor," then:] By Little and Smith. Cincinnati: Printed by J. Pace, No. 106, Main-Street. 1819.

112 pp.; typeset. OC.

EDITION V: [same as Eds. Q and T, except that "Sacred Harmony" is printed in shadowed rather than plain black letter [1820]

127, [1] pp.; typeset. See Table XI. ICU, MiU-C, NcWsMMF.

Table XI

CONTENT CHANGES IN 127, [1]-PAGE EDITIONS

Page	Q	R	T, V, X-AA
20	New Durham, Invitation	*Gilboa	*........
21	Mortality, *Wells	*Wells, *Brighthelmstone	*........ *........
22	Ocean	*Blendon, *Messiah	*........ *........
38	Sherburne	*Christmas, *Chelmsford	*Dundee, *........
45	Delight	*Pensance	*........
102	Exhortation	*Arundel, *St. Ann's	*........ *........

---

* Of European origin.

EDITION W: [same as Ed. S, except that the date has been changed to:] 1820.

126, [1] pp.; typeset. CtY, MWA, N, NN, OClWHi.

EDITION X: [same as Ed. V, except that Daniel Steele's address is given as 435 South Market-street] [1822]

127, [1] pp.; typeset. See Table XI. ICN, MWA.
Daniel Steele was at the street address given in this edition only between April and September, 1822.

EDITION Y*a*: [same as Ed. X, except that the imprint reads:] . . . and D. Steele & Son, . . . and at No. 437 South Market-street. . . . [1824]

127, [1] pp.; typeset. See Tables XI and XII. MnU, MWA.

EDITION Y*b*: [same] [1826]

See Tables XI and XII. CtHT-W, NcWsMMF, OClWHi.

EDITION Z: [same, except that the imprint reads:] . . . and Oliver Steele . . . 1828.

127, [1] pp.; typeset. See Table XI. DLC, MWA, N, NcWsMMF, NNUT.

EDITION AA: [same, except that the imprint is without date] [1830]

127, [1] pp.; typeset. See Table XI. DLC.

EDITION BB: [same, except that the imprint is dated:] 1831.

135, [1] pp.; typeset. MWA, N, NcWsMMF.

An extra signature of music has been added to this, the last edition of *The Easy Instructor*.

Table XII

COMPARISON OF ISSUES, EDITION Y

Page	Points	Ya	Yb
4	First word, second line	ample	example
5	Last word on page	of	persons
61	First letter of word "soft" in relation to letters in "Denmark"	under "D"	before "D"

Table XIII

CONSPECTUS OF EDITIONS AND ISSUES

Edition	Place if other than Albany	Metcalf number	Pages	Number of musical compositions			
				Indexed	Actually printed	Of Amer. origin	Of Eur. origin
Aa [1801]	[Philadelphia]		[2], 105 (i.e., 106)	105	105	100	5
Ab [1802]	[New York]	A	[2], 105 (i.e., 106)	105	105	100	5
B 1805			108	102	102	88	14
C 1806		3	108	102	102	88	14

Edition	Place if other than Albany	Metcalf number	Pages	Number of musical compositions			
				Indexed	Actually printed	Of Amer. origin	Of Eur. origin
Da 1807			108 (i.e., 104)	102	102	88	14
Db 1807		4	108 (i.e., 104)	102	102	88	14
E 1808		5	108 (i.e., 104)	102	102	88	14
F [1809]		6	104	95	95	76	19
G [1810]		7	104	94	94	75	19
H [1810]			104	94	94	75	19
I [1811]		8	104	95	95	73	22
J [1812]		10	112	106	105	75	30
K [1813]		11	112	107	106	75	31
L [1813]		12	112	107	106	68	38
Ma [1814]		13	112	104	105	61	44
Mb [1814]			112	104	105	61	44
Mc [1815]			112	104	105	61	44
N [1815]		15	112	107	108	57	51
Oa [1816]			112	111	113	56	57
Ob [1816]		14	112	111	113	56	57
P [1817]		16	120	124	125	50	75
Q [1817]		17	127, [1]	139	139	34	105
R [1818]			127, [1]	141	141	27	114
S 1818	Utica	22	126, [1]	127	127	49	78
T [1819]			127, [1]	141	141	27	114
U 1819	Cincinnati		112	111	112	49	63
V [1820]			127, [1]	141	141	27	114
W 1820	Utica	23	126, [1]	127	127	49	78
X [1822]		18	127, [1]	141	141	27	114
Ya [1824]		19	127, [1]	141	141	27	114
Yb [1826]			127, [1]	141	141	27	114
Z 1828		20	127, [1]	142	141	27	114
AA [1830]			127, [1]	142	141	27	114
BB 1831		21	135, [1]	142	153	27	126

The Easy Instructor, or

A New method of teaching Sacred Harmony.

Containing the Rudiments of Music on an improved plan, wherein the naming and timing the notes are familiarized to the weakest capacity.— With a choice collection of Psalm Tunes and Anthems from the most celebrated Authors, with a number composed in Europe and America, entirely new; suited to all the metres sung in the different Churches in the United States.

Published for the use of singing Societies in general, but more particularly for those who have not the advantage of an Instructor.

By William Little & William Smith

Copy right secured according to Act of Congress.

22. Edition A*a*. Title page of the 1801 edition of *The Easy Instructor*. Courtesy of the Case Memorial Library, Hartford Seminary Foundation.

THE EASY INSTRUCTOR,

OR, A NEW METHOD OF TEACHING

SACRED HARMONY.

CONTAINING,

The Rudiments of Music on an improved Plan, wherein the Naming and Timing of the Notes are familiarized to the weakest Capacity.

With a choice Collection of Psalm Tunes and Anthems from the most celebrated Authors, with a Number composed in Europe and America, entirely new ; suited to all the Metres sung in the different Churches in the United States.

Published for the use of Singing Societies in general, but more particularly for those who have not the advantage of an Instructor.

By WILLIAM LITTLE AND WILLIAM SMITH.

ALBANY:

Printed by CHARLES R. and GEORGE WEBSTER, and DANIEL STEELE, Proprietors of the Copy-right ; and sold at WEBSTER's Bookstore, corner of State and Pearl Streets, and at STEELE's Bookstore, near the Court House, in Court Street.

1805.

23. Edition B. Courtesy of the New York Public Library.

24. Edition F. Courtesy of the Clements Library, University of Michigan.

25. Edition P. Courtesy of the General Library, University of Michigan.

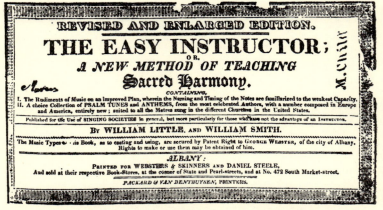

26. Edition Q. Courtesy of the Library of Congress

Appendix C

————— →»» «« ————

A CHECK-LIST OF WRITINGS ABOUT MUSIC IN THE PERIODICALS OF AMERICAN TRANSCENDENTALISM (1835 - 50)

Key

AesP   *Aesthetic Papers* (1849)

BQRe   *The Boston Quarterly Review* (1838-42)

Dial   *The Dial* (1840-44)

Harb   *The Harbinger* (1845-49)

Pres   *The Present* (1843-44)

SpiA   *The Spirit of the Age* (1849-50)

WMes   *The Western Messenger* (1835-41)

1. Anonymous. "Berlioz," *Harb* II, 15 (Mar. 21. 1846), 239–40. Translated from *Deutsche Schnellpost*.
2. ————. "Fanny Cerito in Berlin," *Harb* II, 24 (May 23, 1846), 383–84.
3. ————. "Fanny Elssler in Venice," *Harb* II, 24 (May 23, 1846), 384. Translated from *Deutsche Schnellpost*.
4. ————. "Felicien David," *Harb II,* 19 (Apr. 18, 1846), 304. Translated from *Deutsche Schnellpost*.
5. ————. "Felix Mendelssohn Bartholdy," *Harb* VI, 10 (Jan. 8, 1848), 74–75. From the London *Sunday Times*.
6. ————. "Fourierist Festival in Boston," *SpiA* II, 17 (Apr. 27, 1850), 268–69. Full details of music programs.
7. ————. "Germania Musical Association," *Harb* VII, 26 (Oct. 28, 1848), 204.
8. ————. "Gluck's Monument," *Harb* III, 14 (Sept. 12, 1846), 224.

Translated from *Deutsche Schnellpost.*

9. ———. "Jenny Lind," *Harb* II, 15 (Mar. 21, 1846), 236.
Translated from *Deutsche Schnellpost.*

10. ———. "Jenny Lind," *Harb* II, 19 (Apr. 18, 1846), 303–04.
Translated from *Deutsche Schnellpost.*

11. ———. "Jenny Lind," *Harb* III, 4 (July 4, 1846), 64.
Translated from *Deutsche Schnellpost.*

12. ———. "Jenny Lind," *Harb* III, 5 (July 11, 1846), 83–84.
Translated from *Deutsche Schnellpost.*

13. ———. "Jenny Lind and the Mesmerist," *Harb* V, 20 (Oct. 23, 1847), 309.
From the Manchester *Courier.*

14. ———. "John Simon Mayer," *Harb* II, 24 (May 23, 1846), 384.
An obituary notice translated from the *Deutsche Schnellpost.*

15. ———. "The Juvenile Choirs of Harmony," *Harb* IV, 4 (Jan. 2, 1847), 61–62.
Contains long quotations from Lydia Maria Child. See also No. 26.

16. ———. "Madam Bishop and Bochsa," *Harb* V, 15 (Sept. 18, 1847), 235.
A review of the concert.

17. ———. "Mason's Sacred Harp," *WMes* VIII, 7 (Sept. 1840), 334.
A laudatory review of the "second volume of this work" by T. B. Mason, Cincinnati teacher and brother of Lowell Mason.

18. ———. "Music in Germany," *Harb* IV, 9 (Feb. 6, 1847), 138–40.
Several long letters from an unidentified correspondent in Leipzig.

19. ———. "A Newly Discovered Composition of Mozart," *Harb* II, 18 (Apr. 11, 1846), 287.
Song, "The Nose." Translated from *Deutsche Schnellpost.*

20. ———. "Norma in Boston," *Harb* I, 22 (Nov. 8, 1845), 348–49.
Bellini's opera as performed by the Seguins.

21. ———. "Ostyak Music," *Harb* VII, 10 (July 8, 1848), 75.
From Erman's *Travels in Siberia.*

22. ———. "A Virtuoso on the French Horn," *Harb* II, 16 (Mar. 28, 1846), 256.
Translated from *Deutsche Schnellpost.*

23. ———. "Weigl the Composer," *Harb* II, 18 (Apr. 11, 1846), 287.
An obituary translated from the *Deutsche Schnellpost.*

24. B., D. W. "Musical Queries," *Harb* VIII, 3 (Nov. 18, 1848), 22–23.
A letter from Newburyport, Mass. dated Nov. 12, 1848, about a point in musical theory. Answered by Dwight in No. 51.

25. Bradbury, William B. "Vocal Music in Germany—How Taught," *SpiA* II, 7 (Feb. 16, 1850), 102.
From the *Commercial Advertiser.*

26. Brisbane, Albert. "The Viennese Children," *Harb* IV, 13 (Mar. 6, 1847), 206–07.
    See also No. 15.
27. C. "Church Music," *WMes* I, 2 (Aug. 1835), 134–38; I, 3 (Sept. 1835), 172–74; I, 8 (Feb. 1836), 572–75.
28. C., S. C. "Leaves from a Journal," *WMes* III, 1 (Feb. 1837), 479–81; III, 3 (Apr. 1837), 590–93; III, 4 (May 1837), 665–68.
    Kept by a visitor to Colombia. Contains frequent references to music, including a description of the festival of "La Concepcion" held in New Grenada on Dec. 20, 1833.
29. Channing, W. E. "Popular Amusements From an Address on Temperance," *WMes* IV, 5 (Jan. 1838), 343–49.
    Contains sections on music, dancing, and the theater.
30. Clarke, J. F. "Chapel Hymn Book," *WMes* IV, 5 (Jan. 1838), 353.
    A brief review.
31. ———. "Children's Concert," *WMes* VI, 4 (Feb. 1839), 287–88.
    Describes a concert at the Louisville Unitarian Church on Jan. 14, 1839.
32. ———. "Concert for the Poor," *WMes* VI, 4 (Feb. 1839), 288.
    Describes a sacred concert held in the Louisville Unitarian Church, undated.
33. ———. "Unitarian Church, Louisville, Ky.," *WMes* VI, 4 (Feb. 1839), 284–85.
    Describes music activities in the Sunday school and names the teachers. Embellished by a cut of the church.
34. Cranch, C. P. "The Concert and the Church," *WMes* VI, 5 (Mar. 1839), 339–41.
    A defence of T. B. Mason.
35. ———. "Music in New York," *Harb* I, 4 (July 5, 1845), 59–60.
    Philharmonic Society concerts; the Italian opera company; Ole Bull.
36. ———. "On the Ideal in Art," *Harb* I, 11 (Aug. 23, 1845), 170–71.
    A paper read at a meeting of the Art Re-union in New York in July, 1845. Numerous musical analogies.
37. ———. "Parable VI," *WMes* VI, 4 (Feb. 1839), 269–70.
    A "Transcendental" musical fable.
38. Curtis, George W. "De Meyer in New York," *Harb* II, 11 (Feb. 21, 1846), 173–74.
39. ———. "The Italian Opera in New York," *Harb* V, 9 (Aug. 7, 1847), 136–39.
40. ———. "Music and Ole Bull," *Pres* I, 11–12 (Apr. 1, 1844), 404–10.
41. ———. "Music in New York," *Harb* I, 26 (Dec. 6, 1845), 412–13.
    Philharmonic Society concerts.

42. ———. "Music in New York—No. II," *Harb* II, 9 (Feb. 7, 1846),
          139–40.

43. ———. "Music in New York," *Harb* II, 15 (Mar. 21, 1846),
          235–36.
          Kalliwoda, Cherubini, Weber, Mozart.

44. Dana, Charles A. "The Italian Opera," *Harb* VI, 10 (Jan. 8, 1848),
          78.

45. ———. "The Italian Opera," *Harb* VI, 18 (Mar. 4, 1848), 143.

46. ———. "The Italian Opera in New York," *Harb* VI, 9 (Jan. 1,
          1848), 70.

47. ———. "The Opera at Astor Place," *Harb* VI, 4 (Nov. 27, 1847),
          30.
          Verdi's *Ernani.*

48. ———. "The Opera at Astor Place," *Harb* VI, 12 (Jan. 22, 1848),
          94.

49. ———. "The Opera at Astor Place," *Harb* VI, 13 (Jan. 29, 1848),
          101.

50. ———. "The Opera at Astor Place," *Harb* VI, 16 (Feb. 19, 1848),
          126.

51. Dwight, J. S. "Answer to 'Musical Queries,'" *Harb* VIII, 9 (Dec.
          30, 1848), 70.
          See No. 24.

52. ———. "Beethoven's *Adelaide,*" *Harb* II, 23 (May 16, 1846),
          363.
          A review.

53. ———. "The Boston Academy of Music," *Harb* III, 24 (Nov. 21,
          1846), 381.
          Lindpaintner, Donizetti, Reissiger, de Bériot, Mendelssohn.

54. ———. "Boston Academy of Music," *Harb* IV, 5 (Jan. 9, 1847),
          76.
          Lindpaintner, Mendelssohn, Lachner.

55. ———. "Boston Academy of Music," *Harb* IV, 8 (Jan. 30, 1847),
          123–24.
          Lachner.

56. ———. "Boston Academy of Music," *Harb* IV, 12 (Feb. 27,
          1847), 186–87.
          Beethoven, Auber, Weber.

57. ———. "Boston Philharmonic Society," *Harb* IV, 5 (Jan. 9,
          1847), 77.

58. ———. "Boston Philharmonic Society," *Harb* IV, 12 (Feb. 27,
          1847), 185–86.
          Beethoven, Hummel.

59. ———. "Camilo Sivori," *Harb* III, 23 (Nov. 14, 1846), 363–64.

60. ———. "Chamber Concerts of the Harvard Musical Association,"
          Harb III, 25 (Nov. 28, 1846), 394–95.
          Spaeth, Mayseder, Mozart, Haydn, Beethoven.

61. ————. "Concerts of the Italian Troupe in Boston," *Harb* IV, 25 (May 29, 1847), 394–95.
62. ————. "The Concerts of the Past Winter," *Dial* I, 1 (July 1840), 124–34.
Handel, Haydn, Neukomm; pianists Rakemann and Kossowski; singer Knight; Boston Academy.
63. ————. "De Meyer Again in Boston," *Harb* III, 20 (Oct. 24, 1846), 317–18.
64. ————. "Father Heinrich in Boston," *Harb* III, 4 (July 4, 1846), 58–59.
65. ————. "The Festival Concert in New York—Beethoven's Choral Symphony," *Harb* III, 1 (June 13, 1846), 9–11.
66. ————. "From a Young Composer," *Harb* V, 5 (July 10, 1847), 72–73.
Review of music by H. Auguste Pond.
67. ————. "Great Concert in New York—The Philharmonic Society —Beethoven's Choral Symphony," *Harb* II, 23 (May 16, 1846), 361–63.
68. ————. "Great Festival," *Harb* V, 14 (Sept. 11, 1847), 218–19.
An announcement of a New York festival.
69. ————. "The Handel and Haydn Society," *Harb* VIII, 4 (Nov. 25, 1848), 30–31.
70. ————. "Harvard Musical Association," *Harb* IV, 8 (Jan. 30, 1847), 124.
71. ————. "Henri Herz," *Harb* III, 23 (Nov. 14, 1846), 364.
72. ————. "Henri Herz in Boston," *Harb* IV, 3 (Dec. 26, 1846), 42–43.
73. ————. "Herz, Sivori, and Knoop in Boston," *Harb* VI, 2 (Nov. 13, 1847), 11.
74. ————. "Introductory," *Harb* I, 1 (June 14, 1845), 12–13.
A statement of principles.
75. ————. "The Italian Opera in Boston," *Harb* IV, 21 (May 1, 1847), 331–33.
Verdi's *Ernani*.
76. ————. "The Italian Opera in Boston," *Harb* IV, 22 (May 8, 1847), 346. Verdi's *Ernani*.
77. ————. "Italian Opera in Boston," *Harb* V, 2 (June 19, 1847), 25–27.
Rossini, Bellini.
78. ————. "Italian Opera in Boston," *Harb* V, 19 (Oct. 16, 1847), 299–300.
Verdi, Rossini, Ricci.
79. ————. "Italian Opera in Boston." *Harb* VI, 14 (Feb. 5, 1848), 110.
80. ————. "Italian Opera in Boston—Lucrezia Borgia," *Harb* VII, 7 (June 17, 1848), 47.

81. ———. "The Italian Opera in New York," *Harb* IV, 19 (Apr. 17, 1847), 294–95.
    Verdi, Donizetti.

82. ———. "Italian Opera in New York," *Harb* IV, 25 (May 29, 1847), 395.

83. ———. "Leopold de Meyer," *Harb* I, 25 (Nov. 29, 1845), 396–97.

84. ———. "Madame Anna Bishop," *Harb* V, 14 (Sept. 11, 1847), 217–18.

85. ———. "Maurice Strakosch," *Harb* VIII, 4 (Nov. 25, 1848), 30.

86. ———. "Mendelssohn and His Works," *Harb* IV, 1 (Dec. 12, 1846), 11–13.

87. ———. "Mendelssohn's 'Elijah,'" *Harb* VI, 19 (Mar. 11, 1848), 149–50; VI, 20 (Mar. 18, 1848), 158.

88. ———. "Mendelssohn's 'Songs without Words,'" *Harb* III, 14 (Sept. 12, 1846), 218–19; III, 15 (Sept. 19, 1846), 231–32.

89. ———. "Mendelssohn's Songs Without Words," *Harb* V, 12 (Aug. 28, 1847), 184–85.

90. ———. "More Chamber Concerts in Boston," *Harb* IV, 19 (Apr. 17, 1847), 295–96.
    Beethoven, Haydn.

91. ———. "Mr. Cranch's Address," *Harb* II, 6 (Jan. 17, 1846), 88–90; II, 7 (Jan. 24, 1846), 109–10; II, 8 (Jan. 31, 1846), 123–24.
    Consisting primarily of extracts.

92. ———. "Mr. Edward L. Walker," *Harb* II, 20 (Apr. 25, 1846), 315–17.
    Review of a concert by Walker, who had invented a new type of piano.

93. ———. "Mr. Edward L. Walker," *Harb* IV, 12 (Feb. 27, 1847), 187–88.

94. ———. "Mr. J. L. Hatton," *Harb* VIII, 4 (Nov. 25, 1848), 30.

95. ———. "Music," *AesP* I, 1 (1849), 25–26.

96. ———. "Music in Boston," *Harb* I, 21 (Nov. 1, 1845), 329–32.
    Ole Bull, Beethoven.

97. ———. "Music in Boston," *Harb* II, 5 (Jan. 10, 1846), 76–77.
    Handel and Haydn Society, Boston Academy, Philharmonic Society, Dempster, Burke.

98. ———. "Music in Boston," *Harb* IV, 16 (Mar. 27, 1847), 251–52.
    Boston Academy, Philharmonic Society, Handel and Haydn Society.

99. ———. "Music in Boston," *Harb* VI, 4 (Nov. 27, 1847), 29–30.
    Herz, Sivori, Knoop, the Seguins, Madame Bishop.

100. ———. "Music in Boston," *Harb* VI, 9 (Jan. 1, 1848), 70–71.
    Steyermark Musical Company.

101. ————. "Music in Boston," *Harb* VI, 11 (Jan. 15, 1848), 86.
Musical Fund Society, Italian opera, Burke, Hoffman.
102. ————. "Music in Boston," *Harb* VIII, 10 (Jan. 6, 1849), 79.
Musical Fund Society, Philharmonic Society, Mr. Hatton's concert.
103. ————. "Music in Boston," *Harb* VIII, 14 (Feb. 3, 1849),
109–10.
Bishop, Hatton, Handel and Haydn Society.
104. ————. "Music in Boston During the Last Winter," *Harb* I, 8
(Aug. 2, 1845), 123–24; I, 9 (Aug. 9, 1845), 139–41;
I, 10 (Aug. 16, 1845), 154–57; I, 12 (Aug. 30, 1845),
188–89.
Harvard Musical Association, Boston Academy.
105. ————. "Musical Conventions," *Harb* III, 14 (Sept. 12, 1846),
219.
106. ————. "Musical Fund Society," *Harb* V, 17 (Oct. 2, 1847), 268.
107. ————. "New Chorus and Glee Books," *Harb* VI, 6 (Dec. 11,
1847), 46–47.
White and Gould, *Opera Chorus Book;* Baker, *The Philharmonic;* W. Mason, *Social Glee Book.*
108. ————. "New Collections of Psalmody," *Harb* III, 15 (Sept. 19,
1846), 230–31.
Hamilton, *Songs of Sacred Praise;* White and Gould, *The Modern Harp.*
109. ————. "New Edition of Handel's 'Messiah,'" *Harb* II, 7 (Jan.
24, 1846), 109.
110. ————. "New Music," *Harb* II, 6 (Jan. 17, 1846), 91.
Reviews of music by Donizetti, Dempster, Russell, Templeton,
Brown, Robinson, Hunten.
111. ————. "New Music," *Harb* VII, 4 (May 27, 1848), 30.
Reviews.
112. ————. "New Music," *Harb* VII, 5 (June 3, 1848), 38.
Review of Baker, *Elementary School Music.*
113. ————. "New Musical Publications," *Harb* VII, 15 (Aug. 12,
1848), 111.
Reviews of music by Heuberer, Speyer, Reissiger, Gorca.
114. ————. "New Musical Publications," *Harb* VII, 26 (Oct. 28,
1848), 204.
Reviews of music by Verdi, Donizetti, Voss.
115. ————. "New Publications," *Harb* III, 5 (July 11, 1846), 76–77.
Reviews of music by Chopin, Callcott, Czerny, Mendelssohn,
Knight, Bellini.
116. ————. "New Publications," *Harb* III, 14 (Sept. 12, 1846), 219.
Reviews of music by W. Mason, Hamilton, Weber.
117. ————. "New Publications," *Harb* III, 25 (Nov. 28, 1846), 395.
Reviews of music by Brunner, Blessner.

118. ———. "New Publications," *Harb* IV, 22 (May 8, 1847), 346–47.
     Reviews of music by W. Mason, Wright.
119. ———. "Ole Bull's Concert," *Harb* I, 3 (June 28, 1845), 44–45.
120. ———. "The Opera," *Harb* VIII, 9 (Dec. 30, 1848), 70–71.
121. ———. "The Opera Again in Boston," *Harb* V, 17 (Oct. 2, 1847), 267–68.
     Bellini, Verdi.
122. ———. "The Opera in Boston," *Harb* IV, 26 (June 5, 1847), 408–09.
     Verdi.
123. ———. "Opera in Boston—*Il Giuramento*," *Harb* VII, 8 (June 24, 1848), 62–63.
     Mercadante.
124. ———. "The Prospects for the Season," *Harb* III, 19 (Oct. 17, 1846), 301.
125. ———. "Reed's Publications," *Harb* VI, 15 (Feb. 12, 1848), 118–19.
     Reviews of new music.
126. ———. "Review," *Harb* II, 1 (Dec. 13, 1845), 11–12.
     De Meyer, *Biography*.
127. ———. "Reviews," *Harb* I, 2 (June 21, 1845), 26–27.
     Music by Schubert, Kreutzer, Weber, Beethoven.
128. ———. "Reviews," *Harb* I, 9 (Aug. 9, 1845), 141.
     Music by Forde, Kufferath.
129. ———. "Reviews," *Harb* I, 11 (Aug. 23, 1845), 173–74.
     Music by Bellini, Mozart.
130. ———. "Reviews," *Harb* I, 12 (Aug. 30, 1845), 189.
     Peck, ed., *Boston Musical Review*.
131. ———. "Reviews," *Harb* I, 17 (Oct. 4, 1845), 264.
     Johnson, *Musical Class Book*, and music by Bertini.
132. ———. "Reviews," *Harb* I, 22 (Nov. 8, 1845), 348.
     Music by Barker, Daniell, Brougham, Smith, Czerny, Labitzky, Bohlman, Lemaire, Kreutzer, Neukomm, Bellini, Balfe, Rosellen, Burgmüller, Hunten.
133. ———. "Reviews," *Harb* II, 1 (Dec. 13, 1845), 12–13.
     Music by Spohr, Mendelssohn, Schubert, Lachner, Czerny, Brown, Ordway, Barker.
134. ———. "Reviews," *Harb* II, 3 (Dec. 27, 1845), 43–44.
     Ives *et al.*, *The Beethoven Collection of Sacred Music*.
135. ———. "Reviews," *Harb* II, 5 (Jan. 10, 1846), 77.
     Music by Weber, Wallace, Handel, Pond.
136. ———. "Reviews," *Harb* II, 8 (Jan. 31, 1846), 122–23.
     Holmes, *Life of Mozart*.
137. ———. "Reviews," *Harb* II, 19 (Apr. 18, 1846), 298–99.
     Music by W. Mason.

138. ———. "Reviews," *Harb* II, 20 (Apr. 25, 1846), 317–18.
Ives, *Musical ABC, Musical Spelling Book, Musical Reader, Musical Wreath.*

139. ———. "Reviews," *Harb* II, 21 (May 2, 1846), 333–34.
Music by Heller, Thalberg, W. Mason, Callcott, Bertini.

140. ———. "Reviews," *Harb* III, 9 (Aug. 8, 1846), 140–41.
Music by Herz, Czerny, Flotow.

141. ———. "Reviews," *Harb* III, 10 (Aug. 15, 1846), 152–53.
Darley and Standbridge, *Cantus Ecclesiae*, 3rd ed.

142. ———. "Reviews," *Harb* III, 17 (Oct. 3, 1846), 266–67.
Weber, *Theory of Musical Composition*, trans. Warner.

143. ———. "Reviews," *Harb* III, 20 (Oct. 24, 1846), 317.
Warner, *Rudimental Lessons in Music, The Primary Note Reader.*

144. ———. "Reviews," *Harb* IV, 8 (Jan. 30, 1847), 124–25.
Ives, *Mozart Collection of Sacred Music*, 2nd ed.

145. ———. "Reviews," *Harb* IV, 19 (Apr. 17, 1847), 296.
Music by Maretzek, Adam, Willis.

146. ———. "Reviews," *Harb* V, 2 (June 19, 1847), 27.
Music by Handel.

147. ———. "Reviews," *Harb* V, 12 (Aug. 28, 1847), 185.
Music by Cooke, Yradier, D'Adhemar, Jennerson, Marcailhou.

148. ———. "Reviews," *Harb* V, 14 (Sept. 11, 1847), 218.
Music by Thalberg.

149. ———. "Reviews," *Harb* V, 17 (Oct. 2, 1847), 268.
Music by Liszt.

150. ———. "Reviews," *Harb* V, 19 (Oct. 16, 1847), 300.
Music by Cherubini.

151. ———. "Reviews," *Harb* VI, 5 (Dec. 4, 1847), 38.
Music by Heuberer, Verdi.

152. ———. "Second Week of the Opera in Boston—Pacini's *Saffo*," *Harb* IV, 23 (May 15, 1847), 361–63.

153. ———. "Signora Biscaccianti," *Harb* V, 14 (Sept. 11, 1847), 218.

154. ———. "Sivori and Herz," *Harb* V, 21 (Oct. 30, 1847), 327.

155. ———. "Sivori's Last Concert in Boston," *Harb* III, 24 (Nov. 21, 1846), 379–81.

156. ———. "Songs from Mendelssohn," *Harb* VI, 15 (Feb. 12, 1848), 118.

157. ———. "Songs from 'Sappho,'" *Harb* V, 5 (July 10, 1847), 72.
By Pacini.

158. ———. "The Steyermark Company," *Harb* VII, 26 (Oct. 28, 1848), 204–05.

159. ———. "The Steyermarkers," *Harb* VIII, 4 (Nov. 25, 1848), 31.

160. ———. "Teachers' Conventions for 1845," *Harb* I, 15 (Sept. 20, 1845), 236–37.

161. ———. "Teachers' Conventions in Boston," *Harb* V, 13 (Sept. 4, 1847), 203–05.

162. ———. "The Virtuoso Age in Music; The New School of Pianists and Violinists," *Harb* I, 23 (Nov. 15, 1845), 362–64; I, 24 (Nov. 22, 1845), 378–81.
Thalberg, Liszt, Chopin.

163. Emerson, R. W. "Thoughts on Art," *Dial* I, 3 (Jan. 1841), 367–78.
Includes some mention of music.

164. Fuller, Margaret. "Boston Academy of Music," *Dial* I, 3 (Jan. 1841), 407–08.

165. ———. "Entertainments of the Past Winter," *Dial* III, 1 (July 1842), 46–72.
American music, minstrel songs, Bellini, Haydn, Handel, Spohr, Braham, Beethoven, Elssler, Sloman, Herwig, Nagel, Knoop, etc.

166. ———. "Lives of the Great Composers, Haydn, Mozart, Handel, Bach, Beethoven," *Dial* II, 2 (Oct. 1841), 148–203.

167. ———. "The modern Drama," *Dial* IV, 3 (Jan. 1844), 307–49.
Contains a section on music and ballet.

168. ———. "Review," *Dial* III, 4 (Apr. 1843), 533–34.
A review of Fétis, *Music Explained.*

169. Godwin, Parke. "The Philharmonic Concert," *Harb* VI, 19 (Mar. 11, 1848), 150.

170. Ives, Elam. "Master Burke's First Concert," *Harb* VI, 3 (Nov. 20, 1847), 22.

171. ———. "Music in New York," *Harb* VI, 1 (Nov. 6, 1847), 5.

172. ———. "Review," *Harb* VI, 2 (Nov. 13, 1847), 15.
American Musical Times.

173. ———. "Review," *Harb* VI, 3 (Nov. 20, 1847), 23.
Kingsley, *Harp of David.*

174. King, D. S. "The Philharmonic Institute," *Harb* VII, 15 (Aug. 12, 1848), 111.
Also signed by Alex. W. Thayer and H. G. Barrus.

175. Lane, C. "Popular Music," *SpiA* I, 20 (Nov. 17, 1849), 310–11; I, 21 (Nov. 24, 1849), 321–23; I, 23 (Dec. 8, 1849), 353–55.

176. Osgood, Samuel, "Letter from New-Hampshire," *WMes* IV, 4 (Dec. 1837), 238–41.
Contains a description of church music in Nashua, N. H., in Oct., 1836.

177. Perkins, James H. "Public Worship," *WMes* I, 10 (May 1836), 688–90.

178. Pease, Mary Spencer. "Letter from Philadelphia," *Harb* VI, 16 (Feb. 19, 1848), 125.
A description of singing teacher Signor Dorigo.

179. Ripley, George. "Christmas in Philadelphia," *Harb* VI, 9 (Jan. 1, 1848), 69.

Includes a description of a performance of a Mass by Hummel at St. Mary's Catholic Church.

180. ———. "Death of Felix Mendelssohn-Bartholdy," *Harb* VI, 7 (Dec. 18, 1847), 53.
Translated by Ripley from the *Allgemein Zeitung*.

181. Story, W. W. "Sixth Concert of the Boston Academy," *Harb* II, 13 (Mar. 7, 1846), 204–05; II, 14 (Mar. 14, 1846), 218–20.
Auber, Beethoven, Méhul, Rossini.

182. Tuckerman, J. F. "Music of the Winter," *Dial* I, 4 (Apr. 1841), 539–44.
Boston Academy, Handel and Haydn Society, Wood opera company, Rainer family, Braham, Russell.

183. ———. "Review," *BQRe* III, 2 (July 1840), 332–57.
Fétis, *Biographie universelle des musiciens,* art. "Beethoven."

GENERAL INDEX

INDEX OF TITLES

————— ⇛ ⇚ —————

Including Psalm-books, tune-books, instruction-books, and individual compositions